C000302109

THE
CHELTENHAM
BOOK
OF
DAYS

MICHAEL HASTED

First published 2013

The History Press
The Mill, Brimscombe Port
Stroud, Gloucestershire, GL5 2QG
www.thehistorypress.co.uk

British Library Cataloguing in Publication Data.
A catalogue record for this book is available from the British Library.

ISBN 978 0 7524 6544 9

Typesetting and origination by The History Press
Printed in India

JANUARY 1ST

1966: On this day the beautiful old St James' railway station closed. The first station on this site was opened in 1847, when the Great Western Railway opened a direct line to London via Swindon. Although this was intended to be a temporary building, it was not replaced until September 1894 – nearly fifty years later. Italianate in design, with an impressive covered carriage entrance, it looked like a mini version of many of the great London terminals, being very much like St Marylebone. The arrival of the railway spelled the end for many of the town's established coaching inns, although the improved communications did increase the number of short-term visitors to the town.

Probably the most famous train to operate from St James' station was the 'Cheltenham Flyer'. This was the first train in the world scheduled to run at more than 70mph start to stop, a feat she achieved between Swindon and Paddington in 1932. Today the nameplate of the 'Cheltenham Flyer' is preserved in the National Railway Museum at York. The St James' site is now home to offices and apartments, and much of Waitrose stands on what were the station's sidings. (Various sources, including Rowbotham & Waller, *Cheltenham: A History*)

JANUARY 2ND

2011: On this day the daredevil motorcyclists of the Cheltenham Home Guard Motorcycle Club held their annual New Year Trials at Hazleton Quarry. The ninety-five intrepid riders had to negotiate three laps of the fifteen-section circuit, braving cold and wintery conditions. In fact, they were lucky to be holding the event at all, as only a few days previously the course had been under 2ft of snow and was completely inaccessible. Although the trial was categorised as easy, it nevertheless provided some tricky moments as some of the rocks were still a bit icy. The most successful rider of the day was Tim Wheeler, who lost only one point.

The Motorcycle Club was formed at the end of the war in 1945; the members were drawn from those who had served in the Gloucestershire Regiment's Home Guard. The club was granted the unique privilege of using the Sphinx emblem from the regiment's badge. The badge, worn on the back of the beret, is itself unique to the 'Glorious Glosters'. (Cheltenham Home Guard Motorcycle Club; www.glosters.org)

January 3rd

1915: On this day the celebrated poet, novelist and playwright James Elroy Flecker died of tuberculosis in Davos, Switzerland. His death at the age of thirty was described at the time as 'unquestionably the greatest premature loss that English literature has suffered since the death of Keats'.

His actual name was Herman, but he later decided to call himself 'James'. His father, Revd W.H. Flecker, was the first headmaster of Dean Close School in Cheltenham, where young James was educated. Although perhaps not the best-known poet, his work has influenced many others. His poem 'The Bridge of Fire' is featured in Neil Gaiman's Sandman series, in the volume *The Wake*. The most enduring testimony to his work, though, is perhaps an excerpt from 'The Golden Journey to Samarkand', inscribed on the clock tower of the barracks of the British Army's 22nd Special Air Service regiment in Hereford:

> We are the Pilgrims, master; we shall go
> Always a little further; it may be
> Beyond that last blue mountain barred with snow
> Across that angry or that glimmering sea.

(Various sources, including Gwen Hart, *A History of Cheltenham*)

JANUARY 4TH

1988: On this day the first episode of the Ronnie Barker BBC sitcom *Clarence* was broadcast. It had two connections with Cheltenham: exterior locations for the first episode were filmed in Lansdown Crescent, and the house of the character Jane Travers was in Malvern Road. The series was written by Barker himself under the name of Bob Ferris. He wrote the character Jane Travers especially for Josephine Tewson.

Clarence begins on Coronation Day in 1937 with Clarence Sale, a very short-sighted removal man, clearing the house of a snooty lady who is emigrating. There he meets Jane Travers, her maid. The couple strike up an unusual relationship and soon Clarence proposes to her. Jane decides that they should have a trial period of living together, with a pillow between them to inhibit Clarence's lustful advances. With only two characters there was not much opportunity to develop the plot, and only one series of *Clarence* was made, the last one being shown on 8 February 1988. (Various sources, including BBC)

January 5th

1891: On this day the gaieties of the week commenced with the first of the Tarantella Dances. The round room of the Rotunda had been lightly draped, and the long one more elaborately decorated by Messrs Shirer and Haddon; the colour scheme – amber and green throughout – harmonised well with the deep tones of Mr Cypher's plants. The arrangement of the drawing room was more than ordinarily effective, the slight division produced by the use of screens and plants having a less formal effect than a more rigid separation. That the ornamentation of the room had not been left wholly in the hands of the professional furnisher was proved by the presence of a number of elegant articles which had evidently come from private drawing rooms – possibly from the residence of Colonel Bainbridge, who had carried out the arrangements for the dance. The company, numbering about 170, began to assemble shortly before nine, at which hour dancing commenced. It was kept up until one o'clock with great spirit and without intermission, refreshments being served throughout the evening by Mr Locke. (*Cheltenham Looker-On*)

JANUARY 6TH

2011: On this day, motorbike fanatic John Bliss made his final journey. Instead of a hearse, his body was taken to his funeral at the Cheltenham Crematorium in a motorcycle sidecar. Joy, his eighty-year-old wife, had arranged for the vintage Triumph to carry him to the service. She said: 'He had motorbikes all his life from when he was sixteen.' His son-in-law, Clive Wilson, travelled on the back of the bike to the crematorium.

Mr Bliss had died three weeks earlier at the age of eighty-four after a year-long battle with prostate cancer. He was one of the founder members of the Cotswold branch of the Vintage Motorcycle Club, which met regularly at pubs around the county. Former vice-president of the club, Len Ore, paid tribute to Mr Bliss, whom he had known for forty years. 'He was never happier than when he was building motorbikes and would always help anyone out with spares they needed,' he said. 'He was a keen rider and keen mechanic. All he wanted to do was ride. It is a very sad loss.'

Mr Bliss worked for Dowty Mining for thirty-three years and also served in the army in Egypt during the Suez Crisis in 1951. (*Gloucestershire Echo*)

JANUARY 7TH

1963: On this day the Owe 40 Club held their Junior Squash Rackets Tournament in the Old Bath Road. The lawn tennis and squash club had been founded after the First World War by Henry Holgate Yolland and his wife Katherine. They had bought some land on the Old Bath Road and built a house and four tennis courts. The house was named Longuenesse after the place in France where they had worked together on the Commonwealth War Graves Commission. They then set up the Owe 40 Squash Racquets & Tennis Club, the name deriving from the highest lawn tennis handicap.

After Yolland's death in 1939 the courts and the club declined, but in 1944 Major Albert Edward Millman, who was recuperating from serious wounds he had received in the war, stayed at Longuenesse and, with the help of some German prisoners of war from the camp at Leckhampton Court, set about restoring the courts and reviving the club. Before the war Millman had been a tennis professional, running the Billesley Lane club in Birmingham, and became quite a significant figure in the sport. Several exhibition matches were held at the Old Bath Road club by some of the world's best players. Jack Kramer played there in 1952 and 1965, and Pancho Segura in 1952. The club closed in 1965 when Millman and his wife Elizabeth sold the land to property developers. (CLHS Journal 24)

JANUARY 8TH

1872: On this day Frederick Jones was hanged for the murder of Emily Gardner in Wellesley Road, Cheltenham the previous year. As he could neither read nor write, his confession was written down by the chaplain on the Sunday night before his execution:

> I had been very jealous of her for some time and for a month or more it used to come into my mind very often that if I could not have her, nobody else should. She used to tell me about the larks and bits of fun with this chap and another, and this made me jealous of her and I swore that if I caught her speaking to anybody I would kill her. ... I confronted Emily one evening, she said, 'Don't bother me, I shall do as I like.' I said 'Do you care for me or not?' but she would not tell me. ... I said 'I will make you tell me or I will cut your throat with your father's own razor.' She then screamed murder three times and I said 'I will murder you if I am to hang for it the next minute.' ... I cut her across the throat and she fell against me and knocked me down and we fell together and that was how I was covered with blood. I never knew any harm by her in all my life and I love her now. I should not like to live and do not dread what is before me, and I pray every hour for the Lord to have mercy upon me and forgive me.

(Excerpts from the *Gloucester Journal*, 1872, by Senior Prison Officer White)

JANUARY 9TH

1881: On this day the *Cheltenham Looker-On* reported a packed audience at a Rotunda concert on the previous Saturday. The crowd at the Montpellier event testified once again to the popularity of the Promenade Concerts, of which this was the eighth. Though only one vocalist took part in the programme, the absence of a second – for there had been two singers at each of the previous concerts – was compensated for by the introduction of several instrumental compositions. The most popular of these was a duet for pianoforte and violoncello by Mr von Holst. A pianoforte solo by Mr Teague also afforded the audience great pleasure. Mr Teague's performance was quite an unexpected treat, while Mr von Holst was as brilliant as ever. Miss Lizzie Evans, the sole vocalist, sang four songs all very effectively and was warmly applauded for each, receiving a persistent encore for her rendering of 'When the Heart was Young'. (*Cheltenham Looker-On*)

January 10th

1865: On this day a flight of pheasants was released to enter Cheltenham. Having reached the place prepared for their reception near Regent Street, they flew off in various directions. One brace, for example, headed towards Tivoli Villas, another towards Sandford Place, while a third extended their flight as if making for Leckhampton, but, failing in the attempt, sought refuge behind shrubbery on the side of the road. A fourth brace followed in their wake, but, weaker on the wing, were only able to reach Thirlestaine House, where they came to grief, as did a fifth in the Thirlestaine Road. Several other birds, less confident in their strength, took shorter journeys. One brace sought shelter in the larders of the Queens Hotel, another in one of the Bayshill villas, and a third in Suffolk Square, while some perched in the High Street or crossed over in the direction of Pittville. These aristocratic members of the feathered community were attended on their visit to Cheltenham by others of humbler plumage, who contrived to find their way into the pantries of several of the most respectable tradesmen of the town. (*Cheltenham Looker-On*)

JANUARY IITH

1840: On this day a dastardly attempted murder took place at Coombe Hill, just outside Cheltenham. The victim was Richard Yarworth, a twenty-four-year-old quarryman who had been to Worcester for the purpose of collecting some money owed to his father. He left Worcester by the Wellington coach, in the company of two gentlemen named Pritchard and Sharp. Yarworth explained:

> We came to Tewkesbury, where we all got off at the Bear Inn. Mr. Pritchard was left at Tewkesbury, and the man who was before inside got outside, and took the place [he] had occupied. While proceeding along the road I said I should walk from Combe Hill [*sic*] to Cheltenham and the man said he was going to Cheltenham and would walk with me. When the coach arrived, we both got down. ... We then set out to walk, and after proceeding about 400 yards, he pulled out a pistol and shot me. I fell. He then stood over me, and reloading the pistol, asked me for my money. He than rifled my pockets, and took seven £5 notes, twelve sovereigns and nine shillings, a cheque for £5, a bill at two months for £13, drawn by me, and accepted by Mr Perkes, stonemason, and my watch.

The following Tuesday the bullet was extracted by Mr Gregory, parish surgeon of Cheltenham. Mr Lefroy, the head of the constabulary force, 'used his best exertion to discover the horrid assassin'. (*Cheltenham Free Press*)

JANUARY 12TH

1795: On this day, John de la Bere died. De la Bere was an important man in Cheltenham: a lawyer and Steward of the Manor, and a member of a family that could trace its roots directly back to the early fourteenth century. This branch of the family was based in Southam, a few miles north of Cheltenham. At one point the family owned the land on which the Tivoli area of Cheltenham is built. Not much is known of John de la Bere, but a tablet which used to be in the parish church testified to his importance:

> To preserve the memory of those whose excellences will never be forgotten, this marble records the names of John de la Bere, Esq., who died Jan. 12th 1795. Also of the Reverend John de la Bere, his only son, who died at Burford 1810

The first known Sir John de la Bere appears in 1328. A document of 1397 records that Sir John had died eight years earlier possessed of the castle. His heir was an underage boy, also named John. He may have been a grandson, possibly a younger son of the late Sir Richard of Crécy. The house occupied by the family in Southam, which dates back to 1485, is now the Hotel de la Bere. (Gwen Hart, *A History of Cheltenham*)

JANUARY 13TH

1831: On this day the New Clarence Theatre was opened in St George's Place by Mr Belmont.

The theatre had originally been established as a puppet theatre by Samuel Seward, who had also worked at the Theatre Royal as a scene painter. He named it Sadler's Wells after the theatre in London where he had once worked. His productions were, apparently, as spectacular as anything that the Theatre Royal could offer, except they didn't use live actors. The theatre ran continuously for thirty years until the death of Seward and his wife. Belmont took over the theatre, replacing puppets with live actors and renaming it the New Clarence. The venture did not start well: the company of actors failed to turn up and the opening had to be postponed. Things did not get much better and the theatre closed a couple of years later, becoming Gardner's Academy, privately owned and run by Joseph Gardner. The Church of England Reading Association then took the building over in 1839, and ironically it was Francis Close – who was opposed to most forms of entertainment, particularly the theatre – who inaugurated it.

During work on the St George's Place building in the 1970s, the façade, including the original sign for the theatre, was discovered. It was subsequently demolished and no trace remains. (Michael Hasted, *A Theatre for All Seasons*)

JANUARY 14TH

1865: On this day a brilliant private party was hosted at the Queens Hotel by Mrs R. Bolton and her sisters, the Misses Ireland. The entire suite of rooms forming the north-western angle of the building were appropriated for the reception and entertainment of the guests, who numbered some 150 of the most influential and fashionable residents and visitors of Cheltenham. The large room, in which public dinners occasionally took place, was converted into a ballroom, the walls being covered with white and pink drapery, and ornamented with floral decorations. The drawing rooms of the hotel formed the reception rooms, through which the company entered, and these, also, were most elegantly fitted up and draped with great taste, the curtains separating the apartments being looped up with light festoons of flowers. Here the hostesses received their friends shortly before ten. Dancing began with a quadrille, to the music of Mr Bretherton's Band, at about 10.30 p.m. and continued until 12.30 a.m. Valses, galops and lancers alternated in quick succession. When supper was announced the guests repaired to the large room of the Table d'Hôte, where a sumptuous banquet consisting of every delicacy of the season was set out for their refreshment, with wines of every vintage and variety that the Queens' cellars could provide. (*Cheltenham Looker-On*)

JANUARY 15TH

2011: On this day the Cheltenham Art Gallery & Museum opened an exhibition called Arts and Crafts: Looking Back, Moving Forward to celebrate and raise awareness of the Arts and Crafts Movement, and to draw attention to the important collection that the museum holds.

The Arts and Crafts Movement, which developed in the nineteenth century, was based on simple forms, truth to materials, and the use of nature as the source of pattern. Young London-based architects, inspired by the ideas of John Ruskin and William Morris, founded the Art Workers' Guild in 1884 to break down barriers between architects, artists, designers and makers. The term 'Arts and Crafts' was first used at the suggestion of the bookbinder T.J. Cobden-Sanderson in 1888.

The Cheltenham event, which ran for ten weeks, brought out of storage some works which are not on permanent display. Furniture, ceramics, metalwork and books were on show, with pieces by Ernest Gimson, C.R. Ashbee, Robert 'Mouseman' Thompson, Alfred Powell and the Della Robbia Pottery, plus a selection of private press books from the Emery Walker Library. (Cheltenham Art Gallery & Museum)

January 16th

1932: On this day it was revealed that the Cheltenham General Hospital was experiencing problems finding beds for the victims of road accidents. The cost of treating the increasing number of victims of motorcar accidents was giving most hospitals cause for anxious thought. The article stated that in No. 8 (Accident) Ward at Cheltenham General Hospital, all the beds were occupied by eighteen victims of serious road accidents who had been brought to the hospital during the past few weeks. All were happily on the mend. In addition to the number of people who were kept in hospital for treatment, about sixty others had had their injuries treated, but were allowed to go home afterwards and attend as out-patients until fully recovered.

Undeterred by the situation at the hospital, the Cheltenham and Gloucester Car Mart in Winchcombe Street was pressing ahead with newly equipped workshops and a service station. The company was the county distributer for the famous Austin range, and owners were able to find expert and speedy service for their cars. The garage had installed the latest portable equipment and this, combined with an efficient staff of experienced mechanics, ensured the highest standard of workmanship for repairs of all types and to any make of car. That's what they said, anyway. (*Cheltenham Chronicle and Gloucestershire Graphic*)

JANUARY 17TH

1912: On this day one of Cheltenham's famous sons, Edward Adrian Wilson, reached the South Pole. Wilson was born in Cheltenham on 23 July 1872 at a house in Montpellier Terrace. He attended Cheltenham College as a day pupil and in 1891 went up to Gonville & Caius College, Cambridge where he read natural sciences, obtaining a first class degree in 1894.

Wilson was the chief scientific officer, artist and zoologist on Captain Scott's doomed British Antarctic Expedition of 1910-1913. They set sail on 15 June 1910 from Cardiff on the *Terra Nova*. Wilson perished on the Great Ice Barrier a couple of months after reaching the Pole. Captain Scott said of him: 'He died as he lived. A brave, true man. The best of comrades and staunchest of friends.' A bronze statue, sculpted by Scott's widow Kathleen, was unveiled in the Promenade Gardens by Sir Clements Markham in July 1914. A Gonville & Caius flag, which Wilson took to the South Pole, is preserved at the college. (Various sources, including D.M. Wilson, D.B. Elder, N. Reardon & Edward Wilson, *Cheltenham in Antarctica: The Life of Edward Wilson*)

JANUARY 18TH

1931: On this day an unfortunate accident occurred when a bus turned into the Promenade from the High Street. A policeman on duty had to 'leap for his life' when the new double-decker bus collided with a lorry coming from the opposite direction. Both vehicles were seriously damaged and the road was covered in debris and spilled petrol from the bus's fuel tank. Considerable disruption was caused in the centre of town.

A few weeks later another accident involving public transport occurred in Prestbury. On the night of 25 March, three men travelling in a DeSoto sports car were injured when their car collided with a disused tram. One of the passengers, Mr Frederick Palmer who lived in Shurdington Road, died a few days later from his injuries. Palmer was the heir of Jarrow shipbuilding magnate Sir Alfred Molyneux Palmer. The accident was the result of the car swerving to avoid a motorcyclist. (Appleby & Lloyd, *Cheltenham's Trams and Buses 1890-1963*)

JANUARY 19TH

1853: On this day the *Cheltenham Examiner* announced the appointment of a new sexton for the parish church – a job, it seems, that a lot of people were keen to have.

> From the number of candidates for this office – eighteen or twenty altogether – it would really appear that one half of the parish is actuated with the benevolent desire of burying the other half. Such a prolific issue of addresses and handbills, and such a persevering canvassing as the rate-payers have been subjected to during the last few days, was surely never before known within the memory of 'the oldest (unburied) inhabitant'.
>
> It will be seen by our columns this morning that the Incumbent of the Parish, having ascertained that the appointment lies with him, and not with the rate-payers, has, after consulting with his Church wardens, nominated Mr George Lewis, sculptor, of Clarence Street, to fill the office. Thus, in sporting phraseology, a 'lark horse' wins the stake; and, while the forty-and-one actual have been 'beating the bush', another has quietly bagged the hare. From what we hear Mr Lewis is a very proper person for the office; and, if so, all the harm we wish him is that he may long live to enjoy it – but that the duties and the fees accruing thereafter may (from the proverbial and increasing healthfulness of Cheltenham) 'grow small by degrees and beautifully less'.

(*Cheltenham Examiner*)

January 20th

2010: On this day the body of Martin Bromage was retrieved from the sea off the French coast after a tragic accident ended his attempt to fly to Australia by microlight aircraft.

Martin, who was born in Cheltenham in 1960 and worked locally as a tree surgeon and property developer, had planned the 11,000-mile flight to raise £150,000 for the charity Help for Heroes. The trip was scheduled to take eight weeks, stopping in eighteen counties. He took off from Gloucestershire Airport at Staverton at 10 a.m. on Monday 18 January 2010, but only three hours later it became clear that there had been a problem. Halfway across the Channel he ran into thick fog and, losing his bearings, went off the radar at about 1 p.m., at which time it is assumed he had crashed into the sea. His body was found about 20 miles off the French coast and taken to Boulogne by a patrol vessel sent from RAF Kinloss.

Interviewed at a pre-trip reception at Staverton on the Saturday before he took off, he said, 'I have done a few adventurous trips in Europe in the microlight and I just thought to myself, why not push it that bit further. There is a real sense of freedom – you can feel the wind and smell the atmosphere. You can't do that in a plane.'

A memorial service was held for Martin in Gloucester Cathedral on 5 February 2010. He left two sons. (Various sources, including BBC; *Gloucestershire Echo*)

JANUARY 21ST

1862: On this day Elizabeth Hale claimed that her baby had died from an inflammation of the chest. However, three months later, in April, the body of a three-month-old baby girl was found on the premises of Mr W.T. Smith, at the rear of Brunswick House on the Promenade. Some workmen found a bundle, covered in a coloured pocket handkerchief. The police were sent for and discovered that the bundle contained a partly decomposed body. It was then discovered that twenty-six-year-old Hale, the housemaid of Brunswick House, had given birth to a girl at the house of her former employer, Mrs Hest, in Lower Park Street the previous November, disappearing soon after. Hale told the police that the baby had died of natural causes. She later said that she had hidden it in the house until she would be able to bury it in her home in the Forest of Dean in the summer. She was charged with murder; the baby had been found with a handkerchief tied around its mouth, and the prosecution argued that it had been suffocated to death. But then it was admitted that the chest inflammation could explain other suspicious abnormalities on the child, and Hale claimed that she had tied the handkerchief round the baby's jaw after it had died. Despite the evidence, and the hiding of the body, Hale was found not guilty of murder. (cotswoldhistory.com, Cotswold Murder Walks – Cheltenham, Nell Darby)

JANUARY 22ND

1921: On this day it was reported that the development of St Mark's estate had come to fruition: the first completed houses in Libertus Road and Tennyson Road were officially opened.

At the end of the First World War, Lloyd George made his famous 'homes fit for heroes' speech, which highlighted the dearth of local authority housing. This prompted Cheltenham Council to form a Housing Committee and, by March 1919, they had identified a plot of land belonging to Herbert Unwin of Arle Court. They bought about 100 acres of the land with the intention of building 400 houses. The first sod of the new development was cut on 22 April 1920 by the Mayor of Cheltenham, Alderman Bendall, on what was then known as the National Housing Scheme site. The event was commemorated by the planting of an oak tree at the junction of what would become Byron Road and Milton Road. As you may have already deduced, all the roads in St Mark's were named after famous English poets. (*Cheltenham Chronicle and Gloucestershire Graphic*)

JANUARY 23RD

1928: On this day, a show called *The Golden West* opened at the Coliseum Theatre in Albion Street. It told the story of a pretty young girl who was kidnapped from a farm in Arizona. The girl, Polly, was played by Hilda Baker and the *Echo* described her as being 'a wonderfully versatile artist, and the cleverness of her character studies, as well as the aggressiveness of her comedy, will be appreciated'.

At that time Hilda was twenty-two years old but had been treading the boards since she was ten. By fourteen she had started writing, producing and performing her own shows. Her most famous stage act was as a gossip from the North of England, with a silent, sullen companion named 'Big Cynthia', almost always played by a man in drag. Her act was full of malapropisms and her catchphrase, usually after an innuendo, was 'She knows, y'know!'. By this time she spelled her name Hylda.

Baker came to the attention of the public at large when she appeared in the BBC's recreation of a Victorian music hall, *The Good Old Days*, in 1955. This led to her TV series *Be Soon* (named after another of her catchphrases) in 1957 and a supporting part in the sitcom *Our House* in 1960. This was followed by her own sitcom, *The Best of Friends*, in 1963. She died in 1986 aged eighty-one. (*Gloucestershire Echo*; CLHS Journal 23)

January 24th

1775: On this day a man who had a great influence on the way Cheltenham was developed was born in London. Architect John Buonarotti Papworth set the blueprint for the typical Cheltenham villa. Throughout his career, Papworth's main clients were bankers, industrialists and businessmen, for whom he worked as an internal furnisher, architect, and landscape designer. In the 1820s he turned his attention to Cheltenham. Many of his projects were never realised, or have since been destroyed, but a few of his buildings remain as Cheltenham icons. Papworth did a lot of work for Pearson Thompson and initially designed the Lansdown estate, including Lansdown Crescent, where only one house was built to his specifications before the development ran out of cash and was sold up to the Jearrad brothers. He also designed St James' Church in Suffolk Square, which is now the Zizzi restaurant. However, it is his designs for Montpellier Rotunda and Gardens that are his real monument.

Coincidentally, he has links in London with another of Cheltenham's famous sons. John Nevil Maskelyne, the magician (*see* December 22nd) had a permanent show and exhibition in Egyptian Hall in London's Piccadilly, which Papworth built in 1819. (Rebsie Fairholm, Cheltonia website; H.M. Colvin, *A Biographical Dictionary of British Architects, 1600-1840*)

JANUARY 25TH

1926: On this day, Captain Clive Maskelyne opened his magic and illusion show at the Coliseum in Albion Street. Captain Clive was the son of the famous John Nevil Maskelyne, who was born in Cheltenham in 1839.

Captain Clive was still performing many of his father's illusions, but the advertisement in the local papers for his show promised much more. Billed as being 'direct from St George's Hall, London', it read:

> CAPTAIN CLIVE MASKELYNE, head of the famous Maskelyne's Mysteries, is making his first appearance in the provinces at the Coliseum Theatre Next Monday. His programme will include The Spirits are Here, and Through the Eye of a Needle, one of the most baffling illusions of recent years. Capt. Maskelyne will be supported by a company of Renowned London Vaudeville Artistes. This visit is of more than usual interest, as the Maskelyne family originally came from Cheltenham. The entertainment provided next week will be of an exceptionally high order, and the Cheltenham public are strongly urged not to miss this opportunity.

Captain Clive was also to appear at the Opera House (now the Everyman) in Regent Street in 1939 to celebrate his father's centenary. (CLHS Journal 23)

January 26th

1901: On this day a large consignment of materials for the building of the Cheltenham tramway system arrived in the town from France and America. The shipment had arrived in Avonmouth Docks and was brought up to Cheltenham courtesy of the Great Western Railway.

A year earlier, American tramway pioneer Thomas Nevins had been engaged by the town to build the new public transport system. Nevins brought with him his son, and his nephew Henry J. McCormick was appointed as construction engineer. The Cheltenham and District Light Railway Company's first assignment was to build a light railway the 5¾ miles from Lansdown to Cleeve Hill. Although planning permission was granted for the stretch of line which ran through the countryside, there were objections to the section that passed along Wellington Road. Consequently, the route was changed to run down the lower part of Prestbury Road and then down Winchcombe Street as far as Albion Street. An objection to prevent Sunday working was overruled. (Appleby & Lloyd, *Cheltenham's Trams and Buses 1890-1963*)

JANUARY 27TH

1832: On this day Charles Lutwidge Dodgson, better known by his *nom de plume* Lewis Carroll, was born in Cheshire.

He is said to have based his famous *Alice in Wonderland* character on Alice Liddell, a girl who often visited her grandparents' home in the suburbs of Cheltenham. Her grandfather, Dr Henry Liddell, was Dean of Christ Church College in Oxford. He became a friend of Dodgson, who was a maths teacher at Oxford and who subsequently took Alice and her two sisters on a boat trip. To keep them amused, he told a story about Alice and a white rabbit, later published as *Alice's Adventures in Wonderland* in 1865. This was followed six years later by *Through the Looking-Glass and What Alice Found There*.

The Liddells lived at Hetton Lawn in Cudnall Street, Charlton Kings. The original mirror, or looking glass, is still there. There are several links between Alice Liddell and the heroine in Lewis Carroll's books. Carroll set the story on 4 May, Alice Liddell's birthday, and in *Through the Looking-Glass* the fictional Alice declares that her age is 'seven-and-a-half exactly', the same as Liddell on that date. Carroll dedicated the book to Alice Pleasance Liddell and the poem at the end of *Through the Looking-Glass*, when read downward, spells out her full name. (Various sources)

JANUARY 28TH

1833: On this day Charles George Gordon – 'Gordon of Khartoum' – was born. He is commemorated in one of Cheltenham's most famous monuments, the Gordon Lamp.

The memorial stands in the middle of the road between Montpellier Terrace and Lansdown Road. The residents of Montpellier raised the money to pay for it in 1885, to enhance the area and provide a memorial to General Gordon. The Lamp was unveiled in 1887 and is a fine example of Victorian street furniture. The Aberdeen company Fraser & Son supplied the granite base of the statue at a cost of £200. The lamp post itself has three branches with ornate finials and scrolls. A plaque bearing the inscription 'In memory of Major-General Charles George Gordon CBRE 1833-1885' was added to mark Gordon's centenary in 1933. (Various sources, including Rowbotham & Waller, *Cheltenham: A History*)

JANUARY 29TH

1947: On this day Cheltenham experienced one of its lowest temperatures when the thermometer recorded 22 degrees of frost. Morton-in-Marsh recorded an even lower temperature, with 32 degrees of frost. This year was one of the worst winters since records began and all of the Cheltenham area had suffered heavy falls of snow over quite a long period.

On 5 March, about 500 vehicles were stranded on the road between Andoversford and Northleach in what was said to be one of the worst blizzards the Cotswolds had ever experienced. On the following day Cheltenham was all but cut off, with only two roads into and out of the town remaining open. All the schools in the town were closed. A couple of days later, when the thaw finally set in, most of the rivers in the area, including the Severn at Evesham and Tewkesbury, burst their banks. There was moderate flooding in Cheltenham when the River Chelt was swollen with water coming off Leckhampton Hill. On 15 March the *Echo* declared that the waters had subsided and that the town was free from flooding. (CLHS Journal 23)

January 30th

1941: On this day the Gloucester & Cheltenham Greyhound Stadium raised £450 for the Red Cross. The main event of the afternoon's racing was a match between dogs from the West of England and dogs from London, organised by Mr George H. Flintham. Local greyhounds came out best, with Toftwood Malaga, Clara and Loyal Servant taking the first three places.

The stadium was situated between Cheltenham and Gloucester, with races normally held on Thursday and Saturday evenings. The most prestigious race at the stadium was the annual Grand National of the West, run over 500 yards. The most recent track held its inaugural meeting on 7 March 1975 but only lasted four years, closing its gates on 6 July 1979. (*Cheltenham Chronicle and Gloucestershire Graphic*)

JANUARY 31ST

1891: On this day the *Cheltenham Looker-On* reviewed the Quartette Society's second concert, which had taken place the previous Monday at the Corn Exchange. It was attended by a large and highly cultivated audience, to whose intelligent musical taste the artistic performance of Herr Josef Ludwig and his talented *confrères* evidently appealed. The programme opened with Beethoven's Quartet in B flat, Op. 18, No. 6, each movement of which was very finely played, the utmost grace and delicacy being displayed in the treatment of the *scherzo*, which served to emphasise the pathos with which the fourth movement is replete. Brahms' Quartet in G minor. Op. 25 followed and proved a very distinguished performance, the *intermezzo* especially being invested with the utmost charm of style. The entire movement was listened to with the closest attention, and the executants were enthusiastically applauded. Herr Ludwig played *Romance* (M. Brush) and *Three Original Valses* as solos, the artistic execution of which induced an emphatic recall for the talented artiste. Quartet in C major, Op. 33 No. 3 by Haydn brought to a close a very enjoyable programme. Herr Ludwig was accompanied by Mr Collins (second violin), Mr Blagrove (viola), Mr B. Whitehouse (cello) and Mr A. von Holst (piano). (*Cheltenham Looker-On*)

FEBRUARY 1ST

1925: On this day Cheltenham Spa Malvern Road railway station officially came into being. The station, originally called Cheltenham Malvern Road, was opened by the Great Western Railway in 1908. The station was quite unusual in that its single-island platform was below street level. Access to the platform was by means of a footbridge for the booking hall and then down some stairs. Malvern Road did not have a resident stationmaster but was the responsibility of the St James' stationmaster, who also took charge of Cheltenham High Street Halt and Cheltenham Racecourse stations. Stone from the Cleeve Hill quarries was used in the station buildings, while the platform copings came from Pontypridd.

Improvements in intercity trains led to the decline of the Honeybourne line, which closed for local passenger services in March 1960. Six years later Malvern Road closed completely for goods and passengers. A long stretch of the old Honeybourne line is now a pleasant walking and cycling track. It passes through the site of the old station, of which virtually nothing remains. The goods yards are now Travis Perkins builders' merchants. (Various sources)

FEBRUARY 2ND

1903: On this day Cheltenham witnessed its first cinematic experience. The Winter Gardens, which stood in Imperial Square, presented *Animated Pictures of the Great Delhi Durbar* for one week only, with matinees on Wednesday, Thursday and Saturday at 4 p.m. The film show claimed to be the 'only authentic record' of the event, with 'permission given by His Excellency the Viceroy of India, Lord Curzon'. It showed Lord Curzon himself, as well as the Viceroy's 'gorgeous escort', the 'enthusiastic reception of the 9th Lancers', the Duke and Duchess of Connaught, as well as 'Indian Princes and Rajahs from all climes'. The poster promised 'Line upon line of superb animals – truly an Oriental Dream'. And if that wasn't enough, the supporting features were *Living Cheltenham*, plus fifty other 'humorous and unique films never before seen in this town', with the whole supported by Willow Pattern Serenades, featuring Toy, Li Chang, San and Chin Chin, the 'mysterious musicians'. Tickets ranged from 6*d* to 3*s*, with special rates for schools.

The Winter Gardens cinema, known as The Kinema, was a permanent fixture right up until the outbreak of the Second World War. (Various sources)

FEBRUARY 3RD

1938: On this day a gruesome catch was made by fishermen Sidney Church, Hubert Dudfield and John Bevan when they pulled a headless corpse from the River Severn in their salmon nets near Haw Bridge in Tewkesbury. It has always been generally believed that the corpse was that of fifty-five-year-old Captain William Butt, who lived in the Old Bath Road, Cheltenham with his invalid wife and her nurse, Irene Sullivan.

The captain had gone missing a few days earlier and it was rumoured that he was having a homosexual affair with twenty-eight-year-old Brian Sullivan, the son of his wife's nurse. Brian earned his living as a gigolo and dancer. Two weeks after the torso was discovered, Sullivan committed suicide by gassing himself at his house in Leckhampton. Police found Butt's car keys and bloodstained coat under the flagstones at Sullivan's house. One theory is that Sullivan had been arranging illegal abortions and, when the affair between Captain Butt and Sullivan had turned sour, the captain had threatened to expose him. Local detectives immediately decided to call in Scotland Yard, plus top forensic scientist Sir Bernard Spilsbury, to lead the investigation. The corpse in the river was never officially identified, but no one else was ever arrested or charged in connection with the case. (Richard Whittington-Egan, *The Great British Torso Mystery*)

FEBRUARY 4TH

1805: On this day the *Gloucester Journal* ran an advertisement on behalf of John Boles Watson, owner of the Theatre Royal in York Place, who was trying to raise money for his new theatre of the same name just across the road in Cambray.

The *Journal* advertisement said that the expense of building was greater than estimated and invited subscribers of £100 each, by instalments, at interest. Watson also promised his investors free admission to the Cheltenham theatre, as well as those he owned in Gloucester and Warwick. Three months later, on 13 May, Watson was again asking for money, this time for subscriptions of 150 guineas at £10 a year interest and free admission for the subscribers for each season of six months. Regular patrons of the Theatre Royal were Earl Fitzhardinge and his two brothers, the Hons Frederick and Augustus Berkeley. Lord Byron, too, was a firm supporter. The theatre was destroyed by fire in 1839. (*Gloucester Journal*)

FEBRUARY 5TH

2011: On this day spooky events took place as part of the Cheltenham Paranormal Festival. Four teams installed themselves in that well-known haunted place, the Playhouse Theatre in Bath Road, in the hope of hearing something go bump in the night or feeling an icy shiver run down their spines.

One of the teams, Forest Paranormal Investigations, hosted the hunt on 3 February and made their presentation on the 5th. FPI is primarily a scientific team, set up to investigate paranormal activity using varied proven techniques and methods. With the aid of modern technology, they strive to prove or disprove the existence of life after life, to explain the unexplained, to dispel myths, to put minds at rest and to offer an unbiased insight into all things paranormal. FPI use all sorts of equipment, including Ouija boards, marbles, crystals and tarot cards, not to mention their Ghost Box, complete with a Ghost Box Speaker Booster. Despite their very best efforts, though, investigations at the Playhouse were sadly inconclusive. (The Playhouse Theatre; www.forestparanormal.co.uk)

FEBRUARY 6TH

1897: On this day the first electric street lights in Cheltenham were switched on. The twenty-nine lamps replaced seventy-five of the old gas standards. Examples of Cheltenham's first electric street lamps can still be seen in the parish churchyard, Crescent Place and Trafalgar Street. The onion and dragon lamp standards were designed by borough engineer Joseph Hall and made of cast iron by McDowall, Stevens & Co. at a cost of £9 15s apiece. The town's first electricity-generating station had opened in Arle Road in 1891, and plans to use electricity to light the streets were made in 1896. On the appointed day, the Lady Mayoress turned on the new lamps along stretches of the High Street, Ambrose Street and Clarence Street.

Since 1818 a private company had provided the town with gas for its street lighting, but relations between the town authorities and the company were poor. After a failed attempt to float a private electric light company in 1888-1889, the Corporation decided to provide electric lighting as a Municipal undertaking. In 1895 a second sub-station was completed in Clarence Street, a building that stands to this day. Electric street lighting soon spread to other areas of the town, so that by about 1910 Great Norwood Street had been supplied. (Various sources, including John Roles, *Cheltenham in Old Picture Postcards*)

FEBRUARY 7TH

1973: On this day, television presenter and journalist Kate Thornton was born in Cheltenham. Best known for presenting *The X Factor* and *Loose Women*, Kate started her career at the *Sunday Mirror* in 1992 as an editorial assistant. She later became a pop music columnist for the *Daily Mirror* and was instrumental in the initial success of pop group Pulp when the paper printed a front-page story headed 'BAN THIS SICK STUNT' alongside a story by Kate Thornton which said the song was 'pro-drugs' and called for the single to be banned.

In 1995 she became the youngest-ever editor of pop magazine *Smash Hits*, and in 1997 until 2001 she became a features editor at the *Sunday Times*. She was also a contributing editor for *Marie Claire* magazine, a position she held until 2003. She presented her first TV show, *Straight Up*, in 1997 and has been regularly on our screens ever since. (Various sources)

FEBRUARY 8TH

1844: On this day a very macabre event occurred concerning the incumbent of the parish church, Revd Francis Close, when a coffin containing the body of a baby boy was delivered to him inside a hamper. The *Cheltenham Examiner* reported the story on 14 February under the heading 'Disgraceful Practical Joking'. Who says the Victorians had no sense of humour?

An inquest was held at the Clarence Hotel and was reported in all the local papers. After viewing the body, the coroner, Mr J. Barrett, opened the inquest. The first witness, a Mr Charles Hillier who worked as a clerk at Cheltenham railway station, confirmed that the basket and address had been received at the railway station off the train which had arrived from Birmingham at 9.10 p.m. on 7 February. It had then been forwarded by omnibus for delivery to the Royal Hotel. The hamper – which had been opened – was later returned to the station and was taken into the taproom, where it remained until Hillier received the coroner's orders for its removal. The coroner was not able to draw any conclusions from the evidence. Needless to say, the story was the source of much intrigue and speculation in the town for several weeks. (John Elliott, CLHS Journal 11)

FEBRUARY 9TH

1853: On this day the *Cheltenham Examiner* reported:

A very narrow escape from a serious accident occurred in the Colonnade [the lower part of the Promenade]. It appears that two flys [a single horse-drawn carriage for public hire, i.e. an early taxi] were passing at a rapid rate, in the direction of Montpellier, while another, conveying some ladies to a concert at the Assembly Rooms was coming, at an equally rapid pace, towards the High Street.

Either from the darkness of the night or the careless conduct of the drivers, the three flys came into a violent collision; the shock being so severe, that the two wheels of each side of the middle fly were struck completely off, leaving the body, to the no small terror of the occupants, unceremoniously deposited in the middle of the road. Fortunately no bones were broken and after a good deal of swearing and grumbling two of them were able to proceed to their destination, and, a fresh fly being procured for the party who had been so unceremoniously unwheeled, they reached the concert room without any further mishap.

(*Cheltenham Examiner*)

FEBRUARY 10TH

1928: On this day actor John Henry Ringham was born in Cheltenham. He was educated at Cheltenham Grammar School, and went on to make over 100 screen appearances in a wide variety of roles. Ringham is perhaps best remembered for his leading role as Norman Warrender in the 1980s sitcom *Just Good Friends*. He appeared throughout the BBC's Shakespeare series *An Age of Kings* in the 1960s, most prominently as Humphrey, Duke of Gloucester, the brother of Henry V. He also appeared in *Dad's Army* playing two different characters – Private Bracewell in the pilot episode and then Captain Bailey in four later episodes. Bracewell was set to become a major recurring character in the show, but this idea was later dropped. Ringham appeared in the long-running show *Doctor Who* three times: first as the bloodthirsty priest Tlotoxl in the story 'The Aztecs' in 1964, then returning in the stories 'The Smugglers' and 'Colony in Space' in 1966 and 1971 respectively. John Ringham died on 20 October 2008, aged eighty. (Obituaries in the *Guardian* and the *Independent*)

FEBRUARY 11TH

1854: On this day the dreadful and sad death of a child occurred. The child's mother, Susan Barnett, was a twenty-six-year-old inmate of the Stow-on-the-Wold Union Workhouse.

Susan had given birth to the child in the workhouse on 7 January. At 11 a.m. on Saturday 11 February, Susan discharged herself from the workhouse, telling staff she was leaving for Cheltenham. At 2 p.m., Hannah Allen saw Susan in her public house, but she was no longer carrying the baby. After she had left the pub, a baby's blue bed gown was found at Hannah's door. Another witness later saw a woman matching Susan's description hiding baby's clothing in a field nearby.

On 27 February, an agricultural labourer who was working in a field near Naunton Brook found the naked body of a baby boy, a hole in each side of its head. The following day, Susan Barnett was tracked down to Cheltenham's High Street where she was arrested for murder. At her trial, the jury believed that the poverty-stricken single mother had simply abandoned her child and that the suspicious injuries had occurred later, whilst the child was in the brook. Susan Barnett was found guilty of manslaughter and sentenced to be transported for twenty years. (www.cotswoldhistory.com)

FEBRUARY 12TH

1904: On this day a Cheltenham murderer was sentenced to death in Gloucester Assizes. Sydney George Smith had killed his common-law wife, twenty-one-year-old Alice Woodman, the year before.

Smith, who was not in regular work, had told friends that he was depressed, and had declared it was his intention to 'do' for himself and the girl. He bought a cut-throat razor and was last seen making his way home with Alice to the cottage they occupied together. The next morning neighbours, fearing the worst, entered the house and found the girl dead with a terrible cut in her throat which, in the opinion of the doctor who attended the scene, had been inflicted while she was asleep. Smith was lying on the floor nearby in a collapsed condition, having tried to kill himself with the same razor. He was arrested and, having recovered from his injuries, was tried and found guilty. He was sentenced to death by Mr Justice Ridley and was hanged on 23 March at Gloucester Gaol. (*Gloucester Chronicle*)

FEBRUARY 13TH

1881: On this day Cheltenham was in the midst of its winter season. The local paper waxed lyrical …

Among the Festive Gaieties which have rendered the present Season so exceptionally gay, and contribute to the prosperity of the town, the Private Parties of Mrs Meyricke and of Miss Lutener have certainly not been the least brilliant – considerably over a hundred of *la crême* of fashionable Society responding to the invitations of the former lady to a Ball at Nubie House and nearly two hundred to those of Miss Lutener to a similar entertainment in the Montpellier Rotunda …

The Rotunda itself being reserved for dancing, had undergone but little change; but the long Promenade Room was divided by a light ornamental partition into a Supper Room at one end and a Conservatory at the other … A pyramidal bank of flowering exotics from the hot-houses of Arle Court, extended down the centre of the room, challenged admiration; while a number of oriental looking lanterns hung suspended above them, lighting up the floral exhibition, which, reflected in a series of mirrors placed against the walls, multiplied in a succession of vistas the novel and pictorial scene.

The fair hostess received her friends on their arrival at the entrance into the Rotunda, in which dancing commenced to the music of Mr Pollock's Quadrille Band shortly before ten o'clock, and thenceforward continued uninterruptedly through the night …

(*Cheltenham Looker-On*)

FEBRUARY 14TH

1853: On this day Her Majesty's Inspector of Schools was in town. The *Cheltenham Examiner* reported that he visited 'the capacious school room in Devonshire Street, putting one hundred and forty-six boys through a variety of mental exercises, and eliciting replies to the most abstruse questions, which might well put the most intelligent spectator to the blush'.

According to the *Examiner*, the Devonshire Street Charity School was certainly a great improvement on its predecessor, where 'Those who a few years ago were venturesome enough to ascend the broken stairs leading to a miserable loft, over one of the porches of the Parish Church, might have found a couple of dozen idle and ignorant boys pretending to learn from a drunken and ignorant master'. (CLHS Journal 8)

FEBRUARY 15TH

1908: On this day sporting history was made at the old Athletic Ground in Albion Street. It was here that the deciding game in the very first international Rugby League tour against New Zealand took place. Despite heavy rain, the game was won by the New Zealand team, known as the All Golds, by eight points to five.

Cheltenham had probably been selected as the venue for this important match because the first-ever All Blacks (the New Zealand Rugby Union team) had played at the ground in the 1905-6 season. It was thought that playing the game here would provide a good showcase for the professional rugby game which was struggling to get a foothold in the South of England. Rugby League had separated from the amateur Rugby Union in 1895, and had become firmly ensconced in Yorkshire and Lancashire.

The Athletic Ground was demolished in 1982 to make way for part of the new ring road, known as St John's Avenue. Most of the site of the pitch is now a housing development; the Cheltenham Tigers RFC team found its new home in the Prince of Wales Stadium in Tommy Taylors Lane. (Various sources)

FEBRUARY 16TH

1876: On this day the *Cheltenham Examiner* reported that in 1871 Gloucestershire had been deemed one of eleven counties that were too lenient. They had been told to 'apply the Workhouse Test' and adhere more strictly to the provisions of the orders and regulations. Five years after the 1871 report, changes at the local workhouse were to be made.

The parish workhouse had been established in the Knapp, where inmates made pins and mops to earn their keep. However, the site was considered inadequate and the new Cheltenham Union Workhouse opened in 1841 on Swindon Road. The workhouse accommodated 220 inmates. Families would be separated and an ill-fitting uniform would be issued. The food supplied to the inmates was calculated to provide basic nourishment, with the menus being dictated by the Local Government Board in London, the body responsible for the administration of workhouses.

At the beginning of February 1876 a group of seventeen inmates at Cheltenham complained about the standard and quantity of food, even though it was probably better than they would have eaten if they had been at home. On 9 February the *Cheltenham Examiner* reported that the cost per head in the workhouse had fallen from 4s 1d to 3s 9½d, with a consequent fall in the Poor Rate. (The Poor Rate was a property tax levied on the parish, which was used to provide relief to the poor.) (CLHS Journal 26)

FEBRUARY 17TH

1919: On this day the *Gloucestershire Echo* reported a tragic accident that had occurred at the Opera House in Regent Street. James John French was cleaning the wall in the Upper Circle when he fell from the wooden steps on which he was standing. Pitching on the front rail of the Dress Circle below, he then turned a somersault and dropped on his stomach on the back of the seats in the stalls. A fellow workman ran to his aid and, picking the unfortunate man up, laid him on the floor – only to find that he was dead. It was thought that the steps had been placed upon the seat and had slipped when the man commenced his work, causing him to fall backwards. It is probable, too, that he suffered his fatal injuries in the fall from the Upper Circle to the Dress Circle, and was dead before he reached the stalls. The total drop was 30ft.

The inquest was held on 19 February. French's daughter gave her father's age as fifty-seven and stated that he enjoyed good health and was not subject to fits, and that he lived at Church Place in Charlton Kings.

James French is buried in the local graveyard with his wife, who died six months after him. She was committed to Gloucester Lunatic Asylum soon after his death, being unable to cope with the loss she had suffered. Her death certificate states that she died of 'exhaustion after 14 days of mania'. (*Gloucestershire Echo*)

FEBRUARY 18TH

1915: On this day, Cheltenham soldier Lieutenant John Kearsley Mather, of the 1st Battalion York & Lancaster Regiment, was killed in action in the Ypres area of Belgium. He has no known grave and is commemorated on the Menin Gate Memorial to the Missing. He was born on 25 January 1890 and the *London Gazette* lists him as being commissioned on 17 September 1909.

Tragically, his two brothers were also killed in action and have no known graves. Private Ellis Mather, of the 17th Battalion King's Liverpool Regiment, was killed in action on 11 July 1916 during the Battle of the Somme. He is commemorated on the Thiepval Memorial to the Missing. The other brother, Second Lieutenant Robert Mather, of the 20th Battalion King's Liverpool Regiment, was killed in action on 27 March 1918 in the Folies area of France. He is listed on the Pozieres Memorial to the Missing. Their parents, Arthur and Madelaine Mather, resided at Oakhurst in Parabola Road, Cheltenham; their three sons are commemorated on their gravestone in Cheltenham Cemetery. The three are also commemorated on the Cheltenham War Memorial and the Christ Church Roll of Honour. (Commemorations in Cheltenham Cemetery)

FEBRUARY 19TH

2010: On this day a woman awoke in the middle of the night to find a burglar in the bedroom of her Cheltenham flat. Amy Gill was surprised, but not reassured, when she recognised the thief as Benjamin Urch, the two having been at school together. When the burglar recognised her too, he made his excuses and left. Gloucester Crown Court heard how Urch attempted to escape from the police and assaulted the arresting officer. Recorder Michael Cullum told Urch:

> It was chance that you burgled the home of someone you knew and who knew you. The aggravating feature of your offence is the flat that you burgled was occupied by a young woman. When she was asleep in her bedroom she woke up to find you two metres away from her. That must have been a terrifying experience for her. It will undoubtedly be an experience that she will never forget … and for what? For you to make a few pounds from stealing relatively low-value items. A further aggravating feature is that you were not alone when you committed this burglary. After you had left the flat your colleague emerged from the lounge.

Urch was sentenced and jailed for nineteen months, despite entering a not guilty plea. (*Gloucestershire Echo*)

February 20th

1831: On this day, *Bell's Weekly Messenger* announced the inauguration of Sir Goldsworthy Gurney's steam carriages, which ran between Cheltenham and Gloucester.

The first carriage left the commissioners' yard about 12 o'clock, and was propelled several hours through the principal streets and roads in and about Cheltenham, apparently to divide, as much as possible, the people, and at the same time to gratify their curiosity.

The carriage is elegant and light in appearance, and constructed to carry or draw, or both. On the steam-carriage were ten persons, and in the vehicle attached to it eight more. It continued running through the streets and Montpellier drives until three o'clock, when it returned to the commissioners' yard. The crowd by this time was divided, and after taking in water and coke, the carriage immediately started for Gloucester; it made the distance, 9 miles in 48 minutes; the motion was steady and uniform, the rate scarcely varying perceptibly the whole distance.

After taking in a fresh supply of water and coke at Gloucester, it returned again to Cheltenham, accompanied by several private carriages and gentlemen on horseback. The carriage was regulated, stopped, and turned, with most extraordinary facility, and although it would have been difficult to have driven quiet horses safely under similar circumstances, it is most satisfactory to observe that not the slightest accident occurred during the day.

(*Bell's Weekly Messenger*)

FEBRUARY 21ST

2011: On this day – the start of National Chip Week – the fire brigade in Cheltenham was keen to point out the dangers of kitchen fires. Over the previous six months there had been 175 accidental house fires in Gloucestershire and the most common cause was cooking. The Cheltenham fire brigade issued some helpful tips on staying safe:

> It's important to keep the oven, hob and grill clean and in good working order because a build-up of fat and grease can start a fire. Take care when cooking with oil – if it starts to smoke, it's too hot, so just turn off the heat and leave to cool. Don't cook if you have been drinking alcohol.

Gloucestershire Fire & Rescue Service carried out over 3,770 home fire safety checks last year. This involved a short visit to identify fire hazards and highlight how a fire may occur, and if necessary fit smoke detectors or test existing detectors. (Gloucestershire Fire & Rescue Service)

FEBRUARY 22ND

1941: On this day an unusual double wedding was reported in the local paper. The weddings took place at St Lawrence's Church, Swindon Village, when two sisters named Cooke married two brothers named Cook. The girls were Miss Molly F. Cooke and Miss Lilian Letitia (known as Peggy) Cooke, the daughters of Mr and Mrs Sidney F. Cooke, of South Bank, Alstone. The girls married respectively Mr Alfred Herbert Cook and Mr Reginald Albert Cook, the two sons of the late Mr and Mrs Albert Herbert Cook, of Swindon Gardens. The ceremony was conducted by Revd W.H. Hanna and the girls were given away by their proud father.

The same week, a guard of honour was formed by thirteen lovely ladies of the Auxiliary Territorial Service, or ATS, outside the parish church when their comrade, volunteer Alvira Esther McConnell, daughter of Mr and Mrs R.G. McConnell of No. 15 St Paul's Street North, married Lance-Bombardier Richard Lloyd Tomkins of the Royal Artillery, whose home was in Wrexham. (*Cheltenham Chronicle and Gloucestershire Graphic*)

February 23rd

1842: On this day, Test cricketer James Lillywhite was born. He was the first-ever captain of the English cricket team in a Test match, captaining two Tests against Australia in 1876-77. He later became an umpire.

In 1872 he created the Cheltenham Cricket Festival at the college playing field, with Gloucestershire winning the first match against Surrey. At the time, Lillywhite was the cricket administrator and coach at the college. He was originally from Westhampnett in Sussex, the son of a bricklayer, and had come to work at Cheltenham College when he was thirty years old. He and his family lived in Montpellier, above a shop immediately opposite Brasserie Blanc, an area known as Queens Circus. The family occupied the upper floors of the building while Lillywhite ran a sports shop on the ground floor. He also created the periodical *Cricketers' Companion*, in competition to Wisden.

Cheltenham Cricket Festival is the longest-running cricket festival in the world to take place at a non-permanent ground. (Various sources, including Rowbotham & Waller, *Cheltenham: A History*)

FEBRUARY 24TH

2011: On this day a virulent sickness bug forced the Cheltenham General Hospital to shut its doors to visitors. None of the site's twenty-plus wards allowed patients' friends or family members to visit in any but the most exceptional circumstances. The quarantine was put in place in an attempt to stop the spread of the infamous norovirus bug, which causes severe vomiting and diarrhoea.

One woman complained to the hospital after her seventy-six-year-old diabetic husband was placed in an isolation room which she described as being 'no better than an extension to the gents' urinal. It was tucked away in a corner where no one could see him unless they called in for any reason'. The woman said her husband spent thirty-six hours in the isolation room after contracting the bug. (*Gloucestershire Echo*)

FEBRUARY 25TH

1786: On this day the *Gloucester Journal* recorded the latest episode in a long-running dispute concerning the building of the Assembly Rooms and other developments in Cheltenham's High Street.

The proposed new rooms had caused a bitter dispute between William Miller – one of the main promoters of eighteenth-century Cheltenham and the lessee of the Spa – and Thomas Hughes. Hughes had arrived in Cheltenham from South Wales in 1749 and became articled for five years to local solicitor John de la Bere. After marrying into a wealthy family, he bought a large amount of land on the south side of the High Street and decided to build the Assembly Rooms to replace an old ballroom which had stood on the corner of Rodney Road.

Despite objections, many ancient buildings, like the Corn Market, the Butter Cross and an old building that served as a prison, were demolished; the development went ahead and Hughes opened his Assembly Rooms in 1783. The rooms outshone any other public building in town and were, for 100 years, the focal point of Cheltenham society, being visited by the Duke of Wellington, Jane Austen and Lord Byron, among many others. (*Gloucester Journal*)

FEBRUARY 26TH

1851: On this day William Macready, the greatest classical actor of his day, gave his final performance at the Drury Lane Theatre in London.

Upon his retirement in 1860, Macready moved to Cheltenham and bought a house in Wellington Square. He remained active, giving frequent readings and lectures in the town. Charles Dickens was a close friend and made numerous visits to the house. Macready had made his acting debut playing Romeo in Birmingham in a theatre managed by his father. After the death of Edmund Kean in 1833, Macready became the undisputed leading actor of his time. Macready was not only an actor but also an important theatre manager, having run both the Covent Garden and Drury Lane theatres in London. He died at his house on 27 April 1873. Alfred, Lord Tennyson wrote the following poem in tribute:

> Farewell, Macready, since to-night we part:
> Full-handed thunders often have contest
> Thy power well used to move the public breast.
> We thank thee with one voice, and from the heart.
> Farewell, Macready, since this night we part …

Sir Neville Macready, the actor's son, unveiled a commemorative plaque on the house in March 1927. (CLHS Journal 24)

FEBRUARY 27TH

1915: On this day, the Leckhampton V.A. Hospital (known as Glos. 42) opened to treat the wounded returning from the front of the First World War. The 600-year-old building was very kindly lent to the Red Cross for the purpose by Major Elwes, while he was on overseas service with the Gloucestershire Yeomanry. The hospital was ready for patients by 1 November 1914, though it was not used until the following February. The hospital had 100 beds and, by the time it closed in March 1919, had treated 1,579 wounded soldiers, of whom only two had died. Its commandant was Mrs Ward, MBE.

The situation of the hospital, its glorious views and gardens, its exhilarating air, and homely old-world atmosphere, were particularly successful in all cases of shell-shock and gas-poisoning, while the out-of-door shelters were the means of complete cure in many cases of chest trouble. The average length of stay for each patient was between six weeks and two months.

During the Second World War, Leckhampton Court was a camp for British, American and German (POW) soldiers. The house is now a much-respected Sue Ryder Hospice. (*The Red Cross in Gloucestershire 1914-19*)

FEBRUARY 28TH

1942: On this day Brian Jones, founder of the Rolling Stones, was born in Park Nursing Home in Cheltenham. He spent the early part of his life in a house in Eldorado Road, until his parents moved to Hatherley. Jones, christened Lewis Brian Hopkin Jones, was a pupil at Dean Close School from September 1949 to July 1953, and attended Cheltenham Grammar School from September 1953. The Grammar School at this time was situated in the High Street, on the site of the current Wilkinson store.

Even at an early age Jones was a talented musician who was obsessed with black American music. The most popular music in England around 1960/61 was traditional jazz and Jones played in several bands in Cheltenham led by trumpeter John Keen. Jones had played banjo but switched to guitar. After attending a concert by the Chris Barber Jazz Band at the Town Hall in 1961, Jones went backstage with his friend John Keen to meet Alexis Korner, who had been guesting with the band. Jones moved to London soon after and re-established contact with Korner, who introduced him to Mick Jagger and Keith Richards. The rest, as they say, is history.

Brian Jones drowned in his swimming pool on 3 July 1969. He is buried in Cheltenham Cemetery. (Various sources)

MARCH 1ST

1959: On this day, eminent and influential photographer Hugo van Wadenoyen died in Cheltenham. Although he was born in Holland in 1892, he lived and worked in Cheltenham, having his studio at No. 98 Promenade in what is now part of the Municipal Offices. Van Wadenoyen was a prominent photographer in the years immediately after the Second World War, pioneering the establishment of photography as an art form. He had been elected a member of the Royal Photographic Society in 1918 and went on to become a Founder Fellow of the Institute of British Photographers.

Van Wadenoyen wrote a number of books on photographic techniques, published by the Focal Press. His 1947 book *Wayside Snapshots* was significant in establishing a break from purely pictorial imagery, and portraying the work of individual photographers. He was also the leader of the Combined Societies, an association of photographic societies based in Hereford, Bristol and Wolverhampton. In 1945 the group split from the Royal Photographic Society, which it considered to be out of touch and on the decline. A blue plaque to commemorate Hugo van Wadenoyen was unveiled in 1998 on the site of his studio in the Promenade. (Various sources, including Smith & Rowbotham, *Commemorative Plaques of Cheltenham*)

MARCH 2ND

1852: On this day the *Cheltenham Examiner* recounted the sad story of how a fourteen-year-old local boy, Henry Martin, had been forced to commit a crime through hunger. He was arrested and tried at the Cheltenham Police Court, where he was dealt with rather severely.

The unsympathetic *Examiner* reported how 'a youth on his travels in search of adventure, but who, we shrewdly suspect, is destined one fine morning to travel further and fare worse', was charged with stealing a leg of mutton from the shop of Thomas Hastings, butcher, of St Paul's Street North. The youth evinced his contrition with an abundance of crocodile tears, and said he was 'werry sorry but he was werry hungry'. The Bench sentenced the prisoner to one month's wholesome discipline at Northleach, including a whipping. (*Cheltenham Examiner*)

MARCH 3RD

1796: On this day, at the Court Baron, the following case was heard before Steward Thomas Markham:

> John Jones and his wife Mary, with the consent of Samuel Harward of Cheltenham [a] stationer who had lately contracted for the purchase of the following premises, surrenders for Wakeman Long of Upton-on-Severn, Worcs., gent, a new dwelling house (no. 5) at Colonnade Buildings on the S side of Cheltenham Street, having other new houses of Samuel Harward N and S, the Colonnade street E, and premises of Samuel Harward (lately purchased by him from John Hayward deceased) W, and commencing 128 ft from the corner house of Colonnade Buildings; also right of access. Provided that if Harward pays Long £500 with 5% interest on 3 Sept. next, in accordance with a bond in the penal sum of £1,000, the premises are to be re-surrendered. Heriot 1s., rent 5d.

(James Hodsdon (ed.), *The Court Books of the Manor of Cheltenham 1692–1803*)

MARCH 4TH

1890: On this day the Forth Bridge opened. Its chief designer was Benjamin Baker, who lived at 4 Cambray Place in Cheltenham, a site now occupied by the trendy ivy-covered Tailors bar. The Forth Bridge was one of the wonders of the modern world. It had taken eight years to build, used 54,000 tons on steel and, on its completion, was the biggest bridge in the world.

Benjamin Baker had been born in Frome in Somerset in 1840, but was educated at Cheltenham Grammar School. At the age of sixteen, Baker was articled to Messrs Price & Fox at the Neath Abbey Ironworks on the south coast of Wales, where he stayed until 1860. During his long and distinguished career he designed not only the Forth Bridge but also London's first underground railway line, and the container that brought Cleopatra's Needle to London, as well as being the consulting engineer for the Hudson River Tunnel in New York. He was knighted in 1902 for his work on the Aswan Dam in Egypt and died in Pangbourne, Berkshire on 19 May 1907. In 1922 one of the houses at the old Grammar School was named after him, and remained so until 1971. (Smith & Rowbotham, *Commemorative Plaques of Cheltenham*)

MARCH 5TH

1932: On this day it was reported that the Prince of Wales, the future Edward VIII, Duke of Windsor, had visited the races at Prestbury Park on the previous Wednesday. The Prince was photographed leaning on the railings of the weighing room, chatting, cigarette in hand, to his private secretary, Mr R. Hobbs. Hobbs was also an amateur jockey, and on the day that the Prince visited he rode Belhector, a horse owned by Colonel H.E. Joicey. The horse did not win, but the following day Hobbs rode Chadds Ford, the winner of the Foxhunter Chase Challenge Cup.

On Monday that week, the Duchess of Beaufort was also in town. She opened an exhibition of work by village craftsmen at Cavendish House in the Promenade. The exhibition was designed to promote the work of the Rural Industries Bureau and showed pieces from all over the county. (*Cheltenham Chronicle and Gloucestershire Graphic*)

MARCH 6TH

1933: On this day Cheltenham's smartest cinema opened. The Gaumont Palace in Winchcombe Street was a classic 1930s art deco picture house, the façade resembling an ocean liner with its distinctive fin-like vertical sign. The cinema was built on the site of an old chapel and, apparently, many people refused to visit the venue when it opened for this reason. Despite this, the opening night saw a full house of 1,774 for the film *Rome Express*. The audience was also treated to a recital on the magnificent Compton organ that rose ceremoniously from the orchestra pit. The cinema later dropped Palace from its name and became The Gaumont.

The Gaumont became the Odeon in 1962 and in the 1990s its interior was all but destroyed when it was converted into a multi-screen. The former Screen 7 was said to be haunted. Strange noises were often heard by staff when locking up late at night and seats were also said to move by themselves. The Odeon finally closed on 5 November 2006, soon after the opening of a brand new, high-tech multiplex just down the road, and has stood alone and abandoned ever since. (Various sources)

MARCH 7TH

1865: On this day the Davenport brothers, famous for demonstrating strange and inexplicable 'manifestations', appeared at the Town Hall, which was then in Regent Street.

The matinee was not well attended but in the evening a much larger audience was present at the entertainment, if such it may be called, ensuring that it was exceedingly uproarious. The principal – and indeed almost the only – trick was that of the brothers releasing themselves, when enclosed in their cabinet, from the cords with which they had apparently been securely bound to a chair. They claimed it was spiritual intervention. At the morning show the untying process was accomplished in four or five minutes – but at night their mysterious familiars occupied nearly half an hour in effecting their release, during which prolonged period the patience of the audience became severely tried and the vocal uproar grew well-nigh ungovernable. In fact, not one of the tricks deserved to be placed in the same category as the tricks of Herr Dobler, so recently exhibited in the Assembly Rooms. The American brothers completely cheated their audiences and extracted more half-crowns from the pockets of their victims than any honest conjuror could possibly succeed in doing for so worthless an exhibition. Cheltenham magician John Nevil Maskelyne subsequently built his reputation by exposing the fraudulent Davenports at the same venue a couple of months later. (*Cheltenham Looker-On*)

MARCH 8TH

1865: On this day the competitive plans and drawings for four new boarding houses, which were proposed to be erected for the accommodation of Cheltenham College pupils, were exhibited in the large schoolroom of the Modern Department and were shown again the following Saturday in the same room of the college. There were over twenty sets of designs – several of which were especially noteworthy, combined with considerable artistic skill in the execution of the drawings. The names of the authors of these works were withheld, each set bearing its own distinctive motto, so it was impossible for the mere looker-on to conjecture from whence any of the drawings came. However, the experienced professional eye would, doubtlessly, readily detect the workmanship of some of the town's resident architects, to one of whom the Committee of Selection might feel it their duty to award the first prize, so that Cheltenham could enjoy the credit of at once originating and perfecting the design. (*Cheltenham Looker-On*)

MARCH 9TH

1957: On this day Bill Haley and His Comets hit the stage of the Gaumont cinema (later the Odeon) in Winchcombe Street and things would never be the same again. Fears of the cinema being ripped to pieces by teddy boys incited by this 'devil's music' proved to be unfounded.

Bill Haley, with his famous Brylcreemed kiss curl, is often credited with being the father of rock 'n' roll. His first big hit was 'Shake, Rattle and Roll', which went on to sell 1 million copies worldwide and in December 1954 became the first ever rock 'n' roll song to enter British singles charts. But it is perhaps for the seminal 'Rock Around the Clock' that Haley is best remembered. The song had been written a couple of years earlier and its first release had been a flop. It only became a worldwide hit after it was played over the opening credits of the landmark 1955 film, *Blackboard Jungle*.

Bill Haley was soon eclipsed by the younger, sexier, and more talented Elvis Presley – but Bill Haley was the first, and nobody will ever be able to take that away. He died of a brain tumour on 9 February 1981 aged fifty-five. (Various sources)

MARCH 10TH

1971: On this day the programme for the Everyman Theatre announced the arrival of a new artistic director. The chairman of the Board of Directors, Edward Bradby, made the following introduction:

> Malcolm Farquhar has in recent months been busy in the West End, having directed successful productions of Somerset Maugham's *Lady Frederick* and Julian Slade's adaptation of *Winnie the Pooh*. Earlier in his career he spent two years as Resident Director of the Connaught Theatre, Worthing, and he has also directed at the Alexandra Theatre, Birmingham and the Leatherhead Theatre.
>
> Malcolm Farquhar will be joining us at a time when the new salary-scales recently adopted by national agreement offer a new challenge: by remedying some of the worst deficiencies of the grossly underpaid theatrical profession the new scales will, I am sure, help to raise standards in the long run; in the short run, however, they confront Repertory Theatres with heavy additional expenditure at a time when it is difficult enough to keep pace with rising costs, and there will be need for much cool-headed and careful planning in the coming months.
>
> At this juncture, Malcolm Farquhar's theatrical expertise, wide connections, and boundless enthusiasm will be priceless assets, and the Board looks forward with great confidence to his first season, which will start when the theatre reopens after the summer recess, on 29th June.

(Everyman Theatre programme)

MARCH 11TH

1865: On this day the *Cheltenham Looker-On* announced a forthcoming week of unmissable entertainment in the town:

> A novel entertainment, judging from the published advertisements, is to be produced next week at the Assembly Rooms, Optical Science being rendered subservient to amusement by the introduction of a variety of Spectral Illusions in illustration of phenomena hitherto unelucidated, but which their exhibition in combination with scenic representations and musical accompaniments cannot fail to prove alike entertaining and instructive.

And, if you didn't fancy that ...

> Amateur theatricals are announced to take the place of professional performances at the Old Wells Theatre on Monday evening next, on which occasion Captain Gem, Captain Hudson, Percy Du Cane, Esq. and several other gentlemen connected with the Comedy Club, have selected for representation *A Wonderful Woman*, *Whitebait at Greenwich* and *The Illustrious Stranger*, the part of Crepen in the first-named play being undertaken by Mr Shenton. On Tuesday and following days, Miss Lillie Lonsdale's Company continue their regular performances, including the Burlesque of *Eily O'Connor*, the representation of which has proved very successful during the past week.

(*Cheltenham Looker-On*)

MARCH 12TH

1924: On this day the Cheltenham Gold Cup was first run as a jumps race with a prize of £685. The first Gold Cup took place on Cleeve Hill in July 1819 as a 3-mile flat race. The winner, a horse called Spectre, won the prize of 100 guineas.

The Gold Cup did not take place in 1931 (because of frost) and 1937 (because of flooding), but the five intervening years saw the emergence of the most successful horse in the event's history. All five races from 1932 to 1936 were won by Golden Miller, who also won the Grand National in 1934.

In the mid-1960s the race was dominated by Arkle, who won three consecutive races starting in 1964. Such was Arkle's dominance of the race that in 1966 he commanded odds of an unprecedented 1/10, i.e. a £10 bet would have won £1. He remains the shortest-priced winner in the race's history. The 1990 winner, *Norton's Coin*, became the race's longest-priced winner at 100/1.

The most remarkable feat in the Gold Cup by a trainer came in 1983, when Michael Dickinson was responsible for all of the first five horses to finish – Bregawn, Captain John, Wayward Lad, Silver Buck and Ashley House. (Various sources)

MARCH 13TH

1920: On this day the *Cheltenham Looker-On* published a story about the success of a man and his organ:

> The Coliseum has been besieged this week and if ever a public entertainer deserved the fortune it may be assumed that he is making, it is Mr G.R. Pattman F.R.C.O. for his cleverness in realising the possibility of organ playing as a popular diversion.
>
> There are certainly half a dozen organists in Cheltenham who, in respect of technique and musicianship could hold their own with Pattman. But the local organists might play on their local organs for ever and a day without creating queues a quarter of a mile long and certainly without arousing the enthusiasm that Pattman has done this week. The difference between Pattman and the others seems to rest in the fact that he has revitalised the personality of the organist ... Instead of secreting himself behind a dingy baize curtain in a dim religious light, Pattman brings his console ... right into the limelight, and operates it there in full view of his public ... Pattman further deserves all his success because he has studied his public as assiduously as his organ.

(*Cheltenham Looker-On*)

MARCH 14TH

2008: On this day it was reported that an Irish punter who had gambled with counterfeit euros at Cheltenham's Gold Cup meeting had been banned from betting in England for a year.

Gloucester Crown Court heard that compulsive gambler Patrick Kiely had arrived at the Prestbury Park racecourse for the first day of the four-day festival. He had almost €5,000 in fake notes on him, which he claimed he had bought from a man called Gerry in Ireland for €1,000.

Unemployed Kiely, forty-four, from County Cork, had used two fake €50 notes for two bets on the first race. After one of the bets was a winner, Kiely had returned with his winning ticket but, by then, the police and the bookie's colleagues had been informed. He pleaded guilty to two counts of counterfeiting the day after he was arrested. Lloyd Jenkins, defending, said the offence had been 'clearly out of character' as Kiely had no previous convictions. He added, 'He accepts full culpability.'

Kiely was banned from attending any race meeting, entering any bookies, or placing a bet on any sporting event for a year. He also received a four-month jail term, suspended for one year after he admitted attempting to pass counterfeit currency. (*Gloucestershire Echo*)

MARCH 15TH

1881: On this day Cheltenham's Grand Annual Steeplechase meeting opened at the new racecourse at Southam. The full card for the first day included the Selling Steeplechase, the Selling Hurdle Stakes, the Prince of Wales's Steeplechase (Handicap), the Prestbury Hurdle Race, the West of England Hunters' Flat Race Plate, the Licensed Victuallers' Steeplechase (Handicap), and the Cotswold Hunt Cup Steeplechase. The second day's list of races was no less impressive and included the Selling Hurdle Race, the Selling Handicap Steeplechase, the Cotswold Cup, the Selling Hunters' Flat Race, the Grand Annual Steeplechase (Handicap), the Hewletts Handicap Hurdle Race, and the Scramble Handicap Steeplechase, the day drawing to its end with the United Hunters' Steeplechase. (*Cheltenham Looker-On*)

MARCH 16TH

1901: On this day an advertisement appeared on the front page of the *Graphic* extolling the virtues of the Royal Cheltenham Sausage. This fine delicacy, it was claimed, was supplied to Her Late Majesty Queen Victoria and cost 8*d* per lb, although she probably got hers for free. However, the sausage manufacturer clearly felt that some additional endorsement was needed, so they published a Certificate of Analysis from Granville H. Sharpe, F.C.S. &c:

> I hereby certify that I have submitted to a careful chemical microscopical analysis, specimens of the Royal Cheltenham Sausages, manufactured by Messrs F. Beckingsale & Son, Cheltenham and I find them to be of superior composition and quality and to have been skilfully and judiciously prepared from the best materials only. They are delicate and appetising in flavour, and the result of my investigations prove them to have been made from meat of the primest quality only, the inferior and indigestible portions having been carefully eliminated. I can speak with confidence as to their wholesome, digestive and dietetic properties.

(*Cheltenham Chronicle and Gloucestershire Graphic*)

MARCH 17TH

1846: On this day plans were approved for the new 'Blue Coat' school in Cheltenham, which was to be known as Devonshire Street School. Thomas Haines of Winchcombe Street was given the task of building the new school and the foundation stone was laid on 24 June 1847. The ceremony was attended by our old friend Revd Francis Close, with the pupils, 'about forty in number, being decorated with blue sashes and bouquets of flowers and bearing several flags'.

Earlier that day Revd Close had conducted a service in the parish church, based on the text from the Book of Daniel: 'Many shall run to and fro and knowledge shall be increased.' This sermon was printed and copies were sold to raise funds for the new school. The appeal had already raised £300 and a further £150 was added by the government, which left about £200 still to be found. On 22 November 1847, the trustees formally took possession of the school. With the new premises, a new headmaster was deemed necessary. The incumbent, the seventy-nine-year-old Mr John Garn, was said to be 'incompetent through age', and his son William took over. (CLHS Journal 22)

MARCH 18TH

2007: On this day, Cheltenham comedian Terry Saunders made a hometown appearance, bringing his show *Stories of a Lovelorn Idiot* from the Edinburgh Festival. Saunders took on the character of a fifteen-year-old who communicates the loneliness of love through lyrics by his favourite band, Pulp. He appeared on stage in PVC trousers, a fishnet T-shirt and black eye make-up.

Saunders – Edinburgh fringe stalwart, storyteller, animator, broadcaster, writer, sports pundit and website creator – has won Best Show, Breakthrough Act and the Innovation in Comedy award. *Time Out* called him one of the top ten comedians in the UK. As an animator he's made the hugely popular YouTube series *Six and a Half Loves* and also a new version of *Missed Connections* for BBC Comedy online. As a storyteller, his shows *Missed Connections*, *Pulp Boy*, *Figure 8* and *Six and a Half Loves* have straddled the fringe guides between comedy and theatre. He's had his own Radio 4 show (*Dad Designs*, starring Kevin McCloud), written for the Now Show, and has been a bit of a sports pundit, giving his expert analysis on BBC Radio 5 Live. (*Gloucestershire Echo*; Terry Saunders' website)

MARCH 19TH

1873: On this day an intriguing advertisement appeared in the pages of the *Cheltenham Examiner*. It read:

> The attention of Ladies is drawn to the wonderful efficacy of KEARSLEY'S WIDOW WELCH'S FEMALE PILLS, which have been proved by thousands annually for many years past to be the most effectual remedy for that complaint to which females are liable; Headache, Giddiness, Nervous Depression, Pallor of the Lips and general disability of the system, often accompanied by Palpitation of the Heart. The most obstinate cases (of apparently confirmed invalids) have yielded to a course of these pills. Sold by all Chemists in boxes at 2/9d. Wrapped in WHITE paper. Be sure to ask for KEARSLEY'S as sometimes a spurious article is offered.

There were no testimonials as to its effectiveness, but no one was reported to have died, which is almost a testimonial in itself. For that price, which was the equivalent of 10 per cent of a teacher's weekly wages, it would need to be efficacious, and you could understand why someone thought it worthwhile to come up with a bootleg version. *Plus ça change.* (CLHS Journal 11)

MARCH 20TH

1788: On this day Captain Thomas Medwin was born. The captain was a second cousin and biographer of Percy Bysshe Shelley, and a close friend of Lord Byron.

In June 1812 Medwin served with the 24th Light Dragoons, joining his regiment at Uttar Pradesh in northern India soon after. In September 1820 he went to Geneva and finished his first published poem, *Oswald and Edwin, An Oriental Sketch*. He joined Shelley in Pisa in the autumn of 1820, moving in with him and his wife Mary Shelley, creator of *Frankenstein*.

Following his army service in India Medwin had suffered ill health, and in the summer of 1823 he visited Cheltenham to take the waters for 'attacks of liver'. He stayed at Stiles Hotel in the High Street. The hotel, later known as Yearsley's, was on the site of the old Grammar School and was demolished in 1887 to make way for the school's new Victorian incarnation.

Thomas Medwin died on 2 August 1869, at the house of his brother Pilford in Horsham in West Sussex. (Various sources)

MARCH 21ST

1831: On this day Dorothea Beale, the influential principal of Cheltenham Ladies' College and founder of St Hilda's College, Oxford, was born in London.

She was appointed headmistress of Casterton School in 1856. At about this time, Miss Beale started writing her *Textbook of General History*. The book was considered so significant within the teaching profession that it was no doubt a factor in her being appointed as headteacher of Cheltenham Ladies' College in 1858. Until Miss Beale's arrival the college was not highly regarded, but under her leadership it became one of the most prestigious and important private girls' schools in the country, a position it still holds today. Her emphasis was on academic achievement rather than on music, drawing and other ladylike accomplishments that were the usual subjects of a girl's education at the time.

Miss Beale wrote several books about education, including *Work and Play in Girls' Schools* (1898). She was also an active supporter of the suffragette movement, and in 1865 was one of the co-founders of the Kensington Society, a discussion group that became the London Society for Women's Suffrage. She remained head of Cheltenham Ladies' College until her death on 9 November 1906. She was cremated in Birmingham, but her remains are interred at Gloucester Cathedral. (Various sources, including Elizabeth Raikes, *Dorothea Beale of Cheltenham*)

MARCH 22ND

1775: On this day Jane Cook – a wealthy, well known, but largely forgotten Cheltenham eccentric – was born. Her father was a successful builder who, upon his death, left his daughter (known as Jenny) an extremely rich woman with an annual income of £30,000 – equivalent to about £1.5 million today. Despite her wealth she chose to draw only £300 per year from her income.

Jenny was a good friend of Revd Francis Close, a staunch evangelical Anglican and a keen supporter of many Christian causes both in England and abroad. The Revd Charles Simeon presented her with a twenty-one-volume set of sermon outlines, *Horae Homileticae*, which she later donated to the Bishop's Library in Jerusalem. She worked tirelessly all her life to distribute the Bible and support the poor.

She died on 11 February 1851 in her lodgings at No. 1 Belle View Buildings in the High Street, with one obituary referring to her 'eccentric and penurious life'. During her life she had given away most of her fortune, with the remaining £120,000 being left to various good causes upon her death. She was finally remembered in October 1999 when one of the new halls of residence at the Cheltenham & Gloucester College of Higher Education was named after her. (Alan Munden, CLHS Journal 17)

MARCH 23RD

1879: On this day the first meeting of the Cheltenham Corps of the Salvation Army took place at the new site of the Colosseum.

The Salvation Army had been set up by William Booth in 1865 with the intention of helping the poor and destitute. The main problem the Army had in Cheltenham was finding suitable premises in which to hold their meetings. A conventional church was out of the question as the people whom they were trying to help would not come. They finally built their headquarters, St Peter's, in what was then the poorest part of town. Situated in and around the old gasworks at the beginning of the Tewkesbury Road, the area was known as Lower Dockem. St Peter's was so unpopular that it was soon abandoned and a new location was sought. The Army eventually rented the Theatre Royal at the Old Well on Sundays and the North Ward Hall for week nights. They later used the Colosseum in Bath Road, which backed on to Wellington Street right next to the River Chelt. The Salvation Army meeting place has been on that site ever since. (Various sources)

MARCH 24TH

1556: On this day John Coberley, a tailor from Cheltenham, was burned at the stake as a heretic, becoming one of the group known as the Salisbury Martyrs.

Coberley, sometimes known as William, had been inspired by William Tyndale's translation of the Bible. Tyndale had himself been burned at the stake in 1536. Coberley followed Tyndale's Protestant reformist principles and was arrested along with two Wiltshire men, John Maundrell and John Spicer, for speaking out against the parish church in Keevil and its support for the Pope. They were imprisoned in Salisbury but refused to repent, claiming that 'wooden images were good to roast a shoulder of mutton but evil within the church'. They were executed on 24 March, with Coberley taking a particularly long time to die.

On 17 April 1556, an entry in the Manor Roll for Cheltenham states that John Coberley's land in Westal 'was lately attained and burnt for divers heresies and false opinions … whereby he forfeited his lands to the Lady of the Manor, the Queen'. In fact the land was not forfeited and stayed with Coberley's wife Alice, who had recanted and later married a Robert Ible. (Rowbotham & Waller, *Cheltenham: A History*)

MARCH 25TH

1942: On this day Richard O'Brien was born in Cheltenham. Born Richard Timothy Smith, he is best known as the writer of cult musical *The Rocky Horror Show*.

In 1951, O'Brien and his family emigrated to New Zealand, where his father had bought a sheep farm. He returned to England in 1964 and launched his career as an actor. The horse-riding skills he had acquired on the farm led to one of his very early film roles as a stuntman in *Carry On Cowboy* in 1965.

O'Brien took some method-acting classes and worked in several stage shows as an actor. In 1970 he joined the touring production of *Hair* for nine months, followed by a further nine months in the West End. In 1972 director Jim Sharman cast him as an apostle and leper in the London production of *Jesus Christ Superstar*.

The Rocky Horror Show first opened at the Royal Court's Theatre Upstairs in June 1973. Within weeks it had become the cult show to see in London. O'Brien became the presenter of Channel 4's popular game show *The Crystal Maze* in 1990 and still works on a variety of projects. (Various sources)

MARCH 26TH

1986: On this day the Everyman Theatre reopened after being closed for three years. The closure had been the result of the development of the Regent Arcade, which saw the entire backstage area of the theatre completely demolished and a new one built. When the theatre reopened it was a completely different place. Although the auditorium had remained more or less the same, the front of house had been spoiled. The new, ugly, concrete staircase, more suitable for a football stadium, left the foyer cramped and unattractive. The new façade, however, was a vast improvement on the old-fashioned straight lines, glass and gaudy colours of the '60s. A facsimile of the original brickwork had been reinstated on the first floor and an attractive, Victorian-style, wrought-iron canopy installed along the width of the building. Of the old backstage area nothing remained. It was now all new, clean and efficient. There were spacious offices, dressing rooms with showers, a flying system that did not need three men to operate it, a workshop that did not involve leaving the building to access it, and a stage-door keeper to keep an eye on everything. Gone were the cramped spaces, dusty corners, inadequate facilities and creaky equipment. But gone too was the patina of nearly 100 years. (Michael Hasted, *A Theatre for All Seasons*)

MARCH 27TH

2011: On this day a highly decorated Cheltenham war hero, who kept his cool in Korea despite losing a foot in a landmine explosion, died at the age of eighty-four.

Major Colin Carr, who was born in the town and attended Cheltenham College, was famous for once taking eight wickets in nine balls for the cricket second XI. He served with the 28th Field Engineer Regiment (RE) and was responsible for clearing landmines. In May 1952, after lifting part of an existing minefield, four of his men were wounded by incoming shells. The following day, Major Carr located and neutralised all the remaining enemy mines and, that night, supervised the laying of 300 new mines. On the morning of 13 May he stepped on a mine that had been displaced and buried by shellfire. He lost one foot and his other leg was broken. Despite the great pain, he shouted instructions to his wireless operator. While being carried to the regimental aid post, he gave an accurate account of how the accident had happened and provided the information necessary to complete the mine-clearing task. He was consequently awarded an immediate Military Cross. (*Gloucestershire Echo*)

MARCH 28TH

1930: On this day the first meeting of the Bugatti Owners' Club was held. The club was established in 1929, not only for owners of Bugatti cars but for all those interested in the increasingly popular activity of motor sport. The club purchased land in the Bredon Hills between Gretton and Gotherington, and in 1937 converted a steep, rough track into a smooth, winding racetrack. On Sunday 10 April 1938 the BOC Spring Rally was held in Cheltenham; 130 members and guests converged in the town. After lunching at the Queens Hotel, they drove in convoy to Prescott, led by a Type 18 Bugatti driven by Colonel Godfrey Giles. Lord Howe, the club president, opened proceedings by driving his Type 57 Bugatti up the hill. Ian Craig was fastest in the competition that day, driving his five-litre 'Bachelier' Bugatti over the finishing line in 55.58 seconds. Many famous drivers competed at Prescott or began their careers there, including Stirling Moss.

The Prescott course is 1,127 yards long and rises over 200ft up the wooded hillside through various straights and corners, and a breathtaking hairpin. The fastest modern racing cars currently complete the course in an exciting 36 seconds. There are regular meetings throughout the year. (Various sources, including www.bugatti.co.uk)

MARCH 29TH

1962: On this day a splendid fundraising event for the Cheltenham Literature Festival was held at the Pittville Pump Room. The event, called Victoriana, was organised by Sonia and Tom Rolt. Tom was the L.T.C. Rolt of canal and railway fame, an early champion of our industrial heritage.

Victoriana was described as 'a nineteenth century evocation in sound and vision'. The Pump Room, with its circular dome, is always a difficult space in which to mount any performance, but the Rolts were undeterred. The event, which we would now call multimedia, was very progressive indeed for the early '60s. As the lights dimmed the roar of a jet engine could be heard, which quickly segued into the evocative sound of a genuine old barrel organ. The gallery then transformed itself into a ship taking emigrants to the New World, with ropes being thrown overboard to splash onto the stage below. A girl in Victorian costume then performed as Fanny Burney, along with a boy dressed as a street urchin, against back projections of Victorian life. The event was a great success and was soon followed by *A Scrapbook of the Regency* and *The Elizabethans*, presented at the Everyman Theatre. (Nicola Bennett, *Speaking Volumes*)

March 30th

1808: On this day the first stone of the New Market House was laid in the High Street. The building backed onto St Mary's churchyard, on a site now occupied by Robert Dyas. The Old Market House had been on the next block east, on the corner of Church Street.

Cheltenham had first acquired the right to hold a weekly market during the reign of Henry III in 1226. The first permanent market building is thought to have been built around 1421. In 1610 it seems that this building was also used to store armour and weapons for the local constable. In 1614 Norden's Survey mentioned that there were '... two market houses that standeth in the streets'. It is believed that one was where the armour was kept and the other was Booth Hall, sometimes referred to as Butter Cross.

When Lord Sherborne opened a new market further along the High Street in 1821, the old market became redundant. The building was used by a banker until the late 1820s, after which it became a solicitor's office, with the public offices and magistrates' court upstairs. It became Cheltenham's first Municipal Offices in 1876, and from 1915 until 1960 it was Woolworths. (Caroline Greet, CLHS Journal 24)

March 31st

1961: On this day, 'You're Driving Me Crazy' by the Temperance Seven was at Number 1 in the UK Hit Parade. The band included Martin Fry (from Cheltenham) and Mac White, who was originally from Cirencester, but who hung out in the 1950s with the rest of the jazz crowd at No. 38 Priory Street in Cheltenham. With two local boys in the band, it was quite a big event when the Temperance Seven played the Town Hall for the first time on 30 May 1961.

In pre-Beatles days British pop was dominated by traditional jazz, with bands regularly playing at the Town Hall; as often as not, they would finish up at the impromptu and informal jazz club situated in the basement of the Filby household in Priory Street.

A second concert by the Temperance Seven filled the Cheltenham Town Hall on 7 March 1963. During the interval, Jane Filby and other friends were invited into their dressing room for refreshments. 'Temperance Seven' cigars were handed round to all males present and smoking of the pleasant weed was promptly indulged in. Later that evening, Jane and her mother put on a buffet supper and plenty to drink. Three floors of No. 38 Priory Street were packed with the band, their entourage, supporters and a few neighbours. (John B. Appleby, *38 Priory Street and all that Jazz*, courtesy of Jane Filby-Johnson)

APRIL 1st

1849: On this day the foundation stone of St Paul's College was laid by the Earl of Shaftesbury. The college occupied a 5-acre site in Swindon Road which had been donated by Miss Jane Cook. The architect was Samuel Whitfield Daukes, who had also designed Lansdown railway station, St Peter's Church and Royal Agricultural College.

The teacher-training college had been established by Revd Francis Close in 1847. At first, seven male students were taught in rented rooms and the following year they were joined by twelve women. The building of Francis Close Hall, which housed the male part of the student population, was built in mock-Tudor style. The college was only the sixth Anglican training establishment for elementary schoolteachers in the country. Francis Close Hall now forms part of the University of Gloucestershire. (Various sources)

1974: On this day, under the Local Government Act 1972, the existing borough of Cheltenham was merged with Charlton Kings urban district to form the modern non-metropolitan district of Cheltenham. Four parishes – Swindon, Up Hatherley, Leckhampton and Prestbury – were added to the borough of Cheltenham from the borough of Tewkesbury in 1991. (Cheltenham Borough Council)

APRIL 2ND

2005: On this day a plaque was unveiled to mark the site of H.H. Martyn's Sunningend factory on the corner of the High Street and College Road.

H.H. Martyn, originally a firm of monumental masons, is probably Cheltenham's single most important business. In 1908 the company moved to a 5-acre site next to the railway between Gloucester Road and Rowanfield Road. Inside the grim buildings you would have had difficulty believing that you had not been transported back to Renaissance Italy, such was the sheer quality and breathtaking variety of monumental art that was produced there.

The company undertook commissions to decorate ships (including the *Titanic*), made the Speaker's Chair and the Despatch Boxes for the House of Commons, made the bronze figure of Ariel that perches atop the Bank of England, and made the wood panelling for Court No.1 at the Old Bailey. They produced decorative items for trains, palaces, cathedrals, churches, stately homes and public buildings. Due to the company's incredible versatility and reputation for highly skilled light engineering in various materials, by the early years of the First World War Martyn's was receiving government contracts to build aircraft wings and fuselages. The enterprise was so successful that in 1917 Martyn's formed the Gloster Aircraft Co. Ltd. The Second World War led to its most spectacular development – that of the jet engine. (Various sources, including Smith & Rowbotham, *Commemorative Plaques of Cheltenham*)

APRIL 3RD

2011: On this day work was underway to demolish Cheltenham's fire station in Keynsham Road. The work was part of a £40 million project to improve the fire and rescue service in the county. A temporary station was set up in Kingsditch Lane to accommodate Cheltenham's fire engines until work was completed.

The Keynsham Road station had opened in January 1960. Built on a new site, it replaced the old fire station that had stood in Lansdown Road next to the police headquarters. This fire station was largely a collection of wooden huts, and a block of flats now stands on the site. The town's original fire station opened in St James' Square in 1906. That building has survived more or less intact.

The Cheltenham fire station is responsible for 25,228 hectares and has sixty junior officers and firemen. The station has three pumping appliances, a hydraulic platform, a rescue appliance and a salvage tender, as well as a number of ancillary vehicles.

Although the fire station was at the forefront of the struggle to deal with the dreadful floods in 2007, it was inundated itself when the River Chelt, which runs alongside the Keynsham Road site, burst its banks. (Various sources, including *Gloucestershire Echo*)

APRIL 4TH

2008: On this day a memorial was finally unveiled to commemorate Gustav Holst, who was perhaps Cheltenham's greatest son.

Holst died in 1934 and to Cheltenham's shame it was only with this statue that any sort of memorial was erected to him. The statue, a fountain with the figure of Holst conducting on a plinth in its centre, stands in Imperial Gardens just behind the Town Hall, where Holst conducted *The Planets* in 1927.

The bequest of £45,000, which made the monument possible, came from Miss Elizabeth Hamond, who left a generous legacy to the Cheltenham Civic Society to be used to benefit the town. The Civic Society decided that this would be used for a full-size bronze statue of Gustav Holst, with seven plaques depicting the planets incorporated in the plinth. The statue's sculptor was Anthony Stones, who has completed numerous prestigious public commissions both in Britain and abroad. The figure of Holst and the plaques were cast by the Pangolin Foundry in Chalford. The monument was unveiled by Mark Elder, Music Director of the Hallé Orchestra. (Various sources, including *Gloucestershire Echo*)

APRIL 5TH

1984: On this day one of the most important and controversial figures of the Second World War died eight days before his ninety-second birthday, at his home in Goring, near Henley. Sir Arthur Travers Harris, Marshal of the Royal Air Force, was born at No. 3 Queen's Parade, Cheltenham in 1892, where his parents were staying while his father was on home leave from the Indian Civil Service.

Known as 'Bomber' Harris to the public but as 'Butcher' to other members of the RAF, he commanded RAF Bomber Command during the Second World War and was responsible for the Allies' so-called 'blanket' bombing policy which flattened a number of German cities with a devastating loss of civilian life. So controversial was the man that in 1992 the Queen Mother was booed by protestors when she unveiled his statue outside the RAF church, St Clement Danes, in the Strand in London.

Bomber Harris has been portrayed in many films and television plays – most notably by John Thaw in a 1989 TV film based on his life, with old Cheltenham College boy Robert Hardy playing Churchill. (Various sources, including Dudley Saward, *'Bomber' Harris*)

APRIL 6TH

1910: On this day the opening of the Albert Hall in North Street was celebrated. The hall was originally run by Lawrence Glen Barber and presented 'matinee musicale and tête-à-tête tea'. Music was supplied by Horace Teague, who was also the musical director at the Opera House.

The hall was designed to be multi-purpose, presenting concerts, plays, music hall and new-fangled moving pictures. The first play staged there was *The Importance of Being Earnest*, which opened the second week. The show was a fundraiser for the Charlton Kings crèche.

The Albert Hall was not a great success and was soon taken over by Gillsmith who owned the Hippodrome (later called the Coliseum). The building was renamed the Royal Cinema de Luxe and reopened on 12 April 1911. It changed its name again and became the Theatre of Varieties de Luxe from September that year. Although mainly a cinema, it did put on concerts and other musical events. In the 1930s it became a theatre for three or four years with no great success, and finished up as a garage. The building was demolished in 1988. (Roger Beacham, CLHS Journal 19)

APRIL 7TH

1941: On this day an event shrouded in secrecy took place at the old Brockworth airfield near Gloucester. The Gloster E28/39, also known as the Gloster-Whittle Pioneer, Britain's first jet aircraft, arrived for its first tests.

The aircraft had been built by the Gloster Aircraft Co., which was an off-shoot of the Cheltenham company H.H. Martyn. The engine, designed by Frank Whittle, had been developed in Cheltenham at Regent Motors, a garage on the site where the Regent Arcade now stands. Later, tests were carried out at the Crabtree Garage in Carlton Street.

The E28/39 name comes from the aircraft having been built to the twenty-eighth 'experimental' specifications. The plane's specification had actually required it to carry two .303 Browning machine guns in each wing, but these were never fitted. The experience gained with the experimental E28/39 paved the way for Britain's first operational jet fighter aircraft, the Gloster Meteor. (Various sources, including Frank Whittle, *Jet: The Story of a Pioneer*)

APRIL 8TH

1811: On this day, metallurgist Robert Forester Mushet was born in Coleford in the Forest of Dean. He died in Cheltenham on 29 January 1891 and is buried alongside his wife and daughter in Cheltenham Cemetery. He was apparently not christened with the name Forester, but adopted it in the mid-1840s as a tribute to his place of birth.

Robert learned the business of iron and steel-making at the ironworks his father David had built in the Forest of Dean in 1818. Robert took over the business in 1845 but three years later he moved to a new foundry nearby called the Forest Steel Works. He worked there for the next decade, experimenting with thousands of new techniques and processes. He opened another new foundry, the Titanic Steelworks, in 1862. During this time he developed a cost-effective method of making high-quality steel and invented the first steel alloy that could be produced commercially. He was awarded the highest accolade of the iron and steel industry, the Bessemer Gold Medal, in 1876.

Perhaps Mushet's most far reaching and influential invention was that of steel rails for the railway in 1857. Until then, railway tracks had been made from cast iron which, due to their brittle nature, often had to be replaced every six months. Mushet's rails proved much more durable, lasting years rather than months, and were an important factor in the worldwide development of the railways in the mid-nineteenth century. (Various sources)

APRIL 9TH

1945: On this day a new theatre opened in Cheltenham. The Civic Playhouse in Bath Road was built in a converted swimming pool, with the council providing not only the money for the conversation but also funds for a consultant producer and a resident stage manager. The costs of the productions themselves were to be borne by the individual societies. The only amateur dramatic society that survives from those days is Cheltenham Little Theatre.

With scenery borrowed from the old Winter Gardens theatre that used to stand in Imperial Square, the new theatre mounted its first production. The play was *Arms and the Man*, and the cast consisted of members of several local amateur dramatic societies. The play's author, George Bernard Shaw, even sent a postcard to congratulate those concerned. It read:

> Three cheers for leisured Cheltenham!!! It has trumped the Civic Playhouse of industrial Bradford. May the example of the twain be followed all over the British land.

Other congratulations were received from Sir Ralph Richardson, who at the time was working with Laurence Olivier in Tyrone Guthrie's production of the same Shaw play at London's Old Vic. The thriving theatre is now known simply as the Playhouse. (Various sources)

APRIL 10TH

1912: On this day the *Titanic* set sail for New York on its fateful maiden voyage. One of its passengers was Mr Francis William Somerton from Cheltenham. The ship hit an iceberg and sank five days later and, on 22 April, the *Gloucestershire Echo* ran a story about the disaster:

ALL HOPE OF THE SAFETY of Mr Francis William Somerton, the young Cheltenham engineer, has been abandoned. Mr Somerton, who was only thirty years of age, was a native of this town, and the eldest son of Mr and Mrs Somerton of *Petersham*, Gloucester Road.

He was educated at Christ Church schools and afterwards went through a course to train as an engineer at Whitehead's Torpedo School, near Weymouth. About eleven years ago he went to America and obtained a good appointment at Canastota, New York State. Last December he returned home and brought his young American wife with him … For a short time he was at work in Rugby, but those works were closed down through the coal strike, so he accepted a good offer from the American firm by whom he was formerly employed, and was on his way to take up his duties again in Canastota when the *Titanic* was wrecked and he lost his life.

(*Gloucestershire Echo*)

APRIL 11TH

1931: On this day the Coliseum Theatre in Albion Street closed its doors for the last time as a live theatre. The final plays performed on that Saturday were Noel Coward's *Hay Fever* and *I'll Leave it to You*. The house orchestra was dismissed and the builders moved in. Apart from the installation of the screen and the sound system, only minor alterations were made before the building reopened as a cinema on the following Monday, showing the 1930 musical *Hit the Deck*. Directed by Luther Reed and starring Jack Oakie, the film featured Technicolor sequences and was one of the most expensive productions of RKO Radio Pictures at that time, and one of the most expensive in Hollywood that year. *Hit the Deck* is also considered a lost film. The last known copy was destroyed in a fire at the RKO studios in 1950.

However, there was to be one more live theatre production at the Coliseum, when an amateur dramatic society put on two plays at the end of April: *Sport of Kings* and Agatha Christie's *Alibi*. The Coliseum was demolished in July 2011. (Various sources, including CLHS Journal 23)

April 12th

1945: On this day the long-established Cheltenham firm of F.C. Dodwell & Sons issued the following instruction to members of staff in anticipation of the end of the war in Europe:

> The day the announcement of the cessation of Hostilities is issued, all shops will immediately close. As far as can be ascertained NEWSPAPERS WILL BE ISSUED AS USUAL ON VICTORY HOLIDAY, i.e. the day AFTER the announcement that hostilities may be considered to have ended in Europe. Your shop therefore will be open for the sale of newspapers and close at 11 a.m or when all dailies are sold whichever is the earlier. I leave it to the manageress to decide what staff they shall detail for this work. Signed by Leslie Dodwell

F.C. Dodwell & Sons, or Dodwell's, as it was universally known, was one of the most prominent and well-known shops in town. It had been established in 1883 as a wholesale and retail newsagents, booksellers and stationers. It operated its wholesale newspaper business from No. 333 High Street (later renumbered 252). The High Street shop finally closed in 1983 but a shop bearing the family name continued to trade in Bath Road. (Elaine Heasman, *Images of Cheltenham*)

APRIL 13TH

1949: On this day the idea of creating a Cheltenham Festival of Literature was first mooted. A year earlier the council had set up Cheltenham Arts Festivals Ltd, charged with the 'promotion and encouragement of the Arts and in particular the Cheltenham Annual Festival and to organise, manage and conduct the Festival to include music, drama and such other forms of entertainment'. This approach very much mirrored that of the Edinburgh Festival, which had been created the previous year.

The first official mention of the off-shoot literature festival in Cheltenham was in the minutes of the Town Improvements & Spa Committee, dated 13 April 1949. It reported that speakers would include Compton MacKenzie and C. Day Lewis, both of whom had connections to the town. MacKenzie's family had been involved in the ill-fated attempt to create a repertory theatre in the old Winter Gardens, and C. Day Lewis had been a master at Cheltenham College.

The total cost of mounting the festival was estimated at £300 and the committee felt that this would be 'recompensed by admission charges'. Therefore, with no financial liabilities attached to the scheme, the report was approved and what is now generally considered to be the foremost literature festival in the world got underway. (Nicola Bennett, *Speaking Volumes*)

APRIL 14TH

2000: On this day a commemorative blue plaque was unveiled on Summerfield House in Bayshill Road in memory of a modern-day Cheltenham eccentric and benefactor, Ronald Summerfield. Summerfield had, for many years, run what appeared to be a junk shop on the corner of Montpellier Spa Road and Montpellier Avenue. But when he died in 1989, his collection and stock of antiques sold at a three-day auction which raised £9 million.

Summerfield had come to Cheltenham as a young man in the 1930s, by which time he was already an avid collector and sold pieces from his father's greengrocer's shop. He was known as an eccentric recluse who would often refuse to sell items to customers if he didn't like the look of them. The shop and his house in Bayshill Road became full to overflowing, and to make space and raise money he would often sell items through Charles Fortescue at Christie's Fine Art, who had offices in the Promenade. It was Charles who realised that Summerfield's collection was worth a fortune and, with solicitor Martin Davies, he persuaded him to establish a trust so that after his death his wealth could be used to help worthy causes.

The Summerfield Trust is one of the most important charities of its type in the area, giving to a wide variety of artistic or cultural causes. (Various sources, including Smith & Rowbotham, *Commemorative Plaques of Cheltenham*)

APRIL 15TH

1960: On this day Lillah McCarthy died. Although now largely a forgotten figure, in her day she was one of the most famous and influential actresses in the country.

Lillah was born in September 1875 in the High Street, in a house next to the old Plough Hotel where her father was manager. The site is now a Burger King. She made her first public appearance at the Assembly Rooms and later met Frank Benson, when his company played the Opera House. After hearing her recite, he advised her father to send her to London to train as an actress.

George Bernard Shaw was to take an interest in Lillah's career as well. After seeing her perform, he wrote, 'It is an actress's profession to be extraordinary but Lillah was extraordinary even among actresses.' In 1900 Lillah appeared at the Cheltenham Opera House with the Wilson Barrett Co. She returned three years later, this time with her brother Daniel in the company. In 1905 Shaw asked Miss McCarthy to create the role of Ann Whitefield in his new play *Man and Superman*. This was to be the start of a long association with the Irish playwright and she went on to create five more of his heroines. Lillah married one of the great actor-managers of the day, Harley Granville Barker. (Michael Hasted, *A Theatre for All Seasons*)

APRIL 16TH

1881: On this day the *Cheltenham Looker-On* reviewed a concert given the previous week by the Musical Society. The event, which was:

> ... in furtherance of the movement to found a Scholarship in memory of the late Henry Smart, though supported by nearly all the amateur and professional talent of Cheltenham, was not equally so by the public; that in the afternoon being very sparsely attended, and that in the evening by no means overcrowded. ... The performances deserved better audiences, for they were throughout highly meritorious, the vocal portions principally consisting of Smart's compositions, being rendered on both occasions very effectively, and the instrumental, by local artistes who had volunteered their services, with the most complete success. Notably so the pianoforte solos of Mr von Holst and Ricardo Linter, and a Pianoforte and Harmonium Duet by the latter and Mr Matthews, which were certainly the musical gems of the programme, as the audiences testified by the heartiness of their applause. The *Toy Symphony* in the evening afforded the audience much amusement, and, all things considered, was very cleverly performed. The best songs of the evening were Smart's *Lady of the Lea* and Randegger's *Sleep, Dearest Sleep*, which Miss Bertha Griffiths sang charmingly and were deservedly encored. Mrs Daubeny's *Over London Bridge*, said to be a composition of her own, was also a decided success and was warmly applauded.

(*Cheltenham Looker-On*)

April 17th

2001: On this day the three-day Cheltenham Festival, which had been postponed due to an outbreak of foot and mouth disease, finally got underway.

The meeting had been postponed the previous Wednesday when it was discovered that the course could not meet British Horseracing Board guidelines governing racing during the foot-and-mouth crisis. The new dates meant that the festival would not clash with the Punchestown Festival, should the Irish authorities allow it to go ahead. However, it did coincide with the prestigious Craven meeting at Newmarket. Cheltenham Racecourse managing director Edward Gillespie said at the time:

> We at Cheltenham are only too conscious of the continuing foot-and-mouth crisis and the effect this is having on so many of our customers. However, there is a balance to be struck. We are convinced that we can safely conduct a successful race meeting and that, so long as racing continues and the racecourse remains outside an infected area, then we should make every effort to hold the meeting. We have therefore set dates so that the preparation of the horses and all the arrangements for the meeting can resume.

(*Telegraph*)

APRIL 18TH

1867: On this day one of the most important and influential eighteenth-century British architects died in Cheltenham. Sir Robert Smirke was born in London in 1781, and in 1796 he began his studies at the Royal Academy where he won many awards. From 1801 to 1805 he embarked on the Grand Tour, where he studied architecture in southern Europe.

Smirke's first official commission came in 1807 when he was made architect to the Royal Mint. He was elected an Associate of the Royal Academy in 1808, and made a full Royal Academician in 1811. His important public buildings were numerous and include Covent Garden Opera House, the British Museum, the General Post Office in St Martin's Lane and Lancaster House. Locally he built the County Halls in Gloucester and Hereford, the judge's lodgings in Gloucester, parts of Cirencester Park, and the Gothic Eastnor Castle.

He moved to Cheltenham on his retirement and set up home at No. 1 Italian Villas, now Lansdown Court. He later moved to No. 20 Suffolk Square, at which address he died. He had two brothers, Thomas and Sir Edward, both of whom are commemorated in Leckhampton Church. (Various sources)

APRIL 19TH

1957: On this day the racehorse Arkle was born. Considered by many as the greatest steeplechaser in the history of the sport, many of his greatest triumphs were at Cheltenham.

His first victory at Prestbury was in the Broadway Chase. However, it was in the 1964 Cheltenham Gold Cup that Arkle truly established himself, beating the 1963 winner Mill House by five lengths to claim his first victory in the event. The following year Arkle beat Mill House again, this time by twenty lengths. In the 1966 Gold Cup he was the shortest-priced favourite in history to win the race. Despite his dominance, the horse would often make mistakes going over the jumps. He had a strange habit of crossing his forelegs when jumping a fence. Nevertheless, he went through the season 1965/66 unbeaten in five races. Arkle won twenty-seven of his thirty-five starts. Besides winning three consecutive Cheltenham Gold Cups and the 1965 King George VI Chase, Arkle also won the 1964 Irish Grand National, the 1964 and 1965 Hennessy Gold Cups, and many more races in his short career.

In December 1966 Arkle seriously injured himself going over the open ditch in the King George VI Chase at Kempton Park. After four months in plaster he made a good enough recovery to start training, but he never raced again. He became critically ill and was put down on 31 May 1970. There is a bronze statue of Arkle in the paddock of Cheltenham Racecourse. (Various sources, including Ivor Herbert, *Arkle*)

APRIL 20TH

1877: On this day the splendid new organ at All Saints' Church was dedicated. The original organ in the church, which had been installed a year after the church was built in 1868, was unreliable and a new one had to be found. The replacement organ came from a private house at Dowdeswell and was installed by local organ builder Henry Williams at a cost of £300. The dedication took place at choral evensong and the sermon was preached by Sir Fred Gore, Warden of St Michael's College, Tenbury Wells in Worcestershire and Professor of Music at Oxford University.

This organ was replaced again after the arrival of a new vicar, Revd George Gardner, in 1886. He was an accomplished musician himself and felt that the old two-manual organ did not meet his needs. His new, grand, three-manual organ was unveiled a year later. That organ survives to this day and, on 28 June 1987, the resident organist, Adrian Self, gave a concert to mark its centenary.

The organist at the church from its opening until his retirement in 1895 was Adolph von Holst, father of composer Gustav Holst, who was baptised in the church. (Various sources)

April 21st

1906: On this day a job opportunity arose when the Cheltenham Union Workhouse placed an advertisement in the paper seeking a Public Vaccinator for the District of Cheltenham.

> The Guardians of the Poor of the Cheltenham Union are prepared to receive applications from Medical Gentlemen possessing the necessary qualification as defined by the Orders of the Local Government Board, to perform the duties of Public Vaccinator for the No. 1 Registration District of this Union, comprising the Parish of Cheltenham as it existed prior to the recent extension of the Borough Boundaries.
>
> The remuneration will be by Fees, which are now estimated to amount to about £130 per annum. The person appointed will be required to enter into a Contract with regard to the Office. The appointment will be made subject to the approval of the Local Government Board, and will be held subject to all provisions contained in the Vaccination Acts and the Orders of the Local Government Board for the time being in force relating to Public Vaccinators.
>
> Applications, together with Diplomas, to be sent to me, the undersigned, on or before Wednesday, the 2nd day of May next, endorsed 'Application for Appointment of Public Vaccinator'. – By Order, J. Meek, Clerk to the Guardians.

(*Cheltenham Looker-On*)

APRIL 22ND

1822: On this day a French general who had been the source of a major scandal in Cheltenham drowned at sea.

In May 1812 the *Cheltenham Chronicle* had reported the disgraceful events, 'aggravated by every circumstance that could enhance its baseness' that had recently affected the town. The story concerned a well-respected French officer, General Charles Lefebvre-Desnouettes, usually referred to as General Lefebvre.

Lefebvre had risen from humble beginnings to become a distinguished officer and one of Napoleon's favourites. He was captured at Benavente and brought to Cheltenham as a prisoner of war at the request of Sir John Moore. He was placed, along with two others, under open arrest, having sworn never to venture more than 3 miles from the town. The word of an officer and a gentleman, even a French one, was considered security enough.

Lefebvre's family had been allowed to join him from Paris in 1811. On 2 May 1812 the disguised general and his entourage had left Cheltenham on the post-chaise bound for London, from where they drove to Dover where a boat was waiting to take them to Calais.

There was dismay in Cheltenham. A search party was organised, a reward offered and warrants issues. The scandal reverberated around the town for weeks with conversations always returning to the subject – conversations in which the phrase 'I told you so' probably figured quite prominently. (*Cheltenham Chronicle*; CLHS Journal 22)

APRIL 23RD

1924: On this day, American architect Bertram Grosvenor Goodhue died aged fifty-four. Among his many achievements – and the only one that really concerns us – was the design of the Cheltenham typeface in 1896.

Goodhue became involved in the Arts and Crafts Movement early in his career. In 1902 his font design was purchased by the American Type Founders. Influential type designer Morris Fuller Benton refined the typeface, developing a large variety of condensed and expanded widths for its release. Cheltenham was among the first typefaces to be released as a type 'family'.

Cheltenham enjoyed massive success in the early 1900s and, by 1915, Benton had cut twenty-one variations, leading the typeface to become one of the most widely known in America. It was a favourite among newspapers, and was notably adopted as a headline typeface for the *New York Times* around 1906. For nearly a century, the *New York Times* used Cheltenham in conjunction with at least five other typefaces for front-page headlines. The variety was common for newspapers in the early twentieth century because of the cost of stocking full ranges of metal type within a family. That changed in 2003 when *The Times* settled on a single family, replacing the varied typefaces with roman, italic, and various weights of Cheltenham. (Various sources)

APRIL 24TH

1931: On this day one of the most famous former students of Cheltenham Ladies' College was born. Bridget Riley was one of the most influential artists of her time, almost single-handedly creating a whole new art genre. OpArt was developed during the 1960s when Riley began to paint the black-and-white geometric, optically confusing, works for which she is known. The paintings presented a great variety of geometric forms that produced sensations of movement or colour. In the early 1960s, her works were said to induce sensations in viewers as varied as seasickness and skydiving.

Bridget became an artist of international repute. In 1965 she exhibited in the Museum of Modern Art in New York, which first drew worldwide attention to her work and the OpArt movement. Her painting *Current*, 1964, was reproduced on the cover of the show's catalogue. She later became disillusioned with OpArt because her work was exploited for commercial purposes.

Bridget began working in colour in 1967, the year in which she produced her first stripe painting. She represented Great Britain in the Venice Biennale in 1968 and was the first British contemporary painter, and the first woman, to be awarded the prestigious International Painting Prize. (Various sources)

APRIL 25TH

1871: On this day the Cheltenham Photographic Society made an excursion to Woodchester Park at Nympsfield, near Stroud, to take some pictures. An ideal venue for a photographic expedition, the tranquil wooded valley contains the remains of an eighteenth and nineteenth-century landscape park, with a chain of five lakes.

The society had been co-founded by Edward T. Wilson, father of the Antarctic explorer Dr Edward A. Wilson. When he died in 1918 his obituary stated that 'No man has done so much as he to stimulate and promote the intellectual life of the town of Cheltenham'. Wilson had been a very early exponent of photography, the first pictures having been taken only eight years before he was born. There is a nice photograph of Dr Wilson with his camera and tripod at the Cheltenham Museum. The society, although very popular, did not hold its first exhibition in the town until 1896.

The *Cheltenham Examiner* reported that during the trip to Woodchester, 'some very good pictures were secured in spite of a rather cloudy day'. (CLHS Journal 24)

APRIL 26TH

2011: On this day it was reported that Government Communications Headquarters in Cheltenham had intercepted a large amount of so-called 'chatter' relating to the Royal Wedding between Prince William and Kate Middleton, which was to take place on 29 April. National newspapers claim that security chiefs at the government's listening post in Benhall, who were monitoring electronic traffic, heard the words 'a ceremony' and 'infidels in the big church', and other such inflammatory and provocative words or phrases.

All groups which applied to protest were told by the police that they were likely to be refused permission unless they agreed to postpone demonstrations until later in the day. Sixty people who had been charged with public order offences were banned from the city of Westminster on the day as part of their bail conditions. A spokesman for GCHQ refused to comment, saying that they 'would not comment on speculation regarding our operations.'

More than 5,000 police were deployed on the day of the wedding, with 900 of them lining the route between Westminster Abbey and Buckingham Palace. Helicopters of the Air Support Unit, equipped with thermograph, infrared and video cameras, scoured the crowds before and during the event. (*Gloucestershire Echo*)

APRIL 27TH

2012: On this day, Deputy Prime Minister Nick Clegg visited Spirax Sarco's UK manufacturing site at Runnings Road in Cheltenham.

Spirax Sarco, one of Cheltenham's foremost companies, was established in London in 1888 as an importer of thermostatic steam traps from Germany. The company has recently invested £25 million to improve manufacturing facilities and to expand into a 5-acre site that is linked by an under-road tunnel to its other unit. The company is an acknowledged world leader in the design and manufacture of control valves and other components for steam heating systems and process plants. The other branch of the business, Watson-Marlow, is known for peristaltic and niche pumps.

Sarco is an acronym from the original company name, Sanders, Rehders & Co. They started manufacturing their own products under the trade name Spirax in 1931 and the company was listed on the London Stock Exchange in 1959.

Over the years the Spirax Sarco Group has grown, operating in thirty-four countries with seven large manufacturing plants. In 2010 they completed a new, self-contained plant in Shanghai, China. The company, whose headquarters are at Charlton House in Charlton Kings, announced revenues of £630 million in 2011. (Various sources, including *Gloucestershire Echo*)

APRIL 28TH

1572: On this day William Panton, curate of the parish church, recorded in his register the first mention of Cheltenham Grammar School, with the entry 'the first stone of the schoole howse was laide'.

The Grammar School was founded by Richard Pate, who was a nephew of the Bishop of Worcester. An alumnus of Corpus Christi College, Oxford, he endowed that institution with property, on the condition that they use some of the money to found and maintain a school in Cheltenham. This school was officially founded in 1574 and occupied the same site on the High Street until the mid-1960s, when it moved to Hesters Way. It later merged with Pate's Girls' Grammar School and is now known as Pate's Grammar School. The original High Street building was replaced in the 1890s by a splendid Victorian Gothic building, which was demolished in the late 1960s to make way for Tesco and Wilkinson.

Richard Pate died in 1588 and is buried in Gloucester Cathedral. On his tomb is inscribed *Patebit tum quod latuit*, meaning 'what is hidden will be revealed'. This is also the motto of Pate's Grammar School and the Old Patesians Rugby Football Club. He also has a primary school named after him, the Richard Pate School. (Various sources)

APRIL 29TH

2001: On this day the UK census was held. It established the population of Cheltenham as 110,013 souls, which represents 0.188 per cent of the UK population as a whole. The area of the town is 4,661 hectares, so the population density is 23.6 people per hectare. The most densely populated area of the town is All Saints, with a density of 68.86, and those with the most space live in Battledown, with only 6.58 people per hectare.

The population of the town has risen quickly over the years. Cheltenham began as a Saxon village, and at the time of the Domesday Book in 1086 it was small, with a population of less than 200. However, Cheltenham became a focal point for the surrounding villages. By the seventeenth century it had grown, with a population of about 1,500. The town expanded considerably after discovery of the spa waters and the visit of King George III in 1788. Between 1700 and 1800 its population rose from 1,500 to over 3,000, and by 1850 it was the largest town in Gloucestershire with a population of more than 35,000. In 1901 the population of Cheltenham stood at 49,000, and by 1971 there had been an amazing increase of nearly 50 per cent, bringing it to 74,000. (Cheltenham Borough Council)

APRIL 30TH

1981: On this day a cryptic advertisement appeared in *The Stage*. It had been placed there by Rae Hammond, who was the general manager of the Everyman Theatre and was announcing his resignation.

The advert did not give any reason but, the fact is, there had been a dispute over his salary, and Hammond believed that after all his years of service he was being treated very badly. He had been general manager for fourteen years and had provided the backbone to the theatre during the reign of three artistic directors.

Rae Hammond was an interesting man. In 1946 he had joined the Combined Services Entertainment and spent the next couple of years constantly touring the Far East, first of all with a variety unit and then in revues where fellow artists included Peter Nichols, Stanley Baxter, Kenneth Williams, John Schlesinger and Reg Varney. The company was the inspiration for the hit 1970s television sitcom *It Ain't Half Hot Mum*, and the magician character in Peter Nichols' play *Privates on Parade*, which won the 1977 Laurence Olivier Award for Best New Comedy, was based on Hammond.

Rae Hammond died at his home in Cheltenham of a stroke in 1995, alone but not forgotten. (Michael Hasted, *A Theatre for All Seasons*)

MAY 1ST

1925: On this day a new motor bus service was introduced in Cheltenham. It ran hourly from 10 a.m. until 6 p.m. between the Promenade and Sandy Lane.

This complemented the existing service, which had been introduced at the end of 1923 after successful trials between the then new St Mark's estate and Cemetery Road. This route, using three single-deck Guy motor buses with solid rubber tyres, linked Harp Hill and the Promenade with Lansdown station via Montpellier. The service operated hourly to noon and then half-hourly, alternating Lansdown Road with Tivoli. The first departure from St Mark's was at 8.07 a.m., but by the end of the day it seems there was a great rush to get the buses back to their depot by nightfall. Because of this there were numerous complaints, with passengers claiming that the clock-watching drivers had unloaded them at Lansdown soon after 6 p.m. rather than taking them to the end of the line at the Tennyson Road terminus.

A fourth bus was added in 1924, differing from the other three by having entrances at both the rear and front. (Appleby & Lloyd, *Cheltenham's Trams and Buses 1890-1963*)

MAY 2ND

1860: On this day a Grand Flower Show was held in Pittville Park. Flower shows had played a large part in the social life of nineteenth-century Cheltenham for many years, with the various spas competing for bigger and better public attractions. With their show, Pittville Park sought to outshine their great rivals at Montpellier. In order to do this they enlisted some unlikely support – the army.

To make sure they had enormous crowds, the organising committee sent out free invitations to all the Volunteer Corps. They also obtained the services of the band of the 11th Hussars for the occasion. In order to bring visitors into the town, special excursion trains were laid on from as far afield as Birmingham, Bristol and South Wales.

The 10th (Cotswold) Rifle Volunteer Corps, whose headquarters was in Cheltenham, was responsible for most of the arrangements for the parade. At 11 a.m. a Guard of Honour from the 10th Corps paraded at the Midland station, together with the Corps band, to meet the various contingents. They then all marched to St James' station to meet some more. With all the trains unloaded there were nearly 600 soldiers, and they marched to the Promenade where they assembled near Queens Hotel and from there on to Pittville. Some flower show. (Mick Kippin, CLHS Journal 20)

MAY 3RD

1839: On this day disaster struck when the Theatre Royal, Cheltenham's only full-time and dedicated theatre, in what is now Bath Street in Cambray, was completely destroyed by fire. The cause of the fire is unknown but its effects were devastating. In those days, of course, theatres were lit by candles and oil lamps, and what with all the drapes and bits of flimsy scenery, most theatres were accidents waiting to happen. In fact, between 1802 and 1896, 137 theatres in Great Britain were destroyed by fire with a significant loss of life.

The *Cheltenham Free Press*, reporting on the fire the following day, was at a loss to know how the fire had started, stating that no firearms or naked flames were involved in the performance. The paper also stated that all stage lights and the chandelier had been extinguished at 11 p.m. as the theatre closed.

Performances continued at the Assembly Rooms in the High Street a couple of hundred yards away, and at the old Royal Well Music Hall (which later called itself the Theatre Royal) which opened in Montpellier in 1850. Nevertheless, it was to be another fifty-two years before Cheltenham had another proper, purpose-built theatre in the shape of the Opera House. (*Cheltenham Free Press*)

MAY 4TH

1901: On this day the *Chronicle and Graphic* ran a piece about the recent census:

> Cheltonians are in a state of animated expectancy about the census result and wild horses cannot draw from the authorities the actual mystic figures. Enough, however, has leaked out to dispel all hopes of the Garden Town becoming a county borough by virtue of its possessing a population of fifty thousand. ... I regret my anticipations that the population in the truly rural parishes would show a still further decrease have been realised so far as the available returns go. In the Gloucester, Tewkesbury, Winchcombe, and Stow-on-the-Wold Unions it is all the same sad story. It really seems as if we are fast approaching realisation of Goldsmith's fear: But a Peasantry, their country's pride, / When once destroyed can never be supplied.
>
> As curiosities of the census I notice that the population remains the same total in two parishes, namely, Church-Icomb and Lassington, and it is not a little singular that in this latter village the lads outnumber the 'lasses' by 31 to 26. The name might now be changed to Ladington. Matson shows the smallest proportion of males to females in Gloucester Union, being 18 to 32. Elmstone Hardwicke is evidently not so adversely affected by its proximity to Cheltenham Sewage Farm, as some folk would make believe, for it records one of the few increases (25) of population in the Tewkesbury Union.

(*Cheltenham Chronicle and Gloucestershire Graphic*)

MAY 5TH

1852: On this day a strange phenomenon was reported on Cleeve Hill that could rival the famous White Horse on the Wiltshire Downs.

A story in the *Cheltenham Examiner* revealed the discovery of a Brown Horse that had mysteriously appeared on the hillside overlooking the town. The paper advised its readers as to the precise location of the new landmark, which was 'immediately above Queens Wood and is best viewed from the higher part of Prestbury Park'. The *Examiner* was keen to throw more light on the exciting new attraction, pointing out that 'the head and neck were formed by some freak of nature in the arrangements of the rock and turf'. It was a Mr Yearsley of Clarence Street who first noticed this strange sight from his window and who 'conceived the idea that it would be a good thing to go for the whole animal'. In order to complete his plan, Mr Yearsley sought the 'artistic assistance' of a Mr F.C. Sextie. The pair then proceeded to Cleeve Hill, and 'Under their direction an outline was drawn and a number of men employed to dig out the turf, the completion of this task being commemorated by a good supper, and copious draughts of home-brewed'. (CLHS Journal 8)

MAY 6TH

1556: On this day, some rules governing landowners in Charlton Kings were recorded in the Cheltenham Court Book.

John Stubbes, a local attorney, wrote an almost complete record of the enclosure movement in Charlton Kings. Stubbes wrote that 'heretofore' the land of all the tenants in Charlton Kings had always been thrown open as common pasture at stated times of the year – from hay harvest if pasture land, and corn harvest if arable, until 2 February, a day known as Candlemas. If the land had been lying fallow, as happened every three years, it was to be left open for a whole year.

Stubbes, and many others, objected to this ancient custom because it led to more cattle being allowed into the fields than was considered to be good farming. The agreement of 6 May 1556 stipulated that every tenant, whether freeholder or copyholder, should take up and enclose 1 acre for every 10 acres he held in Charlton Kings and keep it enclosed for the whole of the year. This arrangement, however, was not considered satisfactory by the majority of the tenants, who at the end of three years pulled up the hedges and let their cattle run on the lands which had been enclosed. (Gwen Hart, *A History of Cheltenham*)

MAY 7TH

2011: On this day it was announced that a naturist who preferred doing his gardening in the nude was to stand trial accused of 'insulting behaviour' after complaints from neighbours who had seen him naked. Sixty-two-year-old Donald Sprigg denied three charges, brought under the Public Order Act, alleging that his nude digging and weeding caused 'harassment, alarm or distress'. His solicitor told Cheltenham Magistrates' Court: 'He was initially arrested for indecent exposure. He maintains he is a practising nudist and he does this in his own back garden.'

The neighbours who had complained were apparently over 150m away but managed to take pictures of him in his garden, claiming he was acting in an indecent manner. Sprigg said that he has acted lawfully at all times and taken reasonable care to ensure no one would see him and be offended by his actions. Sprigg argued that his neighbours must have a very good lens to be able to photograph him from that distance. He pleaded not guilty to the three identical charges and was bailed for six weeks. (*Gloucestershire Echo*)

MAY 8TH

1947: On this day, world-famous opera and concert singer Dame Felicity Lott was born in Cheltenham into a family of amateur musicians. She was educated at Christ Church Infants and then Juniors, then went on to Pate's Grammar School when it was exclusively a girls' school.

She took a degree in French and Latin at Royal Holloway College, University of London, intending to be an interpreter. While continuing her studies in France, she enrolled in the Conservatoire de Grenoble and found an excellent singing teacher who encouraged her to pursue her singing studies. She returned to England and was awarded scholarship to the Royal Academy of Music, graduating in 1973 with the Principal's Prize. She made her operatic debut in 1975 with the English National Opera in Mozart's *The Magic Flute*. Since then, Felicity has appeared at all the great opera houses of the world – Vienna, Milan, Paris, Brussels, Munich, Hamburg, Dresden, Berlin, New York and Chicago.

Felicity Lott has received many awards, including Officier dans l'Ordre des Arts et des Lettres in 1990 and Chevalier dans la Légion d'Honneur in 2001 from the French government. In 1990 she was made a CBE and in 1996 she was created a Dame Commander of the British Empire. (Various sources)

MAY 9TH

1906: On this day the Victoria Rooms started a week-long presentation of a spectacular moving pictures show. The 'Stupendous Attraction' was the first visit of the St Louis Animated Pictures and introduced the '*Sensation of the Day – Talking Pictures by the aid of Gaumont's Chronophone ... Pictures that talk, pictures that sing and pictures that live – the human voice reproduced as in life*'.

The quality of the films was questionable. The programme included the 'great American comedian' R.G. Knowles, the great Australian baritone Hamilton Hill, and pantomime favourite Joe Mack. But what they lacked in quality they made up for in quantity, claiming 'over 40 miles of film shown nightly'.

———◆·———

1910: On this day at 12.30 a.m. the new king, George V, was proclaimed from a specially erected platform outside the Town Hall. The proclamation was read by the Mayor, Councillor C.H. Margrett, and Imperial Square thronged, with every vantage point occupied. The boys from Cheltenham College and Glyngarth School were specially assembled behind the platform, whilst the band of the Territorials provided suitably patriotic music. (John Roles, *Cheltenham in Old Picture Postcards*)

MAY 10TH

1834: On this day the new Montpellier Gardens were open for the first time to subscribers. The gardens had been laid out by Robert William Jearrad and his brother Charles, the proprietors of the Montpellier Spa just across the road and developers of much of the Lansdown/Montpellier areas of the town. The gardens had been laid out by another developer, Pearson Thompson, to designs produced by John Buonarotti Papworth.

The gardens soon became the focus of attention for outdoor activities in the town. In addition to the fountain, there was an ornate Chinese pagoda. One early spectacular event was the balloon flight and parachute jump by John Hampton in 1838. Over the years the gardens were used by various theatre companies, which performed on the Pavilion stage; the Archery Club, who stored their bows and arrows and targets under the bandstand; and saw many other strange events, including, in the 1950s, a giant stuffed whale mounted on the back of a huge truck which toured around the country. At one point the Pavilion was extended to make a café and this, in the 1960s, became a table-tennis club whose most celebrated member was Ian Harrison, the then British number one. (Various sources, including Rowbotham & Waller, *Cheltenham: A History*)

MAY IITH

1955: On this day, Gloucestershire and England cricketer Gilbert Laird Jessop died in Dorset.

Jessop, born at No. 30 Cambray Place in Cheltenham on 19 May 1874, was known as The Croucher. He made his Test debut for England on 15 June 1899 against Australia. His final Test match was against South Africa on 12 July 1912.

The Fifth Test at The Oval in August 1902 became known as 'Jessop's match'. Against all the odds, England scored a surprise one-wicket victory against Australia. England needed 263 to win in the fourth innings and, after a disastrous start, Jessop came in to bat. He scored his first fifty runs in forty-three minutes and reached his century in seventy-five minutes. Jessop reached his hundred off seventy-six balls – one of the fastest Test centuries of all time.

He was the Wisden Cricketer of the Year in 1897, during which season he achieved the double of 1,000 runs and 100 wickets. There was a Jessop house in the old boys' Grammar School until it amalgamated with Pate's Girls' Grammar school. (Various sources)

MAY 12TH

1915: On this day Reginald William Cole of Cheltenham was killed in action. He was on sentry duty on the Western Front in Belgium. After putting his head above the parapet, he reported all was clear. A few minutes later he looked again, but this time was shot by a sniper.

Private Cole of 'C' Company, 5th Battalion Gloucestershire Regiment, was aged twenty-two when he died. He was the son of Abraham Noden Cole and Minnie Rosetta Cole of Clarence Square. Private Cole is buried in Ploegsteert (known to the soldiers as Plug Street) Wood Military Cemetery, and is commemorated on the family gravestone in Cheltenham Cemetery and on the War Memorial in the Promenade. His brother, Lance Corporal Norman Frank Ewart Cole, was killed in action on 15 September 1916. Their father, founder of The Famous, a gentlemen's outfitters in the High Street, wrote a poem in memory of his sons entitled 'Lest We Forget'. The first verse reads:

> Shall we ever forget when the boys marched away,
> To fight for their King and their home.
> With a smile on their lips and their faces aglow,
> And no thought of the days yet to come?

(Oxford University Great War Archive)

MAY 13TH

1897: On this day the future King Edward VII visited Cheltenham to review the Royal Gloucestershire Hussars. The visit had been planned for the previous year, but had to be postponed when a smallpox epidemic swept through Gloucestershire.

For the visit, the main streets of the town were impressively decorated with bunting and with Union Flags much in evidence. The Prince arrived at the Midland railway station in the Queens Road at 11.15 a.m. He was then taken by carriage to a small civic ceremony at the Pittville Pump Room, where 4,700 schoolchildren had been assembled in a specially constructed grandstand. A further 1,500 children formed a choir who, with the band of the Rifle Brigade, welcomed the royal visitor.

After the formalities, the Prince paused on the platform erected at the entrance of the Pump Room to allow Mr Philip Parsons to record the event for posterity. In the minute he was allowed, Parsons took four photographs which were produced as a supplement to one of the local papers. (John Roles, *Cheltenham in Old Picture Postcards*)

MAY 14TH

1839: On this day the Cheltenham synagogue in Synagogue Lane, off St James' Square, was consecrated. Noted for its Regency architecture, it was designed by W.H. Knight, who also designed the town's Art Gallery & Museum. The synagogue's chaste, Regency façade features Doric pilasters and a pediment. The interior features a coffered saucer dome – a typically Regency feature at the centre of which is a lantern made by Nicholas Adam to provide natural light. The Georgian Torah Ark and bimah are reused elements of the London New Synagogue of 1761.

A number of unusual elements of the original furnishings survive. Among these are the oldest Ashkenazi furniture (1761) in the UK as well as original rattan upholstery of the pews and bimah seats, and the prayer boards. One board has the Yom Kippur prayers and the other has the prayer for the welfare of Queen Victoria. Victoria's name is superimposed over the names of previous British monarchs, the earliest of which is George II. The synagogue is a Grade II listed building. (John Goding, *Norman's History of Cheltenham*; Alfred Landseer, *A Panoramic Sketch of Cheltenham and its Environs*)

MAY 15TH

1941: On this day the first British aeroplane powered by the turbojet engine invented by Sir Frank Whittle took off from RAF Cranwell on a test flight.

The first prototype of the new plane, known as the Gloster/Whittle E28/39, had been assembled in a shed behind the Plough Hotel, now the site of the Regent Arcade. The shed at one time was used to store scenery and props for the Everyman Theatre. A plaque which had marked the precise locality of the shed was saved before the site was redeveloped and is in storage awaiting the opening of a proposed Jet Age Museum, but there is a permanent commemorative brass sculpture under the Wishing Fish Clock in the Regent Arcade.

Whittle had first patented his turbojet engine in 1929 but it was seven years before development got underway. In September 1939 the Air Ministry asked the Gloster Aircraft Co. at Hucclecote, near Gloucester, to design two prototype aircraft to take the revolutionary new engine. The 15 May test lasted just seventeen minutes and was piloted by Lieutenant Gerry Sayer. The landing gear for the plane was made by another local company, George Dowty. (Gwen Hart, *A History of Cheltenham*)

MAY 16TH

1900: On this day the very last concert was given in the Assembly Rooms in the High Street.

For eighty-four years the Rooms had been the social hub of the town, until succumbing to a dreadful fire in June 1890. The damage was so severe that it was decided to completely rebuild the Rooms and include a new theatre on the premises. Unfortunately for the proprietors, this scheme started a series of events which would lead to the Assembly Rooms' own demise.

The Assembly Rooms Co. had grand plans for the new venue and employed leading theatre architect Frank Matcham to bring them to fruition. However, another company was created at the same time, with the intention of building a brand new theatre in the town. The rival company was successful and Matcham joined them and built the Opera House just around the corner in Regent Street. As soon as the Opera House opened in 1891, the Assembly Rooms went into decline.

The final concert was given by the New Philharmonic Society. The historic building was bought by Lloyd's Bank for a reported £13,800 and was promptly demolished. The bank that replaced it still stands today. As a result of the demise of the Assembly Rooms, the opportunist Town Council immediately started work on the new Town Hall, which would fulfil most of the old Assembly Rooms' functions. (Michael Hasted, *A Theatre for All Seasons*)

MAY 17TH

1749: On this day, the man sometimes referred to as the 'Father of Immunology', Edward Anthony Jenner, was born. Jenner is widely credited as being the pioneer of the smallpox vaccine and his works are said to have 'saved more lives than the work of any other man'.

He was born in Berkeley but for much of his working life he lived in Cheltenham. Jenner and his wife Katherine spent the summer of 1788 in Cheltenham, on account of her health, which was much improved by taking the waters. Consequently, Jenner arranged his professional affairs so that the summer season could be spent here.

On 14 May 1796 Jenner performed the first inoculation against smallpox, treating a young boy who had been deliberately infected with the disease. At the time, smallpox was killing 25 per cent of the population, but by 1980 the World Health Organisation announced that it had finally been eradicated. Not only did Jenner's discovery save millions of lives from that deadly disease but it also laid the foundation for the science of immunology which, in turn, would prevent many other illnesses and diseases.

Jenner died after a stroke on 26 January 1823 aged seventy-three. A small commemorative garden was established just a few yards from St George's Place. (Various sources)

MAY 18TH

2011: On this day it was revealed that Cheltenham had been selected to host an evening celebration event for the visit of the Olympic Flame on 23 May 2012.

As part of its journey through the UK, Cheltenham's residents and visitors had a unique opportunity to see the flame and celebrate all that it stands for. Cheltenham was one of sixty-six evening celebration locations across the UK, confirmed on this day by the London 2012 Organising Committee of the Olympic and Paralympic Games. The evening events offered thousands of people the opportunity to get involved and share in the Olympic spirit. As part of the occasion, LOCOG and the Presenting Partners staged exciting entertainment shows where a cauldron was lit from the Olympic Flame, marking the end of the day's proceedings.

Sebastian Coe, Chair of LOCOG, said: 'We are thrilled that Cheltenham Borough Council has agreed to host the Olympic Flame on its journey right across the UK. The Olympic Flame will shine a light right across Cheltenham, celebrating the culture and heritage of the area and showcasing the very best of Gloucestershire.' (Various sources, including *Gloucestershire Echo*)

MAY 19TH

1924: On this day the railway station at Charlton Kings was flooded. There was a severe and prolonged thunderstorm in the afternoon, resulting in the space between the two platforms becoming a river.

Charlton Kings was one of several railway stations that once existed in Cheltenham. It was a very pretty little station with an attractive wooden waiting room. It stood beside a golf course, and some beautiful Scots pines grew almost on the platform.

The station had opened in 1881 with the introduction of the Bourton-on-the-Water to Cheltenham section of the Banbury & Cheltenham Direct Railway, which was operated and later taken over by the Great Western Railway. Until the late 1930s the station was connected to a branch line from Leckhampton Hill, which brought limestone from the quarries there. This line was very steep, rising 450ft in three quarters of a mile. The station was reduced to 'halt' status in 1956, with goods facilities withdrawn a couple of years before that. Charlton Kings station closed on 15 October 1962. There is no trace of the station today. (Various sources, including *Gloucestershire Echo*)

MAY 20TH

1816: On this day, the first Summer Ball at the old Assembly Rooms in the High Street was held. It is more than likely that the ball was attended by Jane Austen and her sister Cassandra, who were visiting Cheltenham at the time.

The exact dates of the Austen sisters' visit are not known but it is generally considered to be from mid-May to mid-June. The Cheltenham 'Season' ran from May to October but did not really get into full swing until July, when fashionable society arrived en masse. It was then a non-stop swirl of events until September. Jane clearly preferred the quieter period, writing to her sister: 'But how very much Cheltenham is to be preferred in May.' Jane's state of health would probably have ruled out too much dancing but other events, like Card Assemblies, which were held on Wednesdays, would not have been too strenuous.

While in Cheltenham the sisters stayed at Mrs Potter's lodgings, a couple of hundred yards along the High Street and a stone's throw from the original Theatre Royal. Jane complained that the cost of their rooms was high, believing that they were being charged 'for the name of the High Street' rather than the quality of the accommodation. The site is now occupied by the Argos store. (CLHS Journal 23)

May 21st

1891: On this day, the Catholic writer and theologian Edward Healy Thompson died in Cheltenham.

Thompson was born in Rutland in 1813 and educated at Oakham School and Emmanuel College, Cambridge. Having taken Anglican orders, he obtained a curacy at Calne in Wiltshire. After some years in the Anglican ministry, notably at Marylebone in London and at Ramsgate in Kent, he converted to Catholicism in 1846. He is best known for his skilful adaptations of foreign books, which he thought would be of value to English-speaking Catholics. In 1851, jointly with James Spencer Northcote, he undertook the editorship of the valuable, but controversial, series of pamphlets known as the 'Clifton Tracts'. Thompson spent his last years in Cheltenham, where he devoted his time to religious literature.

His wife, Harriet Diana Calvert, also joined the Catholic Church, and, like her husband, devoted herself to literary work. Her chief work is *The Life of Charles Borromeo*, but she also wrote stories of Catholic life as well as articles in the *Dublin Review*. She died in Cheltenham on 21 August 1896. (Various sources, including Joseph Gillow, *Bibl. Dict. Eng. Cath.*; W. Gordon Gorman, *Converts to Rome*)

MAY 22ND

1972: On this day, Cecil Day-Lewis died from pancreatic cancer in the Hertfordshire home of Kingsley Amis and Elizabeth Jane Howard.

Day-Lewis, born in Ballintubbert, County Laois in Ireland, in 1904, was a master at Cheltenham College Junior School in the 1930s. He was constantly in trouble with the headmaster of the college for, among other things, wearing a green shirt while painting his house in Charlton Kings, and publishing erotic love poetry that he had written with his wife. Financial difficulties and a leaking roof forced him to write commercial detective novels, which he did for many years under the pseudonym of Nicholas Blake. He was created Poet Laureate in 1968 and held the post until his death. He was also the first president of the Cheltenham Literary Society, and a keen and loyal supporter of the Literature Festival. He is the father of actor Daniel Day-Lewis and documentary filmmaker and television chef Tamasin Day-Lewis. (Various sources)

MAY 23RD

1891: On this day the *Cheltenham Looker-On* was warm in its praise for a play that had just opened:

> As an antidote to the melancholy induced by the depressing weather of the present week nothing better could be prescribed than the entertainment offered by *Dr Bill* at the Assembly Rooms. Farcical comedies have been many of late years and of varying degrees of excellence, but Mr Hamilton Aide's popular play is so full of bright dialogue, brisk action, and the usual compromising complications as to take a high place among them.
>
> Good as it is in itself, the necessary piquancy and go required to make it a success has to be supplied by the actors and in this respect Mr George Alexander has exhibited a very commendable discrimination. It would be difficult to suppose a better Dr Bill than Mr J.K. Craufurd, a funnier Mr Firman than Mr Wilfred Shine, a more fiery Mr Horton than Mr E.J. Jalyon, or a more enterprising exquisite than Mr Howard Godey. The female characters too are in remarkably able hands. The Mrs Horton of Miss Agnes Thomas is a striking performance and both Miss Trench and Miss Lillie Young are quite at home in very opposite characters.

(*Cheltenham Looker-On*)

MAY 24TH

1890: On this day a letter from Mr A.C. Nicholls of Charlton Kings appeared in the *Cheltenham Free Press*, making suggestions to the newly formed Cheltenham Omnibus Co.

Mr Nicholls' letter noted that, during the initial trials, there was 'overcrowding on the experimental buses' and suggested the use of two horse vehicles plus the addition of second and third-class areas. The company had been registered on 12 April 1890 and, at a meeting at the Corn Exchange Lecture Room, the chairman, Major-General Babbage, said, 'the venture would be run on commercial principles; the first object of the Directors would be to benefit themselves and the shareholders'.

The single horse-drawn omnibuses charged a flat rate of 1*d* for a journey, in direct opposition to the town's hackney carriages which charged anything up to half-a-crown for even a short journey to the railway station. After the successful trials, the first full service between Lansdown station and Pittville Gates started on 2 June 1890. A second route was added between the High Street and Charlton Kings on 28 June. In the first month of operations, the takings were a princely £26 1*s* 4*d*. By August the company's takings were up to £5 per day for the larger vehicles and £2 a day for the smaller ones. (Appleby & Lloyd, *Cheltenham's Trams & Buses 1890-1963*)

MAY 25TH

1935: On this day, the opening ceremony of the Sandford Park Lido took place. The celebrations started at 3 p.m., with a procession of open-top motorcars travelling from the Municipal Offices to the Lido carrying the Mayor of Cheltenham and his wife, along with dignitaries from neighbouring cities and towns. It was a grand day, with special trains and buses laid on to bring people from all over the county to enjoy the warm water in this ultra-modern swimming facility.

The Lido is a fine example of 1930s style, architecture and planning, and, when it opened, it was one of the few outdoor pools to be heated. The cost in 1935 was a mere £15,700. The Lido is set in beautiful lawns and landscaped gardens, and is one of the largest outdoor swimming pools in the UK. It consists of a 50m main pool, a children's pool, and a paddling pool. All the pools are heated to over 21°C. (Various sources, including *Gloucestershire Echo*)

MAY 26TH

1859: On this day a Grand Banquet was given by Charles Schreiber Esq. at the Pittville Pump Room in Cheltenham.

Charles Schreiber, born in Colchester in 1826, was educated at Cheltenham College. He was an academic, fine-art collector and Conservative Party politician who sat in the House of Commons between 1865 and 1884. Whilst at Trinity College, Cambridge, he won the Browne Medal in 1848 and the Chancellor's Classical Medal in 1850, becoming a Fellow in 1852. In 1855 he married Lady Charlotte Guest, the daughter of the Earl of Lindsey. Schreiber was elected MP for Cheltenham in the 1865 general election. He took his seat on 11 July but lost it three years later. In the 1880s he was elected MP for Poole, a seat he held until his death in 1884.

Charles Schreiber died in Lisbon at the age of fifty-seven. He left his collection of English porcelain to the Victoria & Albert Museum. The collection, which bears his name, is considered to be among the finest in the world. There is a fine print of the Pittville Banquet in the Cheltenham Art Gallery & Museum. (Various sources, including Gwen Hart, *A History of Cheltenham*)

May 27th

1819: On this day the *Cheltenham Chronicle* announced that building plots being offered for sale in Wellington Street were 'immediately adjacent to Colonel Riddell's newly-erected and splendid houses'. The street was originally known as Wellington Place and further developments took place there in 1828-33.

Wellington Street, which runs from Oriel Road to Bath Street, was named to commemorate the visits of the Duke of Wellington. The Duke had first come to Cheltenham when it was at the height of fashion in 1805. He had stayed at Colonel Riddell's home, Cambray House, which was soon renamed Wellington Mansion. The Duke's final visit to the town was in 1816, shortly after his triumph at Waterloo.

To mark the famous victory, three arches were erected near to the northern end of the developing Wellington Street to mark the entrance into the fashionable Cambray area of town. The arches were made of wood but were painted to look like stone and carried pictures of the Duke, along with the names of the great battles with which he was associated. The arches were lit on some evenings and proved to be one of the most popular attractions in Cheltenham for the short time they stood there. (CLHS Journal 24)

MAY 28TH

2009: On this day Tewkesbury Borough Council planning committee voted six to five in favour of permitting the demolition of Bank View Farm. This was a decisive decision in a battle involving expansion of the old Staverton Airport near Cheltenham that had been rumbling on for three years.

The problems started on 15 December 2006 when Staverton, now known as Gloucestershire Airport, sought planning permission as part of a five-year plan to improve and expand the airport. However, the plans had come to light some months earlier and in the summer that year a public meeting was held at Chosen Hill School to allow local residents to discuss the future plans with the airport management. This led to the formation of CASE – Concerned [residents] Against Staverton Expansion.

The details of the airport's five-year plan were not initially made public, but a copy was submitted as one of the documents supporting four planning applications that were designed to allow the plan to be implemented. The five-year plan contradicted the airport's public statements, and confirmed many local residents' concerns that the airport wished to significantly increase the number of larger jet aircraft using their facilities. Despite the passion and concern that went into the protest, the battle was lost and work actually started on the airport development at the end of October 2011. (BBC; *Gloucestershire Echo*)

MAY 29TH

2011: On this day the Cheltenham Home Guard Motorcycle Club organised the Barrett Trial, an open, traditional motorbike trial in aid of Help for Heroes. The event took place at Langley Hill in Winchcombe.

The club ran some of the first competitive motorbike events following the end of the Second World War. Since then it has organised many scrambles, grass track races and trials over the years. The Home Guard club continues to run trial events for riders of all abilities, ranging from small, off-road trials to trail bike events using public roads between more challenging sections. The Barrett and Sphinx trail bike events cater for bikes, old or modern, over a course of at least 40 miles through the Cotswold countryside.

The Home Guard club meets at the Cheltenham Motor Club headquarters in Upper Park Street, Cheltenham. (Cheltenham Home Guard Motorcycle Club)

MAY 30TH

1908: On this day the *Cheltenham Looker-On* carried an advertisement announcing the creation of a new variety theatre in the town. The theatre was to be built 100 yards down the road from the Opera House. It was to be known as the Empire and seat an audience of over 1,200 people. The theatre was designed by London architects Wylson and Long, who also designed the Bristol Empire and the Chelsea Palace in London's Kings Road. The advert stated that building was to start almost immediately and that the theatre would be open in time for Christmas. It never happened, possibly because another new theatre was planned at the same time.

To be known as the Palace, the other proposed theatre was situated on the site of the Victoria Rooms, formerly the Corn Exchange, in the High Street. It was due to open on the August bank holiday in 1908 – but this plan didn't happen either. In 1910, local businessman Charles Poole acquired the site and, after a complete refurbishment, opened the Picture Palace, one of the town's first cinemas, on 11 April 1910. (Roger Beacham, CLHS Journal 20)

MAY 31ST

1901: On this day the Cheltenham Habitation of the Primrose League held its annual meeting at the Town Hall. The organising secretary, Mr H. Crowe, gave an address on the Representation of the People Act. Arrangements for the social and political future of the League in Cheltenham were also discussed. The Primrose League was an organisation for spreading Conservative principles in Great Britain. It was founded in 1883 and was active until the mid-1990s, finally winding up in December 2004. The *Daily Telegraph* reported on 16 December 2004:

> ... this week saw a significant event for any observers of political history: after 121 years, the Primrose League was finally wound up. The league's aim was to promote Toryism across the country. 'In recent years, our meetings have become smaller and smaller,' said Lord Mowbray, one of the league's leading lights. Its remaining funds have been donated to Tory coffers. 'On Monday, I presented Michael Howard and Liam Fox with a cheque for £70,000,' added Lord Mowbray proudly.

(Cheltenham Chronicle and Gloucestershire Graphic; Daily Telegraph)

JUNE 1ST

1838: On this day the building that is now Cheltenham's most famous hotel passed its inspection by the Cheltenham Paving Commission. The certificate read:

> I the undersigned, Richard Billings, the Surveyor appointed by the Cheltenham Paving Commissioners for surveying New Buildings within the Limits of the Town of Cheltenham aforesaid, do hereby certify to the said Commissioners that I have viewed and surveyed the *messuage* or hotel called Liddel's Hotel situated in Imperial Square within the Limits of the said Town of Cheltenham, and lately erected by Richard Liddel and Company and that the same hath been completed and finished conformably with the Rules and Regulations prescribed and ordered by the said Commissioners, under and by virtue of the Powers of the Act passed in the Second Year of the Reign of his late Majesty, for Paving and Lighting the Town of Cheltenham aforesaid, and that the Directions of the said Act have been duly complied with in the Erection thereof.

Richard Liddell, who ran other hotels in Cheltenham, initially leased the hotel for £2,100 a year. Despite its luxury accommodation, the hotel did not prosper and in 1852 it was sold for a mere £8,400. It was later renamed the Queens Hotel after Queen Victoria. (Various sources, including *Cheltenham Looker-On*)

JUNE 2ND

1883: On this day Frederick John Knight-Adkin, who was to settle and make his fortune in South America, was born at No. 22 Lansdowne Terrace in Cheltenham.

Frederick was the youngest son of Revd Canon Harry Kenrick Knight-Adkin and Georgina Elizabeth Knight; a brother of the Dean of Gibraltar, W.K. Knight-Adkin; and a cousin of Prime Minister Neville Chamberlain. He was educated at Cheltenham College and New College, Oxford.

On leaving Oxford he went to America for a year, writing short stories for the *Windsor Magazine*. Here he was introduced to New York Society, and made friends who were later very helpful in appointing him to the forestry business. He arrived in Argentina in 1906 as games master to St George's College. In company with three other young masters he then went on an expedition to the Southern Andes, and wrote for the Royal Geographic Society. From 1911 he was appointed general manager of the Santa Fé Land Co. and a Paraguayan Railways company. In a key position, he was denied enlistment despite four attempts to volunteer his service for the army in the First World War. He died in Buenos Aires in 1964. (*The Review of the River Plate*, 1964)

JUNE 3RD

2011: On this day the seventh Wychwood Festival opened at Cheltenham Racecourse. Although it takes place in Gloucestershire, the festival's name originates from the ancient forest that once covered large parts of Oxfordshire.

The Wychwood Music Festival was launched in 2005 and quickly gained a reputation thanks to its eclectic mix of music, creative programming, and family-friendly atmosphere. *Time Out* described the festival as 'an excellent hybrid of the Big Chill, WOMAD and The Cambridge Folk Festival'. The first festival saw performances from Steve Earle, Alabama 3, Show of Hands, Allison Moorer, Eliza Carthy and many others. It was a great success, making it into the *Sunday Times'* Top Seven Festivals of the summer and being nominated for Best New and Best Family Festival. Comedy was added to the programme in the second year and included a show-stopping set from Mark Thomas. The festival received three nominations at the 2006 UK Festival Awards, including Best Family Festival for the second time. The *Oxford Mail* said: 'Wychwood has wasted no time in establishing itself as one of the coolest weekends of the summer.' Since then, Wychwood has continued to grow and has gained a large and loyal following. (Various sources, including the *Oxford Mail*)

JUNE 4TH

1932: On this day, monumental masons E.A. Emms announced that their Hales Road Works had been equipped with the latest power-driven hand tools. These included an electric hammer for drilling granite and an electric saw. It was claimed that these tools would ensure greater efficiency and lower the production costs, making it possible for the company to compete with goods of foreign manufacture. Perhaps anticipating an increase in business, Mr Emms opened a new showroom, 'almost facing the cemetery', in the aptly named Cemetery Road.

Perhaps one of his first customers was Mr George Thomas Robbins, who died in the infirmary this same week aged eighty-five. Known as one of Cheltenham's 'characters', he was the standard bearer for the Liberal Party in the old political days and used to carry the Keys of the Borough in the processions of long ago. Mr Robbins was of great height and of considerable physical strength and always went by the name of 'Cock Robin'. (*Cheltenham Chronicle and Gloucestershire Graphic*)

JUNE 5TH

1915: On this day George Raymond Dallas Moor, an old boy of Cheltenham College, displayed an act of gallantry that won him the Victoria Cross – the highest and most prestigious award for gallantry in the face of the enemy that can be awarded to British and Commonwealth forces. George was only eighteen years old. The *London Gazette*, 23 July 1915, reported:

> South of Krithia in Gallipoli, Turkey, when a detachment of the battalion which had lost all its officers was rapidly retiring before a heavy Turkish attack, Second Lieutenant Moor, realising the danger to the rest of the line, dashed back some 200 yards, stemmed the retirement, led back the men and recaptured the lost trench. This brave act saved a dangerous situation.

George Moor's was one of fourteen Victoria Crosses that have been won by Old Cheltonians. Another of the recipients was Duncan Gordon Boyes, who was born at No. 3 Paragon Buildings in Cheltenham on 5 November 1846. Midshipman Boyes, of HMS *Euryalus*, won his VC aged seventeen, for his part in action at Shimonoseki, Japan on 6 September 1864. He carried the Queen's colour into action, with the leading company attacking the enemy's stockade. He kept the colours flying in spite of direct fire which killed one of his colour sergeants. (Register of the Victoria Cross; *This England*, 1997; *London Gazette*)

JUNE 6TH

1932: On this day the 'Cheltenham Flyer' broke all railway speed records, travelling at an average speed of 81.6mph between Swindon and Paddington. Such a journey speed had never been recorded and this became the fastest railway run in the world. The train was hauled by 'Castle' Class 5006 *Tregenna Castle* and was crewed by Driver Ruddock and Fireman Thorp.

The train, more correctly called the 'Cheltenham Spa Express', was known, rather quaintly, as the 'Tea Car Train' service from Cheltenham to Paddington, which called at Gloucester and Stroud en route to Swindon. From here it was able to make use of the superb main line laid out by Brunel in the 1830s. Its scheduled times over the 77 miles to Paddington were successively cut during the 1920s and 1930s. (*Great Western Railway Magazine*, July 1932; *Great Western Railway Engines* 1938; and others)

JUNE 7TH

1847: On this day the celebrated artist Hector Caffieri was born in Cheltenham. He studied in Paris under Bonnat and Lefebvre, and worked in London and Boulogne-sur-Mer, often painting fishing scenes. He also painted flowers and some sporting subjects, but he is best known for his typically Victorian country and woodland scenes.

He became a member of the Royal British Society of Artists in London and a member of the Royal Institute of Painters in Watercolours. He displayed his work at most of the major London and French exhibitions, including the Royal Academy between 1875 and 1901, and the Salon exhibition of the Société des Artistes in Paris in 1892 and 1893. Caffieri died in 1932. (Various sources, including Smith & Rowbotham, *Commemorative Plaques of Cheltenham*)

———◆———

1977: On this day the nation celebrated the Queen's Silver Jubilee. Colesbourne Road in Benhall staged a magnificent street party on the Saturday before the official Jubilee holiday, while the street party at Clyde Crescent was one of the largest in town, with knobbly knees competitions for dads. Shortly before the Jubilee day, workers at the Royal Mint went on strike; this resulted in commemorative coins being in short supply and many children received a commemorative mug instead. (*Gloucestershire Echo*)

JUNE 8TH

1886: On this day a gentleman was arrested for stealing money in a cricket pavilion. Players had noticed for some time that small amounts of money had been going missing from the changing room at the Charlton Park ground of the East Gloucestershire Cricket Club. A trap was set during a match: marked coins were left in various items of clothing and a police sergeant observed the room from a hiding place. A man was seen taking the money, an act he freely admitted when he was arrested. He was sentenced to twenty-eight days' hard labour in Gloucester Jail.

The man was thirty-three-year-old Walter Raleigh Gilbert, a well-known amateur cricketer who had played for England. This was in the days when most top cricketers were amateurs or 'gentlemen'. Pavilions would have two separate entrances: one for 'gentlemen', the other for 'players' or professionals. Gilbert, obviously in need of money, had actually turned professional only a few months before, at the beginning of the season. Following his release from prison Gilbert moved to Canada, where he died in 1925. (CLHS Journal 12)

June 9th

1877: On this day the first championship of the All England Lawn Tennis and Croquet Club took place at Wimbledon. In those days lawn tennis was regarded as a frivolous game for suburban back gardens and it was croquet that was the main game. And it was at croquet that a Cheltenham man would prove to be pre-eminent.

Professor Bernard Neal from Cheltenham was British Croquet Champion an impressive thirty-seven times between 1963 and 2002. He only failed to retain the trophy in 1964, 1974 and in 2001. 'It's not a very great achievement,' he claimed. 'These were the club championships for members only and not many members of the All England Club play croquet at all.'

Croquet was soon relegated into a very modest second place at Wimbledon after tennis became established, but the game is still played there. A croquet lawn was created in 1957 and was in use until 2007 when the new Court No. 2 was built over it. However, the sport can still be played on two of the practice courts, which together form a full-size croquet lawn. (BBC News; The Croquet Association)

JUNE 10TH

2003: On this day, the notorious Johnson Gang from Cheltenham carried out one of their most audacious burglaries at Waddesdon Manor near Aylesbury in Buckinghamshire, where antiques valued at over £5 million were taken. The gang, who specialised in stealing fine art and antiques from English country houses, were active over a period of twenty years. They staked out properties for several weeks before the crimes and used 4x4 vehicles to ram heavily bolted gates.

The goods they stole were estimated to be worth between £30 million and £80 million. In October 2005 the police launched Operation Haul, which led to the arrest and conviction of many of the gang members, who were sentenced to a total of forty-nine years in prison in August 2008. In addition to the thefts from stately homes, the gang were involved in thefts from shops, cash machines and metal merchants.

Since the arrests in 2006, Thames Valley Police has seen a 90 per cent reduction in offences attributable to the group, and across all areas there has been a dramatic decrease in country house burglaries, and cash machine and metal thefts. (Various sources, including *Gloucestershire Echo*)

JUNE 11TH

1881: On this day the *Cheltenham Looker-On* reported on Whitsun Week in the town:

Whitsun Week has been a week of unwonted activity. Rarely indeed, if ever, has its programme proffered so much entertainment to all classes of the community or its *Sayings and Doings* been so generally approved.

Excursionists by road and rail were, consequently, enabled to perfect their arrangements, and to indulge in whatever Sports and Pastimes they had planned for their recreation in remote localities, while the friends they left behind them were no less fortunate, participating in the amusements catered for them at home; and what with Industrial Exhibitions, the Fete at the Montpellier Gardens and the performances at the Theatre, were at no loss for wherewithal to celebrate their traditional holiday, which was moreover enlivened this year by a much larger influx of visitors than usual from all points of the compass.

The new Railway from Bourton contributed a very considerable contingent, and the old lines brought quite their customary battalions. The Town, consequently, presented an especially animated appearance and Hotels and Coffee Taverns did a large stroke of business.

(*Cheltenham Looker-On*)

JUNE 12TH

1915: On this day, Naunton Park V.A. Hospital (Glos. 106) opened its doors to care for wounded soldiers returning from the First World War. The hospital treated a total of 2,751 patients until it finally closed on 29 December 1919.

Naunton Park schools were placed at the disposal of the Red Cross by the Cheltenham Education Authorities. All the local detachments were already at work when the new hospital was opened, but a few members were taken from each and formed into a detachment under Miss Geddes as Commandant. The Medical Officers were Dr E.J. Tatham, Dr A.G. Foljambe Forster, Dr S.T. Pruen and Dr R. Kirkland. A special massage centre was established and the hospital also specialised in Carrel Dakin treatment and pathological and bacteriological work.

The hospital was inspected on various occasions by the Commander-in-Chief, Southern Command, and also by Lord French. In February 1918 Miss Geddes was succeeded by Miss Holland, who continued as Commandant to the end.

The buildings are still in use today as the Naunton Park School. (*The Red Cross in Gloucestershire 1914-19*; www.angelfire.com)

JUNE 13TH

1887: On this day the Cheltenham chemists Beetham's ran a very attractive advertisement in the *Illustrated London News* for their proprietary Glycerine and Cucumber potion. The potion claimed to preserve the complexion from the effects of hot sun, wind and hard water. Bottles cost 1*s*, 1*s* 9*d*, and 2*s* 6*d*. Customers were urged to 'beware of injurious imitations'.

Beetham's had been established in Cheltenham around 1846 by Michael Beetham, who came from Doncaster in Yorkshire. The company continued trading until the early 1960s, when it is thought to have merged with another local chemists, C.&P. James, who are still trading in St George's Road. (CLHS Journal 24)

———◆———

1945: On this day, the first concert of the first-ever Cheltenham Music Festival took place only a few weeks after VE day. The first performance featured the London Philharmonic Orchestra. The festival has taken place in June/July every year since, and is the oldest music festival of its type and one of the most prestigious.

JUNE 14TH

2010: On this day Cheltenham Borough Council reported that violent crime in the town had fallen yet again, according to the latest figures. Gloucestershire Constabulary reported that violent crime figures for the town centre had fallen by 17.1 per cent over the previous year, which was the biggest drop in seven years. The figures also showed a 38 per cent reduction since 2005/06, coupled with an increase in detection rates. These figures demonstrated that the town centre was an increasingly safe place to visit at night, which might have appeared contrary to public perception. Martin Quantock, who co-ordinates crime-reduction scheme 'Cheltenham Safe', said:

> These statistics go to show how far we have come by working in partnership with local retailers, the police and other stakeholders in managing crime within our town centre. If you are thinking of opening a new retail or hospitality outlet in Cheltenham, these figures underline Cheltenham Safe's impact to managing crime since its inception four years ago, and that the town centre is a safe place to be both day and night. Cheltenham is not a violent place in the evenings, and I hope that this can go someway to restoring consumer confidence back into the high street after 7pm.

(Cheltenham Borough Council)

JUNE 15TH

1881: On this day, the second flower show of the season took place in Pittville Gardens. The show was organised by the Royal Horticultural Society and Cheltenham's Mayor, W. Nash Skillicorne. By permission of Colonel Ewart, the splendid band of the 2nd Life Guards, under the direction of M.W. Winterbottom, had been engaged to play for the visitors as they strolled around the various exhibits.

Entrance for pedestrians was the first gate by the bridge, and those arriving by carriage were directed to the gate near Beaufort Villas. Gates opened at 2 p.m.; admission between then and 4.30 p.m. was half-a-crown, and 1s thereafter. Pupils of the college, and indeed all schools, were charged 1s, but if you were unlucky enough to be in a wheelchair you would be charged an additional shilling. Political correctness had obviously yet to raise its head. (*Cheltenham Looker-On*)

JUNE 16TH

2010: On this day, Alexander Ffinch gave an acclaimed organ recital in the chapel at Cheltenham College where he is resident organist. As well as teaching and playing the organ, Mr Ffinch directs the College Chamber Choir, whose 2010 CD entitled *Coeperunt Loqui* received positive reviews in the *International Record Review* and *Organists Review*.

Ffinch studied at the Royal College of Music, and then became an organ scholar of Keble College, Oxford. He gave over 100 recitals at Lancaster Town Hall in the 1990s, where he was resident organist. He regularly gives organ recitals around the world. Additionally, he was appointed Director of Music of St Catharine's College, Cambridge in 2001. Here he conducted the choir's 2003 CD *Videte*, featuring works by sixteenth-century English composer Thomas Tallis. His other performances on disc include *Salve Puerule*, a collection of Christmas choral music with Andrew Swait and the Trinity College Chamber Choir. (www.alexanderffinch.co.uk)

JUNE 17TH

2011: On this day the brilliantly quirky and surprising Ukulele Festival of Great Britain opened in Cheltenham. Ukulele players and star performers from all over the world attended and could be seen strolling round the town carrying their dinky instrument cases and sometimes giving impromptu concerts to passers-by. Although the ukulele is associated with George Formby, it is a versatile instrument, and music ranging from Jimi Hendrix to Beethoven was played. There were soloists playing virtuoso instrumentals, singers accompanying themselves, and mini ukulele orchestras.

The main venue for the festival was the Town Hall, where there were workshops, demonstrations and concerts, as well as dealers and makers selling a wide variety of ukes. But it was in Imperial Square that all the enthusiasts overflowed to try out their new instruments, and find a partner to jam with and compare notes.

In the afternoon they formed a procession and marched strumming down the Promenade, where hundreds of young and old musicians congregated by the hare statue outside Waterstones for a mass Uke-in. Afterwards they trooped up to the Exmouth Arms in the Bath Road to continue the party. (Ukulele Festival of Great Britain)

JUNE 18TH

2010: On this day Malcolm Mitchem, a decorated RAF war hero from Cheltenham, died aged eighty-nine. The young Malcolm came to Cheltenham when his parents moved from Cardiff and set up home in Pilley Crescent.

A former pupil of Cheltenham Grammar School, Malcolm joined the RAF in 1937 as a technical apprentice. At the start of the Second World War he was serving with a squadron of Vickers Wellesley bombers as an airframe fitter.

After serving in Ethiopia, Sergeant Mitchem was posted to Bomber Command 218 Squadron, based at Downham Market. During a mission over the Italian city of Turin in August 1943 his aircraft was badly damaged, resulting in the death of the navigator and serious injury to the lone pilot. Despite this, the crew attempted to make it to the North African coast where, after several attempts, the aircraft eventually made a crash landing. The pilot, Flight Sergeant Arthur Aaron, was rescued from the wreckage but later died of his injuries. He was awarded a posthumous Victoria Cross and Malcolm Mitchem received a Distinguished Flying Medal. He remained in the RAF until 1972, when he left with the rank of Flight Lieutenant.

Following his death, Mr Mitchem's son-in-law, Wing Commander Barry Simon, said, 'The RAF was his life and he was very proud of what he did.' (Various sources)

JUNE 19TH

1826: On this day, the *Cheltenham Journal* reported on a fabulous new fountain which had been opened at the Sherborne or Imperial Spa at the top of the Promenade:

> Mr Henney has just erected a curious playing fountain, to add to the fascinations of this sweet retreat. The fountain is cut out of the purest marble, and has been very judiciously placed at the lower end of the grand promenade, where it forms an object of great attraction to the admirers of art. It is evidently taken from the antique, and is a chef d'oeuvre of its kind. It was brought over from Italy, during the time that Buonaparte and his army robbed that country of its most celebrated monuments.
>
> The fountain formed part of the cargo of a vessel on its way to France, which was taken by one of our cruisers in the Mediterranean. The carving on every part is of the most exquisite workmanship, representing three heads of Bacchus, crowned with ivy, pouring from their mouths water into three shells, which are supported by three dolphins with their tails reversed. At the upper part of the font are other emblematic devices, and the water which is poured from various openings is received into a large circular basin. The whole is surmounted on a pedestal of marble, in which are cut curious figures of shells, snakes, tortoises etc., forming altogether an object of great attraction.

(CLHS Journal 5)

JUNE 20TH

1982: On this day *The Times* ran an interview with artist Kit Williams, who designed one of Cheltenham's most recent and most popular attractions, the Wishing Fish Clock.

In 1985 Williams designed the clock as a centrepiece to the Regent Arcade. Standing over 45 ft tall, the clock features a duck that lays a never-ending stream of golden eggs and includes a family of mice that are continually trying to evade a snake. Hanging from the base of the clock is a large wooden fish that blows bubbles every half hour. Catching one of these bubbles entitles you to make a wish, hence the name of the clock.

In his interview with Susan Raven, Williams said, 'I became a painter because I was a painter.' He was almost put off art at school, but said, 'I always knew I could do it. When I left school … my mother was so fed up she sent me off to join the Navy.'

Kit started painting on board the aircraft carrier HMS *Victorious*. To keep steady when the ship was moving, he used to tie down the canvas and the seat he was sitting on; he even tied his arm to an armrest. 'They thought I was very strange, but my divisional officer somehow understood. He gave me a tiny compartment to paint in.' (*The Times*)

JUNE 21ST

1887: On this day the foundation stone of Cheltenham's public library was laid in Clarence Street, then known as Manchester Street. Large crowds massed to watch the ceremony, which was part of the local celebrations of Queen Victoria's Golden Jubilee.

The opening of the public library signalled the end of a thirty-four-year campaign to establish a free library in the town. Earlier attempts in 1855-56 and 1873 had failed to persuade the authorities to adopt the Public Library Act, and although a public meeting in 1878 had narrowly voted in favour, a town poll later reversed that decision. Only in October 1884 was a free library finally opened in temporary premises in Liverpool Place.

The 8ft-high statue of Shakespeare above the library entrance was added in 1911. It was presented by Mr R.W. Boulton of the local stonemason's firm. (John Roles, *Cheltenham in Old Picture Postcards*)

JUNE 22ND

1974: On this day the fine old Coliseum cinema closed its doors for the very last time, having been a popular place for entertainment in Cheltenham for over sixty years. The final screening was the 1967 Arthur Penn film *Bonnie and Clyde*, starring Warren Beatty and Faye Dunaway.

The cinema, formerly a music-hall theatre, had been built in a converted Conservative Club in Albion Street. Although the original Georgian façade of the club remained, the building had gone through so many changes that it was clearly considered not worth preserving. When the cinema closed, the building became a bingo hall for many years, but at least most of the interior structure was kept intact. Its last incarnation was as the Springbok disco, by which time all recognisable remnants of the old theatre had been ripped out to make way for bars and dance floors.

After many schemes and plans for the building, demolition finally started in June 2011. The only recognisable features from the original theatre were the stairs on the back wall that led to the dressing rooms, and some moulding high on the foyer ceiling. Within a few weeks nothing remained but a hole in the ground. (Various sources, including Michael Hasted, *A Theatre for All Seasons*)

JUNE 23RD

1936: On this day an award for bravery was given – for the first time – to a policewoman. WPC Marion Sandover was appointed to the Gloucestershire Constabulary on 6 May 1919, and worked under the same conditions as police reservists. She was posted to Cheltenham as a clerk, and in 1921 was posted for duty at Gloucester City. There she also acted as Inspector of the Female Domestic Servants Registries.

On the day in question, WPC Sandover went to the assistance of another constable who was struggling violently with a man he was attempting to arrest. Although at that time she would not have been expected to give assistance, she joined the constable and provided help in securing the violent prisoner. She was highly commended for her actions and became the first and only policewoman in the force to be awarded the Chief Constable's Silver Braid for Gallantry.

Marion went on to serve for thirty years with Gloucestershire Constabulary. During her service she was commended on seven occasions, and received the King George V Silver Jubilee Medal in 1935 and the Defence Medal following service in the Second World War. (Gloucestershire Police Museum)

JUNE 24TH

1840: On this day, Cheltenham's Lansdown Road railway station was opened by the Birmingham & Gloucester Railway (B&GR). The station has undergone many changes over the years. Designed by architect Samuel Whitfield Daukes, it was originally built with a splendid Gothic Doric portico, which was sadly demolished in 1961. Much of the rest of the building has remained intact.

The station was enlarged and redecorated in August 1891 to cope with the greater number of passengers that were expected once the Midland & South Western Junction Railway was allowed to operate from the station. It was renamed Cheltenham Spa (Lansdown) on 1 February 1925 by the London, Midland & Scottish Railway, and again renamed Cheltenham Spa by British Railways in 1948.

It is now Cheltenham's only railway station and, in spite of all the changes, it has retained many of the original features, including some fine ironwork. (Various sources, including Steven Blake, *Cheltenham: A Pictorial History*)

JUNE 25TH

1964: On this day the Council of Repertory Theatres held its conference in Cheltenham. The seventy-second conference, along with the twenty-first Annual General Meeting of CORT, was held at the Everyman, with speakers including Harold Clurman of the Lincoln Centre Theatre in New York and Cheltenham Town Clerk, Mr F.D. Littlewood.

In those days the council represented the British repertory system, whose dozens of theatres brought live theatre, employing a permanent company of actors, to large and small towns the length and breadth of the British Isles. For the conference to be held in Cheltenham was a bit of a coup for the Everyman and its Director of Productions, Ian Mullins. Mullins had created the first cohesive repertory company at the theatre only three years before. Before his arrival, the Everyman had only been in existence for eighteen months, having previously been known as the Opera House.

Mullins brought actors like Josephine Tewson, William Gaunt and Penelope Keith to the theatre early in their careers, and established a company that could hold its own with any of the bigger, longer-established repertories like Birmingham, Coventry and Liverpool. (Michael Hasted, *A Theatre for All Seasons*)

JUNE 26TH

1903: On this day the War Memorial at Cheltenham College was unveiled by General Sir Power Palmer. Originally known as the Old Cheltonians South African War Memorial, it commemorated the dead of the Boer War who had attended the college. The memorial had first been suggested in 1901, and by the end of that year it was decided to install a special reredos in the College Chapel and an Eleanor Cross on the front lawn.

Over the years the college has had strong links with the military and produced many distinguished soldiers. Six-hundred-and-seventy-five Old Cheltonians were killed in the First World War and 363 in the Second World War. Cheltenham's military past is recognised by the fact that it is one of only three schools in England (the others being Eton College and the Duke of York's Royal Military School) to have its own military colours.

The names of those Old Cheltonians killed in the First World War are recorded in the College Chapel and those killed in the Second World War are displayed on the memorial in the dining hall. In total, fourteen former pupils have been awarded the Victoria Cross. Seven of the College VCs are on public display, but that of Midshipman Boyes was sold by the college in 1998 to raise scholarship funds. (Various sources, including John Roles, *Cheltenham in Old Picture Postcards*)

JUNE 27TH

2009: On this day, casual visitors to the Brewery precinct in the centre of Cheltenham would have been surprised to see a menacing, 8ft-tall silver robot wandering around, hobnobbing with the crowds and amusing young children. Titan, the rather frightening-looking android, was there to promote the latest *Transformers* film showing at the nearby cinema complex.

Titan was designed and built in Cornwall by Cyberstein Robots and frequently appears alone, or with one of his two siblings, at events around the world. How the robot works is a closely guarded secret, but on this day a 'demonstrator' was close at hand, as was Titan's so-called 'docking station' – a sort of shopmobility vehicle that he uses to get around when his knees begin to squeak and his batteries need recharging.

Titan seems to be a very popular fellow (or are robots gender neutral?), having appeared on the cover of several newspapers and magazines, although it must be said that these were either in the Far or Middle East, where he even met royalty. If you were unfortunate enough to miss Titan at the Brewery, you can see him on one of the 1,000-plus clips on YouTube, or on his own website. (Various sources, including the Brewery website)

JUNE 28TH

1838: On this day the Gloucestershire Zoological, Botanical and Horticultural Gardens opened in a 20-acre piece of land in Leckhampton. The attractions included an ornamental lake cut in the shape of Africa; a second was planned in the shape of America. The proprietor of the zoo, local solicitor Thomas Billings, had plans to show elephants, pelicans, monkeys, kangaroos and polar bears. Unfortunately the whole scheme was a little too ambitious and failed before it was completed. The site was bought up by local architect Samuel Whitfield Daukes.

Daukes reopened the gardens in 1842 as public pleasure grounds to be known as The Park, for which he charged 1s admission. The Park also included the grounds of the Cheltenham & Gloucester Cricket Club, but even the chance of seeing matches played there could not save the zoo. It closed and in February 1844 all the animals were auctioned off at the Assembly Rooms in the High Street. Much of the stock, including an aviary in the shape of a Chinese pagoda, was sold to Jessop's Nursery Gardens, another pleasure garden in St James' Square. (Rowbotham & Waller, *Cheltenham: A History*)

JUNE 29TH

1850: On this day the *Illustrated London News* printed a fine engraving and review of the Grand Horticultural Exhibition which had been held on 20 June at the newly opened Royal Well Walk and Pump Room. It was described by the organisers as 'monster floral exposition' and 'the most brilliant display of the kind ever produced in the provinces'. According to the newspaper, the show attracted 6-7,000 people, who were 'a galaxy of beauty, rank and fashion rarely equalled'.

The new venue had been created on the site of the Royal Old Well in Montpellier by George Rowe, a printer and artist, and architect Samuel Onley. They promised their new hall would house the old spa and be a place for 'respectable amusements'. But it seems that the establishment of the Pump Room and the mounting of the flower show was a clever ruse by Rowe and Onley to open a new theatre without anyone noticing. Our old friend Dean Francis Close had forbidden the opening of places of entertainment, but obviously a flower show would not be frowned upon. However, immediately after the event, the building was converted and renamed the Royal Well Music Hall. The Ladies' College took over the lease in 1887, finally buying it outright in 1890. The college's Princess Hall was built on the site in 1897, where it still stands today. (CLHS Journal 26)

JUNE 30TH

1903: On this day Buffalo Bill's Wild West Show came to Cheltenham, appearing on land in Cemetery Road, now known as Priors Road.

About 8,000 people saw the show, which included Indians 'engaged at their toilet', according to an account in the *Echo*. The poster for the event announced that Colonel W.F. Cody was touring the provinces in his own special trains with a company of 800 people and 500 horses. The troupe would arrive at about 4.30 a.m. and be ready for the show at 2.30 p.m. After the evening show at 8 p.m. they would pack up their tented city and disappear into the night, en route for their next venue.

Acts that were promised included Mounted Warriors of the World – 'A gathering of extraordinary consequence to fittingly depict all that Virile, Muscular, Heroic Manhood has and can endure'. There was also a mystery performer in the show. Billed as The Blue Man, Fred Walters claimed to have come from Cheltenham, where he attended the Grammar School, and said that his mother was buried in St Mary's churchyard. However, investigations at the time could find nothing to substantiate his claims. (James Hodsdon, CLHS Journal 19)

JULY 1ST

1939: On this day the familiar and long-established Cheltenham District Traction Co. parted company with Balfour Beatty Ltd and became part of the Red & White United group. Soon after this, Britain was plunged into the Second World War and the buses would be affected as much as anything else.

Although Cheltenham was not in the front line of aerial bombardment, the problems that arose were much greater than those that had been experienced in the First World War. The trams during the First World War had run on electricity generated by home-produced coal, but twenty years later the buses depended on imported oil.

Notices were stuck on to bus windows announcing curtailed services and other emergency measures. Lighting on both decks was reduced from twelve lamps to three, each with dimmed bulbs. The windows were covered with blue paint to minimise the light escaping from the buses, and the headlamps were masked to reduce the beam. In order for the buses not to be completely invisible to other road users and pedestrians, white paint was liberally applied to mudguards and all corners of the vehicles. (Appleby & Lloyd, *Cheltenham's Trams and Buses 1890-1963*)

JULY 2ND

1910: On this day the Cheltenham & North Gloucestershire Boy Scouts Rally took place in Charlton Park (entrance by the gate on the Old Bath Road, by kind permission of R.V. Vassar-Smith, Esq.). The event opened at 3 p.m. and, soon after, the Scouts were inspected by Major-General Sir Francis Howard, the Scout Commissioner for the county. The inspection was followed by displays given by the various Scout troops and patrols. Admission was *6d* and tickets were available from Scoutmasters or Commander Dillon, who lived at No. 4 Priory Street. Tea was on sale for *6d* a cup.

The following weekend the Scouts were in action again, this time at the Great Annual Carnival which was held in Montpellier Gardens. They once again gave their famous display but the crowds were probably more interested in the star of the show – the first visit of Mr E.T. Willows' amazing airship. During the day, the airship was kept in its hangar but could be seen for *2s*. Mr Willows had promised to make an ascent on the condition that the weather was favourable. (*Cheltenham Looker-On*)

JULY 3RD

1920: On this day the Annual Choral Festival at St Luke's Church, which had taken place on the previous Wednesday evening, was reviewed in the *Cheltenham Looker-On*. The paper reported that the concert had produced good music and as much money for the choir and organ fund as could be expected. The festival, which was held in the church, was crowded to its utmost limits and some were content to stand or sit on the gallery staircase.

The melodious and not-too-exacting oratorio of Sir William Sterndale Bennett, 'The Woman of Samaria', was rendered and Mr Ernest Dicks directed about 100 voices with the capable support of the young organist, Mr Leslie Betteridge. The soloists were Madame Rita Rabone-Beales, Miss Enid Rhodes, Mr E.T. Evans and Mr Sydney Rayner. The latter had never been heard to better advantage, but Miss Rhodes depreciated her nice contralto voice by a marked liking for the tremulous effect. In the lovely unaccompanied quartet, 'God is a Spirit', pitch was not well sustained. At the final rehearsal on the previous Monday, Mr Dicks had been presented by the festival choir with a leather despatch case in commemoration of the twenty-first anniversary of the festival at St Luke's. As the vicar, Revd C.C. Petch, said, all the members of the choir, and indeed all associated with St Luke's, had a sincere affection for Mr Dicks and his abilities as composer, organist and conductor. (*Cheltenham Looker-On*)

JULY 4TH

1816: On this day new regulations came into force concerning sedan chairs, which were the equivalent of modern taxis. The chair consisted of a box, about the size of a telephone kiosk, with a seat inside. It was carried by two men, one in front, the other behind, by the means of two poles which went along each side of the chair. The regulations of 1816 set out the places, equivalent to taxi ranks, where the chairs could wait for fares. These sites were Cambray Street, near to Mr Rous the watchmaker; Winchcombe Street; Colonnade Road, between the houses; and near the prison in New Street. (CLHS Journal)

1884: On this day Arthur Inglis was born. After being educated at Cheltenham College, Inglis established a unique position in the history of tank warfare. Inglis, who had joined the Glosters at the outbreak of the First World War, was the first man ever to lead tanks into action and he did so on foot, the traditional way for cavalry commanding officers. The event took place in 1916 at the Battle of Flers Courcelette in the Somme sector. Remarkably, Inglis survived this ordeal, but was injured in 1918 and died a year later from his wounds. Major Arthur Inglis is buried in Prestbury churchyard. (www.firsttankcrews.com)

JULY 5TH

1858: On this day two splendid cannons were mounted on iron plinths at the top of the Promenade by Imperial Gardens. These two Russian guns had been captured at the Siege of Sebastopol during the Crimean War and were given to the town in 1856 by the then Minister of War, Lord Panmure. Although a site was soon agreed, the cannons were stored in the Queens Hotel's stables for over eighteen months as no one would agree to pay for the cost of displaying them. Eventually, the hotel's owner, Mr W.S. Davis, offered to pay and the guns were taken out of storage and raised onto the new plinths, which were inscribed with the names of the fallen from the town.

Within a year of the ceremony, the plinths were painted to resemble granite and an arch of laurel leaves supporting a globular lamp, complete with Queen Victoria's initials, was added to improve the appearance of the memorial. The cannons remained on this site until the Second World War, when they were removed for salvage along with many of the town's fine iron railings. Today only one plinth remains, and that is utilised as a flowerbed. (Various sources, including John Roles, *Cheltenham in Old Picture Postcards*)

July 6th

1908: On this day the Gloucestershire Historical Pageant took place in Pittville Park. Such large historical spectaculars were very popular in Edwardian times and were really an excuse for a display of municipal pride. Despite initial fears that Cheltenham, because of its supposed lack of antiquity, was not a suitable location, the pageant was planned as a mammoth spectacular, with 2-3,000 performers enacting various episodes from British history; these included William Rufus installing Anselm as Archbishop of Canterbury and Queen Elizabeth I being royally entertained.

Spectators watched from a specially erected 4,000-seat grandstand built on one side of the lake, while a band provided the necessary accompaniment to the chorus who floated on the lake in four decorative barges. A number of evening events were held in conjunction with the pageant to help raise money for charity, including fancy-dress balls at the Town Hall and Winter Gardens. The proceeds went to the Veterans' Relief Fund, a charity which aided soldiers and sailors who had been members of Her Majesty's Armed Forces prior to 1860. Despite some inclement weather, the pageant appears to have been a success. (Various sources, including Steven Blake, *Cheltenham: A Pictorial History*)

JULY 7TH

1841: On this day the Hon. Craven Berkeley, younger brother of the notorious Colonel Berkeley of Berkeley Castle, was re-elected to Parliament. He had been the first Cheltenham MP elected after the Reform Act of 1832, and held his seat in the 1835 election made necessary by the accession of Queen Victoria.

By the time of the 1841 general election, Liberals had held power for eleven years; the public wanted change and some realistic opposition began to show its head. The Cheltenham Conservatives nominated James Agg-Gardner from a well-known family who had recently bought the manor from Lord Sherborne. The Radicals put up another distinguished candidate, Colonel Peyronet Thompson, who had fought in the West Indies and the Peninsular War.

The election was held in a field at Bayshill. Agg-Gardner's platform was that he owned so much of the town that its interests would always be very close to his heart. The whole event degenerated, with a bucket of water being thrown. In the final vote, Craven Berkeley received 764 votes and Agg-Gardner 655. Poor old Thompson received only four votes and consequently the Radicals fielded no further candidates. The following day a great banquet and procession was held to celebrate Berkeley's victory. But Berkeley's days were numbered and Agg-Gardner would eventually be elected to represent Cheltenham in Parliament, a seat he held for forty-three years. (Gwen Hart, *A History of Cheltenham*)

JULY 8TH

1826: On this day, perhaps the best known of Cheltenham's shops, the department store Cavendish House, opened for business at No. 3 Promenade. The store's origins go back to 1818, but in fact it was only in 1826 that Thomas Clark and William Debenham of Wigmore Street, near Cavendish Square, in London, opened a branch of their drapery business in Cheltenham.

The store was by far the largest and smartest in Cheltenham, and had all the airs and graces of a Harrods or Fortnum & Mason. The premises were refurbished a few times in the 1800s, whilst remaining largely on the same location. The most substantial refurbishment was in 1931, with the creation of its distinctive art deco pre-Brutalist 287ft frontage on the Promenade. The entrances on Regent Street retained the older Victorian and Art Nouveau styles.

The inside of the building remains a rabbit-warren of steps and rooms, a legacy of the various expansions. The once-famous food hall, which sold a wide range of delicatessen items, has now sadly disappeared, along with the uniformed concierges at the main entrance who kept 'undesirables' from entering the premises. The store was taken over and became part of House of Fraser in 1970. (Various sources, including John Roles, *Cheltenham in Old Picture Postcards*)

JULY 9TH

1914: On this day a bronze statue of Edward Adrian Wilson (*see* January 17th) was unveiled by Sir Clements Markham. This part of the Promenade, the Long Gardens in front of the Municipal Offices, has three other statues of interest.

One of Cheltenham's most famous landmarks is the Neptune Fountain which stands at the south end of the gardens, on the corner of St George's Road. The magnificent statue was designed by borough engineer Joseph Hall and was constructed in Portland stone by the town's leading monumental masons, R.L. Boulton & Sons, in 1892-3. The statue shows Neptune, the god of water, holding a trident as a symbol of his power over the sea. The fountain draws water from the River Chelt, which flows below it through a large culvert, and is said to have been inspired by the Trevi Fountain in Rome. It was officially unveiled on 3 October 1893.

In the centre of the gardens is Cheltenham War Memorial. This 24ft-high simple cenotaph was unveiled on 1 October 1921. At the other end of the gardens is a statue commemorating local men who died in the Boer War. This statue was unveiled in 1907. (Various sources)

July 10th

1858: On this day the town band took part in a great procession to mark the arrival of the Sebastopol guns. Brass bands were, and still are, very popular and gave frequent concerts in the various bandstands in the town.

In 1834, the *Cheltenham Looker-On* wrote: 'For the last ten years Cheltenham has been almost as famous for its musical amusements as for its waters.' Certainly the various spas jostled to have the best music. Soon after the Montpellier Spa opened, the *Looker-On* in 1833 mentioned its band in nearly every issue. There was a concert nearly every night during the season, which was held either in the Spa Promenade, in Montpellier Gardens or in the Rotunda. Most of these bands were predominately woodwind bands but in 1836 the first brass band was reported. The band had almost a monopoly until 1841, when the owner of the Pittville Spa announced the creation of his own band. These and other spa bands rather died out in the 1860s, with the falling popularity of the spas themselves. (CLHS Journal 9)

JULY 11TH

1958: On this day Mark Lester, best remembered as the cherubic, blonde boy who played Oliver Twist in the film *Oliver*, was born. The 1968 film won six Oscars and made Mark an international star at the age of ten.

After drifting away from his acting career, Mark trained at the British School of Osteopathy and opened his osteopathy and acupuncture clinic in Cheltenham in 1993. Asked why he chose Cheltenham, he replied:

> My dad had a weekend place near Cirencester and I used to come down from London while I was training. I was looking for somewhere in Gloucestershire to set up an osteopathy practice after I qualified. We … found our way into Cheltenham. I'd grown up in London so coming here was a breath of fresh air.
>
> Cheltenham proved to be ideal. We drove past this house by chance. There was a large 'For Sale' sign outside and the property was pretty dilapidated. … We restored it and established my clinic and were ready to go. I love Cheltenham; it's a beautiful town, so much happening; so many good restaurants, festivals, a great theatre and fantastic countryside only five minutes away. I love it here and I'll never leave.

(Interview by Michael Hasted in *The Cheltonian* magazine)

JULY 12TH

1788: On this day King George III and Queen Charlotte arrived in Cheltenham to take the waters. They were to stay nearly five weeks. Overnight, the King's visit transformed Cheltenham into one of the most fashionable and exciting towns in England. The press covered the visit in great detail, with lengthy articles in the *Gentleman's Magazine* and the *Morning Post*. The visit was also chronicled in the works of Peter Pindar, the leading satirist of the time.

The *Morning Post* was keen to link Cheltenham with as many fashionable things as possible – there was the Cheltenham cap, the Cheltenham bonnet, Cheltenham buttons and Cheltenham buckles. One could be dressed from head to foot in eighteenth-century Cheltenham merchandise. It is not known if there were any tee-shirts, though a good slogan would have been *SPAced Out*. Journalists were keen to hype up the town, declaring that Well Walk was on a par with Pall Mall in London.

During their visit the royal party stayed at Lord Fauconberg's newly built house Bayshill, and the King rose at 6 a.m. most mornings to take the waters. (Various sources, including the *Morning Post*)

JULY 13TH

2011: On this day, the death of rock guitarist Michael Burston was announced. He had been born in Cheltenham on 23 October 1949 and was perhaps better known by his stage name, Würzel.

Before joining Motörhead in 1984 at the age of thirty-five, Burston had been a corporal in the army, serving in Germany and Northern Ireland with the 1st Battalion of the Gloucestershire Regiment. It was in the army that he earned the nickname Würzel, as in Worzel Gummidge, because of his West Country accent and dishevelled appearance.

He once said, 'I knew deep down that the only thing I would really be happy doing was playing rock 'n' roll.' After hearing that Brian Robertson had left Motörhead, Michael sent a demo tape to the legendary founder of the group, Lemmy. Würzel became the madcap court jester and counterfoil to Lemmy's sterner image.

One of his first performances with the band was in an episode of the cult comedy *The Young Ones*. Between 1984 and his departure from the band in 1995, he played on nine studio and live albums. Much of Würzel's popularity came from his unaffected good nature and his expert musicianship. (Various sources, including *Gloucestershire Echo*)

JULY 14TH

1956: On this day Cheltenham became linked with Annecy, one of the most beautiful towns in France, nestling, as it does, under the Alps and beside one of the cleanest and most spectacular lakes in the world. The town formally became twinned with Cheltenham when the Protocol of Friendship was signed on the French national holiday: 14 July.

Annecy has a population of 115,000 and is situated in south-east France, close to the Swiss and Italian borders. Lake Annecy covers an area of over 10 square miles and is central to many of the leisure activities that take place in the town. It provides a haven for water-sport enthusiasts in the summer, with the mountains providing a skiers' paradise in the winter. The town is one of three candidate cities for the 2018 Winter Olympic Games. The many bars and restaurants in the lakeside villages and old town are a gourmet's delight. Running along the lake is the Promenade Cheltenham, where there is even a red British telephone box. Annecy is a centre for the arts and has hosted the Annecy International Animated Film Festival since 1960. (Various sources)

JULY 15TH

2010: On this day it was reported that a Cheltenham Gold Cup, one of horseracing's most famous trophies, had been stolen from Raymond Mould's house in Wormington, Gloucestershire.

The cup had been won in 1988 by Charter Party, who was trained at Cheltenham by David Nicholson and was ridden to Gold Cup success by Richard Dunwoody. Gloucestershire police said it was one of a number of trophies stolen, with a combined value estimated at more than £150,000. They added that a new Gold Cup is cast every year and that the owner keeps the cup he has won. A Challenge Cup trophy and a Britannia Handicap Cup trophy were also stolen. In addition, bronze ornaments in the shape of a hare, a spaniel with a pheasant in its mouth, and two horses being ridden by jockeys were stolen, along with a dark wooden clock with gold sides and a gold mechanism, two silver trophies, a silver fisherman ornament and a cigarette case. (*Daily Mail* online)

JULY 16TH

1853: On this day a Grand Exhibition of Plants in Cheltenham's Pittville Park was reported in the national press:

On Tuesday the county of Gloucester and Cheltenham Horticultural Society held their annual Exhibition at Cheltenham. The fete was distinguished by a variety of splendid plants, fruit, flowers etc. from the Continent – this being the first occasion of foreign contributions being received at such exhibitions in this country: and the success which has attended the experiment promises great additions to the attractions of our Horticultural Societies.

The fete was given in the beautiful grounds of Pittville. The display of fashionably-dressed ladies, in the light summer costume, gave great gaiety to the scene. The banks of the lake, with its fountains playing, formed an agreeable promenade for the company, after gratifying the sight with the lovely flowers of all kinds, and from distant countries.

The Customs in London and Dover very politely forwarded the plants from the Continent without opening them, and sent down an officer to inspect them on their arrival. ... The bands of the Highlanders and 1st Royals played throughout the day.

(*Illustrated London News*)

JULY 17TH

1907: On this day, General Sir Ian Hamilton unveiled the South African War Memorial which commemorates the sixty Cheltenham men killed during the Boer War. The statue stands at the northern end of the Promenade Gardens in front of the Municipal Offices.

The figure of the soldier standing in the 'arms reversed' position (i.e. his rifle is upside down) was modelled by R.L. Boulton's head modeller, Ambrose Neale. The statue was produced in bronze rather than stone as had been originally intended. The impressive figure is dressed in the British Army uniform of the turn of the century, with his head bent, only a few yards from Cheltenham's main war memorial.

The Promenade Gardens in which the statue stands were the result of one of the municipal improvements carried out in 1893, when a loan was raised to purchase the Montpellier Gardens and to renovate the previously unkempt gardens in front of Harward's Buildings. (*Cheltenham Looker-On*)

July 18th

1914: On this day a society wedding at Christ Church was reported. The wedding had taken place on the previous Thursday afternoon between Major G.D.P. Swinley and Miss Harriet Lamb. The bride was a daughter of the late Mr William Wilkin Lamb and Mrs Lamb of Mockerkin, Cheltenham. The bridegroom's father was Major-General G. Swinley of No. 2 Fauconberg Villas, Cheltenham.

The bride wore a beautiful dress of softest white chiffon over white satin. The skirt was draped, revealing an underskirt of silk net embroidered with pearls. Honiton lace was used to enrich the dress, and the full court train was draped with old Brussels lace. The veil, arranged over a coronal of orange blooms, was lent by the bride's cousin. Her only ornament was a diamond and pearl pendant and she carried a white exotic shower bouquet, both gifts from the bridegroom. Captain McCloughin supported his brother officer as best man.

The bride's mother subsequently held a reception at the Pittville Pump Room. Major and Mrs Swinley spent their honeymoon touring through the New Forest by motor. (*Cheltenham Looker-On*)

July 19th

2002: On this day a commemorative green plaque was unveiled to honour the famous Montpellier caryatids.

The caryatids had first appeared in 1843 in Montpellier Walk near to the Montpellier Spa. There were originally three terracotta statues, loosely based on the ancient figures on the Acropolis in Athens. The sculptor was Henry Rossi from London. The other statues were added between 1843 and the 1850s, said to have been carved by local sculptor William Giles Brown. However, it has since been established that they were carved by his father, James Brown, at his Tivoli Studios, where William was an apprentice. One of Rossi's original caryatids was removed in 1969 in order to make a cast for the production of more statues.

The plaque, on No. 1 Montpellier Walk, was co-sponsored by the Montpellier Traders' Association and unveiled by the Mayor, Councillor Kenneth Buckland. The plaque had originally been proposed by Revd Brian Torode, who had written a history of Tivoli in 1998. John Henry, chairman of the Civic Society, stood alongside the reverend and, following the ceremony, Dr Stephen Blake gave a talk on the history of Montpellier. One of the original statues can be seen in the town's museum. (Smith & Rowbotham, *Commemorative Plaques of Cheltenham*)

July 20th

2007: On this day Cheltenham saw some of the worst flooding in living memory. Despite new flood defences having been put in place only a year or two earlier, after torrential rain the River Chelt burst its banks and whole swathes of the town ended up under a foot or two of murky water. The worst affected areas were around the Playhouse Theatre in Bath Road, the Promenade by the Neptune Fountain and some streets in St Luke's.

Although the Chelt appears to be a small and inoffensive river, it has unleashed its venom on many occasions previously. The problem appears to be that the Chelt falls very rapidly, and in the hills above Dowdeswell several small steams feed into it. At this point the so-called river corridor is about 5.5 miles wide but, as it enters the built-up areas of Charlton Kings and Cheltenham, it rapidly narrows to 1.5 miles. If water through this bottleneck builds up, flooding can occur within a couple of hours.

There have been frequent floods in the town since the earliest recorded one in June 1731. The most recent, before the 2007 inundation, had been in August 2004. (Mick Kippin, CLHS Journal 23)

JULY 21ST

1831: On this day a commotion took place in the High Street and a world-famous musician was embarrassed. The renowned Niccolò Paganini was in town to give two concerts at the Assembly Rooms, one on the Wednesday evening, the 20th, followed by a second on the Thursday afternoon. Both concerts were sell-outs. Not to be outdone, the proprietor of the Theatre Royal, Mr DeVille, pulled off a major coup when he visited the maestro at the Plough Hotel and persuaded him to give a third concert at his venue. This would be for 'the lower classes', who could not afford the Assembly Rooms concerts.

In spite of DeVille's efforts to drum up an audience, at the appointed hour not enough tickets were sold to cover Paganini's agreed fee and he refused to play. The crowd got angry and marched along the High Street to the Plough chanting 'Piggy Ninny, Piggy Ninny'.

The violinist was persuaded to change his mind and even waived his fee, saying it should be given to Cheltenham's poor. However, it soon became clear that the mob in the street were not in fact people who had bought tickets for the Theatre Royal, but just a rowdy mob. Paganini was not pleased, and as soon as the concert was over he left town post haste on the 11.30 post chaise to London. (Michael Hasted, *A Theatre for All Seasons*)

JULY 22ND

1914: On this day a grand flower show took place in Montpellier Gardens. It had opened the day before, and on the previous weekend a local newspaper had announced that it:

> ... will, if the magnitude be less, be quite on the lines of the old days when these pretty functions were the chief events or each season; when Society put on its best bib and tucker, took a genuine interest in the orchids and the onions, and paraded its prettiest frocks in the neighbourhood of the band.
>
> Few Flower Shows nowadays seem to get on without extraneous attractions and I for one have little faith that any Horticultural Society could be revived on the old plan of three shows a year. As far back as 1853, there was a British and Foreign Horticultural Exhibition held at Pittville, the profits of which were over ninety pounds. This emboldened the then Society to extend its scope with unsatisfactory financial results the next year when a 'Great Exhibition' was held in the Old Wells Walk for six weeks.
>
> The Committee, however, consoled itself with the consideration that its 'Great Exhibition of Horticulture, Works of Art and Design' had rendered much service to Cheltenham by 'causing it to be honourably known as the first and hitherto only provincial town in the kingdom which has followed the example of the Metropolis in opening an Exhibition for cultivating the taste and improving the minds of the people'.

(*Cheltenham Looker-On*)

July 23rd

1932: On this day a full-page advertisement appeared in the local paper extolling the benefits of property investment. It read:

> In times of severe financial stress the value of Real Property is not liable to the violent fluctuations which frequently occur in Stocks and Shares. On the contrary if judiciously purchased in selected areas, it maintains a comparative stability in value unattainable in any other form of investment and remains always a tangible security realisable at will, in the meantime yielding varying rates of interest according to the nature of the holding.

The advert then went on to list some of the available properties in Cheltenham. For example, it was possible to buy a modern, red-brick detached villa with six bedrooms in Christ Church for £1,300. For £1,150 you could buy a detached, double-fronted residence in Tivoli Road with seven bedrooms. If these were a bit out of your league, you could buy a nice little five-roomed cottage in Leckhampton for £300. For slightly more, there was a pair of modern villas on sale in Charlton Kings with seven rooms and a garden. They were offered as 'good value to a Lady willing to purchase sound property showing a small, safe return' of £32 per annum in rent. (*Cheltenham Chronicle and Gloucestershire Graphic*)

JULY 24TH

2011: On this day, Lord Jones unveiled two pieces of art at the Cheltenham branch of the Samaritans. The ceremony took place during a 'Take tea with Samaritans' event, which was part of the national Samaritans Awareness Day.

Local artist and Samaritan volunteer, Judy Richards, produced a painting of forget-me-not flowers. She said that the theme of forget-me-nots worked on a number of different levels. It could relate to remembering a loved one, or remembering that Samaritans are available to support those in distress twenty-four hours a day. The event also hoped to encourage people to remember Samaritans by way of a legacy or through donations made during their lifetime. In 2010 the Cheltenham Samaritans gave support to 40,000 callers.

Tasked with creating an image celebrating Samaritans, Cheltenham was one of 119 of the charity's branches across the UK to submit a piece of artwork. Using all of the images, Samaritans commissioned artists Grit Hartung and Marilou Rabourdin to produce a national piece of artwork. The final creation was a flexible structure spelling out the words 'Call US' and 'Join US'. (Cheltenham & District Samaritans)

July 25th

1758: On this day the *Gloucester Journal* described some of the amusements that were available to visitors at the nearby Cheltenham Spa:

> For the entertainment of these visitors there were the country pastimes [of] cock-fighting and bull-baiting with dogs in the Street ... In one of the lanes leading from the High Street a very small malt-house had been converted into a primitive theatre. It was here that the young Sarah Siddons appeared in *Venice Preserved* and so moved some members of the audience that they reported her performance to David Garrick. Shortly afterwards she began her famous career on the London stage. Travelling companies moving between Stratford and Warwick also played in the little Cheltenham theatre.
>
> There were balls and card parties and billiards in the newly built rooms at the Spa and bowls on the green at the back of the Plough. There is a great appearance of gentry at the Balls every Monday and Thursday and at the Card Assemblies every Tuesday, Wednesday, Friday and Saturday.

(Gwen Hart, *A History of Cheltenham*)

JULY 26TH

1855: On this day a flash flood severely damaged Jessop's Nursery, one of the town's most visited attractions.

Jessop's Nursery Gardens, opened around 1821 by Charles Hale Jessop, stood on a 20-acre plot of land that later became St James' railway station and is currently the new development in St James' Square. The extensive gardens attracted huge numbers of visitors, who came to see the bananas, rice and breadfruit plants. A broad gravelled path led through the gardens, crossing the Chelt by a rustic bridge. The gardens were accessed through St George's Terrace in the east, linking St James' Square to St George's Place and the Royal Crescent. In the 1840s Jessop was obliged to sell a significant amount of land to the Great Western Railway for their station.

The dreadful flood, said to be the worst for 273 years, occurred when the River Chelt burst its banks and caused damage worth in excess of £800, depositing tons of bricks, wood and mud over the ground. The nursery never fully recovered and in 1858 Jessop was declared bankrupt and the gardens were put up for auction. (Mick Kippin, CLHS Journal 23)

JULY 27TH

1906: On this day the boys of Cheltenham Grammar School presented their retiring headmaster, Mr Style, with an album containing all their autographs and inscribed with a Latin text. For those of you who think the tone of this book would benefit from a better class of narrative, here it is in its original:

Ad virum streuuum, justum. constantem, Johannem Style, Artium Magistrum, Scholae Grammaticae Patesianae apud Cheltonicnses per annos viginti quattuor Archididasculum. Nos Scholae ejusdetn alumni tui mox altcuutis desiderium mocsti prospicientes verbum 'Vale' raro sine dolore dicendum, sed optimis nostris pro tua felicitate precibus et votis, sincero cordis affectu cupimus pronuntiare. / Per multos annos nos quorum nomima sunt subscripta te probe novimus non solum in Litteris Humanioribus eruditum sed etiam studiis recentioribus et hodiernis et scientiae naturali aeque faventum; novimus etiam semper erga omnes tuae curae commissos, ad quodcumque vitae propositum praeparandos, amicissimum, et quo modo eis maxime prodesses serio et perpetuo studentem. / Quantum in hoc officio et opere, tam gravi, tam necessario, tu, vir dilecte, Scholae nostrae, Rei-Publicae, ne dicam Imperio nostro, profecisti, Registrum eorum qui in largiore arena Universitatum nostrorum vel in vita et negotiis cujuscumque genens honores adepti sunt et bene profecerunt satis indicat. Certissimum vero documentum quam feliciter tu, non solum ingenio et moribus verum, etiam studio, doctrina, conscientia, tuum munus obiisti, restat notandum; crescens scilicet eorum numerus qui, sub tuo regimine, Scholae nostrae alumni facti, eam, sicut nos ipsi, dilexerunt, diligunt et diligent in futuro. Te, vir honorande, jam deponentem officium tuum tam digue, impletum, honos. memoria, desiderium prosequitur araicorun.

(*Cheltenham Looker-On*)

JULY 28TH

1906: On this day the Vagabonds gave their final performances in Montpellier Gardens. The party was organised by Mr Harold Montague, under whose capable direction they had already met with much success in London and various parts of the provinces. Mr Montague took an active part in the programme as a humourist; many of the items were of his own composition and sufficiently illustrated his versatility as an entertainer.

He was ably supported by a number of capable artistes, among whom mention must be made of Miss Belle Green, who was an old favourite, having appeared there in another company last year. The reputation she then made was more than sustained during the week. Miss Merita Leclair sang nicely and received numerous recalls, while Mr Percival Mackenzie's cartoons were distinctly amusing, his sketches being particularly effective and executed with astonishing rapidity. With a few strokes he was able to turn the most common objects into something totally different, and he was able to draw sea or landscape views upside down with equal facility. Mr Mackenzie also excelled as a banjoist. Mr Ernest Devereax sang in an acceptable manner and Mr David Norton played a number of piano solos, as well as acting as accompanist. (*Cheltenham Looker-On*)

JULY 29TH

1816: On this day the new Assembly Rooms opened in Cheltenham on the corner of the High Street and Rodney Road.

Public rooms (then known as the Lower and Upper Rooms) had existed on the site since 1784. The new venue opened with a magnificent Grand Dress Ball, attended by the Duke and Duchess of Wellington. In addition there were upwards of 1,400 'personages of distinction in society' in attendance, who had paid an admission of 7s 6d (men) and 5s 6d (ladies). A month later, on 29 August, the Duke and Duchess of Orléans, the future King Louis-Philippe and Queen Marie-Amelie of France, attended a harp recital in the hall. They had recently taken up residence in nearby Cambray House after the Duke of Wellington had left Cheltenham.

Mr J.K. Griffith wrote in his 1818 guide to the town that 'The new Assembly Rooms may now be ranked among the most elegantly finished piles of building in the Empire. ... The entrance hall is neat and very extensive being upwards of 120 feet in length, terminated by an elegant bar.' (CLHS Journal 5)

JULY 30TH

1795: On this day the first troop of the Gloucestershire Yeomanry was raised at the Plough Hotel in the High Street. This was in response to Prime Minister William Pitt's fear that invasion by Napoleon Bonaparte was possible. The cavalry troop, which consisted of volunteer gentlemen and yeomen, was under the command of Captain Peter Snell of Guiting Power. Troops were to be formed around the country under the control of each county's Lord Lieutenant. Their role was to control any civic unrest or riots, and provide home defence in an invasion. Several other troops were created in the area, including Minchinhampton, Wotton-under-Edge and Stow-on-the-Wold. Following the end of the Napoleonic Wars in 1802, all but the Cheltenham troop were disbanded. In 1803 the war re-erupted and twelve troops were reconstituted. However, it seems the only time they saw action was quelling a riot in Gloucester between the citizens and a group of Irish militia.

In 1834 the Gloucestershire Yeomanry troops amalgamated with the Gloucestershire Yeomanry Cavalry, and in 1841 they were granted the title 'Royal' by Queen Victoria. In 1847 the regiment became the Royal Gloucestershire Hussars. You could often tell a local hussar as moustaches were compulsory. Soldiers who were unable to grow a moustache were supplied with one by the regimental barber. (Smith & Rowbotham, *Commemorative Plaques of Cheltenham*)

July 31st

1958: On this day a handwritten notice appeared on a popular café's glass door. It stated 'Closed for Alterations'. The door was that of El Flamenco, Cheltenham's most popular coffee bar and focus of the local in-crowd, including the young Brian Jones. For three years El Flam had been the place to go and be seen by the jazz and skiffle-loving, art-school crowd of semi-beatniks in Cheltenham. In the 1950s young people used to hang around coffee bars celebrating rock 'n' roll and drinking the newfangled espresso coffee. El Flam in the High Street (now The Strand bar) was only one of the many 'in' places in Cheltenham at the time. The Tiffin in Royal Well Crescent was another, as was Geraldine's near the old Regal cinema.

When El Flam closed, in fact never to reopen, it didn't take the kids long to find a new place to go. The Studio Coffee Lounge had opened a few doors along, above Dewhurst's butcher shop in the Strand. Here the proprietor, Eric Baylis, a well-known local society photographer, served coffee and real beef steak baps in pleasant surroundings in two rooms on the first floor. Later, other trendy venues included Bar-B-Q and the Waikiki in Queens Circus, at the side of the Queens Hotel. (John B. Appleby, *38 Priory Street and all that Jazz*, courtesy of Jane Filby-Johnson)

AUGUST 1ST

2011: On this day an interview with Vicky Tuck, the principal of the Cheltenham Ladies' College, was published. After running the college for fifteen years she was about to start a new job in charge of the International School in Geneva, Switzerland, which has nearly 4,000 pupils of both sexes, aged three to nineteen.

She is probably the most successful girls' school head of her generation, strengthening the college's reputation and keeping up the numbers when neither single-sex education nor boarding is in fashion. During her time at the college, it is reputed that pupils coined the expression 'chav', this being their snooty way of putting down the local proletarian youth. The Ladies' College is often cited as the 'female Eton', but this is a concept Tuck has refuted, claiming that girls still have far fewer opportunities in politics and business than boys in spite of alumnae that include two ministers, a deputy governor of the Bank of England and one national newspaper editor (Rosie Boycott).

Ms Tuck was the first principal of the college to have been married. In fact, its most famous head, Dorothea Beale, was immortalised along with the first head of North London Collegiate in the rhyme: 'Miss Buss and Miss Beale / Cupid's darts do not feel. / How different from us, / Miss Beale and Miss Buss.' (*Guardian*)

AUGUST 2ND

1972: On this day the Everyman Theatre acquired the status of a Grade II listed building. Its listing citation describes it as:

... red brick in Flemish bond where original with ashlar dressings and terracotta and concealed roof.

Exterior:- 2 storeys, five bays. Facade articulated by pilaster strips to ends and between bays through ground and first floors, with moulded lintel band and cornice over first floor windows (missing to right), depressed over windows to 2nd and 4th bays, with *ogeed* arches above *voussoirs*; moulded panels with masks; further moulded string with plaque to centre inscribed 'EVERYMAN'; moulded cornice as second-floor sill band; pediments to second and fourth bays with ornate scrolls to tympana. Ground floor has wide opening to left, otherwise C20 glazed doors and mainly large windows. ... Attic: outer casements and central tripartite window with ½ columns between. Crowning ornate frieze and cornice, pediment set back to centre has scroll decoration.

Interior:- a sumptuous and intact scheme with 2 galleries and a further gallery set behind the upper one. Boxes at circle level, shallow domed ceiling. Very elaborate rococo decoration to fronts of galleries, and wood and plaster decoration to boxes. Of principal interest for the interior, a good example of the provincial work of one of Britain's two major theatre architects.

(British Listed Buildings)

AUGUST 3RD

1990: On this day the highest temperature ever recorded in the UK at the time – a scorching 37.1°C – was registered in Cheltenham. There was once a small meteorological station in Montpellier Gardens near Montpellier Walk, surrounded by iron railings. This contained equipment for measuring such things as temperature, rainfall, wind speed, and air pressure. This little patch of ground, known as Station 4967, was the domain of Frank Ford, who lived in The Lodge up by the tennis courts. Before retiring in 2003, Frank took five readings every day over a thirty-three-year period – a grand total of 60,265 readings, including leap years.

The equipment was removed from Montpellier Gardens in 2001 and a small plaque that marked the spot was later moved to the refreshment kiosk a few yards away. The official meteorological thermometer used by Frank was set up at a new meteorological station at Gloucestershire Airport.

In August 2003 Cheltenham lost its record to Gravesend in Kent, which notched up a new high of 38.1°C. On 24 July 2004 Frank Ford unveiled a new plaque on the refreshment kiosk which was sponsored by the Civic Society and Friends of Montpellier Bandstand to commemorate his achievement. The Cheltenham Brass Band played and a good time was had by all. (Smith & Rowbotham, *Commemorative Plaques of Cheltenham*)

August 4th

2011: On this day, community-spirited bosses of a Charlton Kings shop announced that relief was at hand and that they were stepping in to help run a village toilet. Managers of the Co-operative had agreed to lock the Church Piece public convenience each night. The move meant that Charlton Kings Parish Council, which had recently taken over the running of the facility, could be excused. Parish council chairman, Martyn Fry, said: 'We were having trouble finding somebody to open and close the toilets, so this is a great relief. If the Co-op had not offered, the parish councillors would have had to take turns fulfilling the role.' Some council members did seem a little flushed but were glad to be able to wash their hands of the whole thing.

The deal was struck by parish councillor Rob Reid after talks with the store. Borough bosses had recently agreed to hand over the toilet and adjoining Stanton Rooms in a bid to save maintenance costs because, it seems, they were not willing to spend a penny. (*Gloucestershire Echo*)

AUGUST 5TH

1818: On this day the building of a Masonic temple in Cheltenham was proposed by Brother Baynes. A month later, at a meeting of the Foundation Lodge held at Sheldon's Hotel in York Passage, it was agreed to start making plans for the new building. In May 1820 the plans were sent to HRH the Duke of Sussex, and the contractor, local architect Mr G. Underwood, was engaged.

The Masonic Hall in Portland Street is believed to be the second oldest purpose-built lodge in England. It is one of the few temples in the country which has continuously been used as a lodge room for considerably over 100 years. It is also the oldest public building in Cheltenham, other than the churches, still used for the purpose for which it was designed.

The external appearance of the building is an impressive stone structure, with deep recesses in the walls. There are a few Masonic ornaments carved in the solid stone and two pillars on the main front. At the four corners of the building are heavy tower-like projections which appear to contain what are possibly secret chambers. (W. Bro. Paul Dyke, *Foundation Lodge 1753 to 1965* (privately printed history); Records of Foundation Lodge, Gloucestershire Public Record Office)

AUGUST 6TH

1932: On this day the opening of the new Black & White coach station in St Margaret's Road was celebrated. When the local paper visited, it found fifty coaches in the station at the same time and said the scene resembled a busy London railway terminus.

St Margaret's Road became the hub of Associated Motorways, a consortium formed by six motor coach operators in 1934. The aim was to pool their services between the Midlands and the South and West of England, and between London and South Wales. The consortium was formed as a result of the Road Traffic Act 1930, which encouraged competing coach operators to co-ordinate their services. Associated Motorways did not own or operate any coaches. Each member company committed itself to providing an agreed mileage of coach journeys for Associated Motorways, which took a share of the profits.

At a peak summer weekend the consortium could have over 800 coaches on the road. Every day, coaches from all over England and Wales converged in Cheltenham and exchanged passengers with each other. At 2 p.m. sharp, an inspector blew his whistle and the coaches departed en masse. The coach station closed in 1984. (*Cheltenham Chronicle and Gloucestershire Graphic*)

AUGUST 7TH

1901: On this day the first Cheltenham tram service was inaugurated. The No. 7 tram was bedecked with flags and bunting and conveyed invited guests, including the Mayor, Alderman G. Norman.

Work had been completed on the line a month earlier, but a trial run on 29 July had ended tragically when a car descending Cleeve Hill had overturned, killing two workmen. It was found that the brakes had been incorrectly fitted, but public confidence was restored when a second trial took place. The tram, attended by numerous bicycles and other vehicles, ascended the hill with no mishap. The Board of Trade issued a certificate of safety and two days later the first passenger service started, with trams running between Lansdown and Southam.

The trams were an instant success and within the first week carried 44,000 passengers. The *Gloucestershire Graphic* waxed lyrical: 'At last the trams are here; round the corner comes the huge mass like a small town hall on wheels and the quiet respectability of Cheltenham is challenged by the sharp "Ting-Tang" of the gong and the grinding of the wheels in the rail grooves ...' (Various sources, including Steven Blake, *Cheltenham: A Pictorial History*)

AUGUST 8TH

1838: On this day a grand centenary fête was held to celebrate the founding of Skillicorne's Well, an act that was to set Cheltenham on the path to becoming one of the most fashionable towns in Regency England.

Henry Skillicorne, a retired Manx sea captain, could be described as the father of modern Cheltenham. The first well or spa had been discovered in 1716 by Skillicorne's father-in-law, on a site in Montpellier on which now stands Princess Hall at the Ladies' College. It was Skillicorne who saw the potential of the spa and developed the site from 1738 onwards; he was aided by his wife, who laid out Well Walk which led from the spa to the parish church.

There is a memorial to Henry Skillicorne, said to be the longest in England, in the parish church. One of Cheltenham's hidden secrets is the Skillicorne Garden directly at the back of the Town Hall in Imperial Square. The garden is kept locked but it is possible to see it by peering through the iron gate. It contains a bas-relief bust of the great man by local sculptor Percy Braisby. (Various sources, including Rowbotham & Waller, *Cheltenham: A History*)

AUGUST 9TH

1841: On this day an exhibition of Works of Art and Science opened in the Promenade. The show had been planned at a Special General Meeting of the Cheltenham Literary & Philosophical Institution on 27 May. Although for decades Cheltenham had been known as the Pleasure Town, the Institution (founded in 1833) was keen to promote 'a spirited attempt to disseminate a knowledge and love of the arts and sciences among the town's people'. Their plan was to hold the exhibition for at least two months. The venue for the show – part of Promenade Villa near the Queens Hotel – was to be their headquarters.

The exhibition consisted of four areas. In the Institute's lecture room there was a display of Ancient and Modern Buildings, with paintings, drawings and models, as well as some sculpture. Many of the 200 paintings had been loaned by local families. There were works by Veronese, Poussin, Canaletto and Velázquez alongside English artists Sir Joshua Reynolds and Thomas Gainsborough. Cheltenham had never seen anything like it. Two of the other rooms housed a Museum of Natural History, and in another was the Archaeological Museum or Museum of Antiquities. (Gwen Hart, *A History of Cheltenham*)

August 10th

1868: On this day inveterate diary writer William Swift, a schoolteacher from Badgeworth, wrote about a walk he had taken in Leckhampton. Swift was a keen rambler, often combining his walks with visits to local churches and frequently covering 20 miles in a single day. On this fine summer's day he made a trip to Leckhampton Church and remarked on the many fine new graves to be seen there, including some 'very old wedge-shaped stones with full length crosses'.

Swift ate his picnic lunch in a field a short distance from the church and then climbed the hill. Apparently it was a very warm day and the teacher found it quite hard-going. Feeling rather parched by his exertion, Mr Swift eagerly anticipated the cool spring he would find at the so-called 'diamond of the desert' on Charlton Common. Unfortunately, a large herd of sheep had passed that way a little earlier, rendering the track rather messy. Unwilling to dirty his boots, Swift made a detour down Sandy Lane and drank from a trough there.

William Swift kept a journal all his life, from at least 1859, recording many interesting events and locations around Cheltenham and Gloucester. He died in February 1915, an event not mentioned in his diary. (CLHS Journal 8)

AUGUST 11TH

1741: On this day a great sporting event was held. In the days before television, radio and video games, people had to make their own entertainment. Very often they did this by hitting each other on the head.

On the Thursday in question, a cudgel match was advertised which was to take place outside the Plough Hotel in Cheltenham High Street: the first to 'break the most heads in three bouts to win a good hat and a guinea'. Possibly the ones with the broken heads would need the hat more, in order to cover their bandages.

Violent, unpleasant sports were common in the streets in those days. Bull-baiting was popular, as was cock-fighting. Bare-knuckle fighting was keenly followed and Cheltenham had its own champion pugilist in the muscular shape of James 'Earwig' Edwards, who was born in Rutland Street in 1822. Edwards was the local champion in the ring and was known nationally as 'the king of the lightweights'. During one fight, which lasted for 167 rounds, Edwards broke his arm but carried on fighting. The contest was declared a draw when night fell. Perhaps that's what was meant by 'knocking the daylights out of each other'. (Rowbotham & Waller, *Cheltenham: A History*)

AUGUST 12TH

1990: On this day the Gloucestershire Warwickshire Railway held an open day. Thousands attended the event at Toddington station, where many old railway engines were on view and rides could be taken along the old Honeybourne line towards Cheltenham.

The GWR runs along a part of the former Great Western Railway's main line from Birmingham to Cheltenham. The line commands wonderful views of the sleepy hamlets and villages as it passes through the beautiful Cotswold countryside. It was built between 1900 and 1906, primarily to improve through services from Birmingham to Bristol and the West Country. It also carried fruit from the highly productive farming areas both in the Cotswolds and the Vale of Evesham. The line closed to local passenger traffic in March 1960 but continued in use for goods services until an incident at Winchcombe in August 1976 effectively closed the line.

Following early work primarily aimed at trying to keep the line open, the Gloucestershire Warwickshire Railway was formed in 1981 with the aim of one day restoring this line from Stratford Racecourse to Cheltenham Racecourse to its former glory. By 1984 work had advanced sufficiently to allow the first public train to operate over a ¼ mile of track, and, on Sunday 22 April, Nicholas Ridley MP, the Secretary of State for Transport, cut the ribbon to mark the official opening. (Various sources, including *Gloucestershire Echo*)

AUGUST 13TH

2011: On this day a very unusual and rare event took place when a professional presentation of Shakespeare's comedy *Much Ado About Nothing* was staged at the Lido in Cheltenham. The aptly named Rain or Shine Theatre Co. presented the play, directed by James Reynard, at a variety of open-air venues across the county, as well as other UK locations throughout the summer.

Sitting in deckchairs with a blanket and a thermos of hot tea on their laps, theatregoers had the chance to enjoy one of the greatest romantic comedies of all time. The review in *The Stage* said:

> Rain or Shine is real fit-up theatre with a small and very adaptable set, and a van. This eight-strong company certainly earns its money, which is probably loose change to their more illustrious London counterparts. They play 14 parts between them and, on several occasions, it must be a quick-change tent routine.

(Various sources, including *The Stage*)

AUGUST 14TH

2011: On this day a youth was photographed vandalising one of the life-size horse sculptures that was displayed on the streets of Cheltenham.

A trail of horse sculptures had been created around the town to celebrate the centenary of the Cheltenham Festival. They were also used as a way of maintaining public awareness of the museum during the two-year period it was closed for development. The ten horses were designed by local artist P.J. Crook and painted by local businesses, schools and other artists. After the incident, a police spokesperson said:

> We need to speak to this man in the images and also the woman who is seen photographing him. I realise this damage may have happened as a result of silly behaviour going wrong, but damage was caused and this is a criminal offence. We would urge the people in the picture or anyone with information that could help the investigation to come forward.

The exhibition, called Horse Parade, was organised by Cheltenham Art Gallery & Museum and ran until 16 October. All the horses were then moved to the racecourse and auctioned off for charity. (*Gloucestershire Echo*)

AUGUST 15TH

1803: On this day, a lady by the name of M. Nevill sent a letter to Lady Reade at Shipton, Burford. The letter gives a very personal account of life in Cheltenham at its most fashionable period. Here are some extracts:

> And now let me beg of your Ladyship to accept our sincerest acknowledgements for the many civilities we have repeatedly received at Shipton and where we so lately spent those pleasant days, which so agreeably broke the length of our journey ... we had a comfortable morning drive to Cheltenham, which had been remarkably full and gay ... The Ball for the Master of ceremonies was uncommonly thin, only 200 were at it; 50 more intended going but were prevented by the bad news from Ireland and one of Lord Longford's family being wounded at St Lucie ... Mrs [Sarah] Siddons seems to have behaved here with less politeness than usual both she and Cooke were gone before we came; and though here is at present a very indifferent set of actors, the house fills especially when plays are bespoke ... We have not been one evening in public, but preferred rural walks to crowded rooms.

(Various sources, including *Jones' Views of the Seats, Mansions, Castles, etc. of Noblemen and Gentlemen etc. etc.*)

AUGUST 16TH

1788: On this day King George III and the royal party left Cheltenham after a five-week visit. The night before their departure, the King and Queen attended a gala performance at the theatre. The upper boxes were crowded with all the fashion that Gloucester, Worcester and the county could send. The playbills for the evening were printed on white satin.

During his visit the King, along with the Queen and other courtiers, made several visits to the theatre, thereby entitling it to be called the Theatre Royal. Those who accompanied the King were very impressed with the theatre, one of them noting:

Mr Penn's *Don Juan* deserved the encomiums of the whole house, and Mr Kelly, brother to the gentleman of the same name at Drury Lane, pleased much in a soft song. … The theatre is a very elegant and commodious structure, erected by Mr Watson, the proprietor and manager. There are two rows of boxes, one in the form of a gallery, behind which in a most ingenious manner is erected another gallery for the servants, etc. The whole of the theatre, scenery, etc. is above mediocrity and the performers are equal to the task of doing their parts justice.

(Michael Hasted, *A Theatre for All Seasons*)

August 17th

1854: On this day a gruesome murder took place in what was then Rutland Street, one of Cheltenham's most notorious slums.

Earlier that year, local resident Mary Killanan, who lived in one of the overcrowded houses in Long's Court, had been charged with assault, grievous bodily harm and attempted murder after attacking one of her neighbours, a fellow Irishwoman named Ellen Carey. Killanan was jealous of Carey, and had previously threatened to murder her. The two had quarrelled again on 16 August and Carey had gone out to look for new accommodation. But when she got back, Killanan picked another argument. At 7 a.m. on the 17th, whilst Carey was asleep, Killanan poured boiling water over her, before beating her with a gardening tool. Naked, Carey escaped to a neighbour's house, but was followed by an angry Killanan. The neighbour shut Killanan out, and Carey collapsed on the floor. She was so scalded that flesh was dropping from her arms, and the blanket the well-meaning neighbour had wrapped round her had quantities of flesh stuck to it. Her head and throat were swollen, and she had severe injuries to her side and back from the beating Killanan had given her. (cotswoldhistory.com, Cotswold Murder Walks – Cheltenham, Nell Darby)

AUGUST 18TH

1961: On this day footballer Mark Buckland was born in Cheltenham.

Buckland started his football career with Cheltenham Town in October 1979, when he scored two goals on his debut match. After moving to AP Leamington, for which he made fifty appearances, he signed for First Division Wolves in 1984. His first match for them was a local derby against Birmingham City on 11 February, a match that resulted in a goalless draw. Mark went on to make fifteen appearances during the remainder of that season as the club dropped out of the top flight. He made forty-one appearances during the 1984/5 season – his only full season at Molineux – scoring five goals. After the club was again relegated, manager Tommy Docherty left and Buckland was released.

He then played for non-league club Kidderminster Harriers, later returning to play once more for the Robins at Cheltenham. He also played for Gloucester City, Moreton Town and several local teams in the Cheltenham area.

His son Alec plays for Bishop's Cleeve and Mark, who coaches the team, turned out as a substitute for their third team on his fiftieth birthday in 2011. To celebrate the occasion, he was presented with a scrapbook containing memorabilia from his long and distinguished career and a fine birthday cake. (Various sources, including *Gloucestershire Echo*)

AUGUST 19TH

2009: On this day, Lloyds Banking Group declared that they were reviewing their decision to close all 164 branches of the Cheltenham & Gloucestershire Building Society.

The previous June, Lloyds, who had taken over the Society in the mid-1990s, had stated their intention to close the branches by November that year. It was estimated that around 1,660 jobs would be lost. However, Lloyds announced that the C&G brand name would still be used to issue mortgages and for managing customers' savings. Society clientele would also be able to access their accounts through the numerous branches of Lloyds TSB.

During the first half of the nineteenth century the population of Cheltenham had risen substantially. In the thirty years from 1820 it doubled, settling at more than 35,000. The lower echelons of society subsequently suffered due to a dire lack of housing for working people in the town. As a result, there were large areas of sub-standard accommodation in Cheltenham, with many people living in appalling conditions. The Cheltenham & Gloucestershire Permanent Mutual Benefit Building and Investment Association was set up in 1850 to help alleviate the situation. The company changed its name to the Cheltenham & Gloucester Building Society in 1918 and by 1990 had a staff of almost 2,500, more than a million investors, and 265,000 borrowers. (Various sources, including Lloyds TSB; Cheltenham & Gloucestershire Building Society)

AUGUST 20TH

1932: On this day the *Graphic* announced the forthcoming week's cinematic entertainment. At that time there were only three cinemas in town plus the Opera House (which had temporarily gone over to films) and the Winter Gardens. The town's two big cinemas, the Gaumont (later the Odeon) and the Regal (later the ABC) would open soon after.

The Palace, which was opposite the Regent Arcade in the High Street, had four programmes during the next seven days, including three spectacular musicals: *The Vagabond King*, *The Big Pond* and *The Love Parade*, the last two starring Maurice Chevalier. The Coliseum in Albion Street was showing *Honor of the Family* starring Bebe Daniels, while the Daffodil was proud to present *The Beast of the City* with Jean Harlow and Walter Huston.

The Opera House in Regent Street had been adapted to a cinema in 1929 and equipped to show the first talkies. For this week it was showing Frederick Lonsdale's most charming romance *Lovers Courageous* starring Robert Montgomery. Its supporting feature – in those days you got two films for your money – was *Hotel Continental*, promising 'Love, Intrigue, Crime' and an optional bag of popcorn. (*Cheltenham Chronicle and Gloucestershire Graphic*)

AUGUST 21ST

1865: On this day an unfortunate Cheltenham grocer discovered the malevolent nature of some varieties of American cheese.

The singular accident occurred at the establishment of Mr Williams, a tea dealer whose shop was in Clarence Street. It appears that two or three very large American cheeses were placed in a slanting position in the window. No doubt Mr Williams thought this made a very attractive window display, but unfortunately he seems not to have taken enough care with it. Consequently, from some unexplained cause, one of the cheeses threw an involuntary somersault over a heap of Portugal onions, demolished the sheet of glass, and made its way with some of the Portugal esculents to the pavement outside. Apparently, Mr Williams had only a few weeks previously taken the precaution to insure his window. Perhaps if he'd stuck to a good old Double Gloucester or a nice Cheddar, the accident could have been avoided. (*Cheltenham Examiner*)

AUGUST 22ND

2011: On this day BBC Newsbeat technology journalist Dan Whitworth reported on his visit to the Government Communications Headquarters in Cheltenham. Better known as GCHQ, the complex is one of the most top secret sites in the UK.

Top secret it may be, but if you were up to no good, or even just a tourist, you certainly would have no trouble finding it. Behind 2m-high razor wire fences guarded by platoons of security guards, CCTV cameras, and half a dozen vehicle checkpoints, the building looms in the western suburb of Benhall like a glimmering, metallic football stadium. In fact, it is roughly the same size and dimensions as Wembley.

Known affectionately to the locals as 'The Doughnut', GCHQ's thousands of staff work with MI5 and MI6 to protect the country's national security interests. They monitor radio signals, emails, satellite and phone communications, and the flow of all electronic data around the world.

Before The Doughnut, the site had consisted of dozens of barrack-type buildings and could easily have been mistaken for a military depot. Its current high profile is due to the increase in electronic communications, television series like *Spooks* and, by no means least, due to the magnificent silver doughnut itself. (Various sources, including BBC Radio 1's Newsbeat)

AUGUST 23RD

1957: On this day Tommy Steele, England's first rock 'n' roll star and our answer to Elvis Presley, attended a private dinner party at the Hop Pole Inn at Tewkesbury after an appearance in Cheltenham. Tommy provided a reason why Cheltenham and its immediate area was so popular with touring bands and musicians. He confided, 'What I like about the crowd around here is that they treat me not as a pop star but as one of their number, free to drink and be merry without being torn to shreds by autograph collectors and souvenir hunters.' As midnight approached, the party sat down to a celebration meal of asparagus soup, roast Cotswold chicken and fresh vegetables, fruit salad, cheese and biscuits, coffee, wines, champagne and finally liqueurs, after which Tommy made a brief felicitous speech. Certainly he appeared to enjoy himself that night, and later coaxed a number of guests into the garage at the rear of the hotel to view his latest car, bought that day from Bob Walker and with the ideal number plate RAD 101 ('Radio-One'). (John B. Appleby, *38 Priory Street and all that Jazz*, courtesy of Jane Filby-Johnson)

AUGUST 24TH

1943: On this day André Gilbert Kempster (né Coccioletti), a former pupil of Cheltenham College, was posthumously awarded the George Cross for an act of gallantry in Algeria during the Second World War. Kempster had died a few days earlier, on 21 August. The official description of his act of bravery read as follows:

> On August 21st, 1943, near Philippeville [Skikda], Major Kempster was carrying out grenade throwing practice with two others in the same pit. A grenade which was thrown by Major Kempster rolled back into the pit. Major Kempster attempted to scoop the grenade out of the pit but failed to do so. By this time detonation was due. Without hesitation Major Kempster threw himself on the grenade just before it exploded and received fatal injuries. By his self-sacrifice, Major Kempster undoubtedly saved the lives of the two other occupants of the pit. Major Kempster's act meant certain death, and he must have known this at the time. His was a supreme act of gallantry. He was born in Westminster in London on 26 October 1916.

(*The Times*)

AUGUST 25TH

1906: On this day the *Looker-On* reported that, on the previous Thursday, the residence of Mr Hubert O. Lord had been the scene of festivity. The festivity in question was a grand cricket match that Mr Lord had arranged between the Cotswold Hunt and the Beaufort Hunt.

Mr Lord was, for many years, a keen supporter of cricket and was a good bat in his time. Among the many improvements carried out on his Lilley Brook estate was the making of a fine cricket ground, delightfully situated, overlooking the Dowdeswell Valley and the Vale of the Severn. Upon this spot, tents were erected for luncheon and the band of the Royal Gloucestershire Hussars, under their veteran conductor, Mr J.P. Hatton, played sweet music at appropriate intervals. The wicket was in excellent condition and a close and interesting game was played, resulting in favour of the Cotswold Hunt by the narrow margin of two runs on the first innings. (*Cheltenham Looker-On*)

AUGUST 26TH

1903: On this day William Henry Corfield, a scientist who revolutionised hygiene and household sanitation in Victorian England, died in Sweden. He was born on 14 December 1843 and was a pupil at Cheltenham Grammar School, where a house was later named after him. After leaving the Grammar School, Corfield pursued an academic career, going to Magdalen College, Oxford.

He was appointed Professor of Hygiene and Public Health at University College London in 1869. That same year he was elected to the British Association for the Advancement of Science to report on the treatment and utilisation of sewage. He established the first hygiene laboratory in London in 1875, and a museum of practical hygiene in London in 1876. As a result of his success in diagnosing the causes of illnesses, Corfield enjoyed a large consulting practice. At his death, he was President of the Epidemiological Society, Past President of the Society of Medical Officers of Health, and Vice-President of the Sanitary Institute. (Corfield, *The Corfields: A History of the Corfields from 1180 to the Present Day*)

AUGUST 27TH

1881: On this day a Cheltenham local paper described a week of terrible weather:

> Unsettled and unseasonable weather during the past week has sadly damped the hopes of the Agriculturists throughout the rural districts of Gloucestershire, and seriously interfered with the few engagements of a public character which proffered occupation or amusement ... six hours of heavy, uninterrupted, rain on Sunday, continued also, at intervals, throughout the night ... and suddenly lowered the temperature of August to that of April for the following day, which, although more favourably disposed, inspired no confidence in its prolongation through the morrow.
>
> The morrow, indeed, proved a dismal disappointment ... for it rained unceasingly as though it had never rained before, keeping everybody confined to the house who was not actually compelled by business to face the inclement visitation. A fresh breeze on Wednesday drove off much of the accumulated moisture, and dispersed the ominous clouds which, ever and anon, darkened the heavens, threatening to discharge their contents upon the already saturated earth. Threatenings which were carried into lamentable effect long before day-break next morning when the rainfall of Tuesday recommenced and continued through the whole of Thursday, scarcely ceasing for an hour from sunrise to sunset. Yesterday the weather cleared up and continued fine until evening, when the sky became again overcast foreshadowing another wet night.

(*Cheltenham Looker-On*)

AUGUST 28TH

2010: On this day, people relaxing in Montpellier Gardens were entertained by Sharpness & District Silver Band, who played a programme of popular tunes.

The sounds of free open-air jazz and big band concerts filled the air in Montpellier Gardens and Pittville Park throughout the summer, as Cheltenham residents were treated to a string of open-air concerts courtesy of some of Gloucestershire's favourite local bands, at two of Cheltenham's prettiest parks.

The bandstand in Montpellier Gardens has been a favourite since it was built in 1864. Before the bandstand there had been a Chinese pagoda in the gardens as part of the original 1831 designs. From this pagoda the celebrated Spa Band played on a regular basis. The bandstand did not only function as a platform for music. The Cheltenham Archery Club held its meetings in the gardens and used the space under the bandstand to store its targets and other equipment. The club was established in 1856 and archery was considered a perfectly respectable activity for the ladies; in fact, one of the club's members was Queenie Newall, who was Olympic Champion in 1908. (Various sources, including Rowbotham & Waller, *Cheltenham: A History*)

August 29th

1883: On this day William Henry Drake was born in Charlton Kings in Cheltenham. In 1907 he joined the 1st Battalion of the Gloucestershire Regiment and three years later he became a policeman.

In 1914 William was recalled to the army and, less than a month later, he landed in France. At Zillebeke, in Belgium, the Glosters were ordered to clear the Germans out of the wood just east of the town, but they were held up by barbed wire and machine-gun fire and had to withdraw. At 9 a.m. the next morning a further attack was ordered, but this failed for the same reason. At roll call that night only 213 men answered and it was estimated that about 300 casualties had been sustained, mostly killed and missing. William Drake was never found.

On 7 November 1914, less than three months after arriving, William Drake was officially reported as missing in action. He was thirty-two years old and has no known grave. He is remembered on the Menin Gate Memorial at Ypres. His name also appears on the Cheltenham, Charlton Kings, and St Mary's Church War Memorials. (Gloucestershire Police Museum)

August 30th

1994: On this day an award-winning film director with strong links to Cheltenham College died.

Lindsay Anderson, the son of an English army officer, was born in India in 1923. He was sent to school at the college, returning in the late '60s to make his most famous film, *If...*, satirising English public school life. Notorious for its depiction of a savage insurrection at a public school, the film features surrealist sequences and ends with schoolboys machine-gunning the staff from the roof of the school. The film starred Malcolm McDowell in his first screen role and many of the boys attending the college acted as extras. *If...* was mainly shot in and around the college, but some sequences were filmed at the Rotunda roundabout and elsewhere in the town – although some scenes were shot at Aldenham School in Hertfordshire. The film won the Palme d'Or at Cannes Film Festival in 1969. (Various sources)

AUGUST 31ST

1939: On this day the Redgwell family moved into the new house they had built in an orchard on the outskirts of Cheltenham. War was declared on Sunday 3 September. Jo Redgwell recalls:

> I remember an atmosphere of anxiety during the day, but greater consternation arose at dusk, when it was realised that all the houses had blackout and we had large windows and no blackout. Blankets were hastily strung across windows in two rooms and we camped out. The next day a visit was made to the Miss Shills' drapery shop in the Bath Road to buy bales of dark green material and vital hangings were quickly sewn. Later shutters were made for some windows.
>
> To add to the chaos, my aunt arrived with my cousin. My father's brother was in Denmark and she was convinced she was a widow. This was not to be. He arrived later in the week and instead of beginning to create a garden, my father and he dug an air raid shelter. ... Railway sleepers lined the walls and made the roof; benches were constructed on either side; steps led down to a door and a pipe placed at the far end for ventilation and all of it turfed over. It was never used. Sometimes I feel guilty that I had an easy war. There was no chance of being evacuated, or having a father or near relation in one of the armed forces. There were no sleepless nights or being bombed. I was lucky to have lived in Cheltenham.

(Jo Redgwell, BBC's WW2 People's War)

SEPTEMBER 1ST

1862: On this day the High Street railway station opened in Cheltenham. It was built by the Midland Railway to serve the north-western part of Cheltenham and was situated on the main Birmingham to Bristol railway line. Originally known as Cheltenham Tewkesbury Road Bridge station, a month later, on 1 October, it was renamed Cheltenham High Street station.

There was another station on the High Street nearer the town centre. This was the Cheltenham High Street Halt, which opened in 1908 and closed in 1917 due to the First World War, never to be reopened. The Halt had a pagoda-style shelter on each platform and was unstaffed. (Various sources, including Gloucestershire Warwickshire Railway)

SEPTEMBER 2ND

1784: On this day an important hot-air balloon flight took place. Soon after lunch on this Thursday afternoon, exactly a year after the Montgolfier brothers had made the first ascent in a hot-air balloon in France, one of Gloucestershire's most famous sons, Sir Edward Jenner, who developed the smallpox vaccination in Cheltenham, made his own leap into the unknown. The thirty-five-year-old Jenner launched his balloon from the courtyard of Berkeley Castle at 2 p.m. The wind carried it 10 miles north-eastwards, when it finally came to rest in a field at Kingscote, just to the south-west of Nailsworth. The balloon was relaunched and the breeze, which had now changed direction, carried it north, along the line of the hills, for a further 14 miles. The excursion finally ended when Jenner's balloon came down in a field on Crickley Hill at Birdlip, a site commemorated by the famous public house that now stands there: the Air Balloon. (Various sources, including the Jenner Museum)

SEPTEMBER 3RD

1943: On this day, musician, journalist and author Michael Anthony 'Mick' Farren was born in Cheltenham. His name is always closely associated with the London underground scene of the 1960s and '70s, of which he was a leading figure.

Mick Farren is probably best known for his pre-punk band The Deviants, who, between 1967 and 1969, released three successful albums. In the following decade he released the solo album *Mona – The Carnivorous Circus*, which also featured eminent musicians Steve Peregrin Took, John Gustafson and Paul Buckmaster. Farren later released the EP 'Screwed Up', the single 'Broken Statue', and the album *Vampires Stole My Lunch Money*. He collaborated with many luminaries of the 1960s, including Barry Miles on the seminal *International Times*. He also worked with Lemmy when the latter was in Hawkwind, co-writing 'Lost Johnny' for the band as well as co-writing songs with Motörhead and several other bands.

Mick worked for *Los Angeles CityBeat* between 2003 and 2008, and has written over twenty works of fiction and a dozen or so non-fiction titles. (Various sources)

SEPTEMBER 4TH

1894: On this day, the bodies of fifty-seven-year-old Rebecca Hartland and her youngest son, thirteen-year-old George, were found at their home at No. 303 Lower High Street, Cheltenham. They had been murdered by Rebecca's drunken husband, sixty-year-old greengrocer Job Hartland.

Job had frequently threatened his wife with violence, causing their older children to move out, and, by 1894, only George was left living at home. The previous Friday, Mrs Hartland had woken during the night to find her husband standing above her brandishing a hatchet. She had refused to stay another night in the house, sleeping at her daughter's for the next two nights. However, on the Monday morning, 3 September, she had to return to run the grocer's shop and so she slept at home that night. The next morning, her body was found in her bed, together with that of her son.

Job had attacked his family with a coal hammer and a butcher's knife, nearly severing his wife's head and slitting his son's throat, in addition to beating them both round the head. Job subsequently boasted of what he had done, telling the barmaid of the Clarence Hotel that he had just murdered two people. The police soon found Job, drunk, in a lane behind Clarence Street. They had to wait for him to sober up before they could charge him with murder. He was executed at Gloucester on Thursday 13 December 1894. (cotswoldhistory. com, Cotswold Murder Walks – Cheltenham, Nell Darby)

SEPTEMBER 5TH

1643: On this day the English Civil War reached Cheltenham.

On 26 August 1643, the Earl of Essex had left London with an army of 15,000 men to relieve the City of Gloucester, which had been besieged by 25,000 Royalist troops who were devastating the area, pillaging for food and supplies. Meanwhile, the Royalist army began tunnelling to place a mine under the East Gate, but a sudden spell of bad weather flooded the tunnel, leaving enough time for the Earl of Essex to arrive and reinforce the city.

Essex had spilt his forces into two so as to avoid the Royalist stronghold at Oxford, and reunited in Northamptonshire. His army was attacked at Stow-on-the-Wold by Prince Rupert, who commanded most of the King's cavalry. But, in spite of this setback, Essex was able to regroup and carry on towards Cheltenham. They reached Prestbury on the outskirts of the town on 5 September. Because of the imminent threat from Essex, the King's forces lifted the siege of Gloucester and retreated to Sudeley Castle at Winchcombe. The siege was lifted just in time. By its end, Colonel Massey, who was defending the city, had only three barrels of gunpowder left. (Various sources, including Phyllida Barstow, *It Happened in Gloucestershire*)

September 6th

2003: On this day a plaque was unveiled to commemorate comedian Norman Wisdom's connection to Cheltenham.

In 1943, Wisdom had been billeted at the Moray House Hotel in Parabola Road. The hotel later became the Carlton and, finally, the Hotel du Vin. Wisdom was a member of No. 2 Company, War Office Signals; the establishment to which it was attached, the highly secret CWW-Cheltenham Network, was, to a certain extent, a forerunner of GCHQ.

When Wisdom organised a concert party at the Town Hall, it was seen by Rex Harrison, who encouraged him to take up show business professionally. He subsequently made about fifty films, starring as the downtrodden loser, Norman Pitkin, in a cloth cap and ill-fitting suit. Wisdom was at his peak in the 1950s and his first film, *Trouble in Store*, earned him a BAFTA for Most Promising Newcomer to Film. His career declined in the '60s, although he remained an enormous star in Albania, where he was one of the few entertainers whose work was not banned.

Norman Wisdom and his former comrades held annual reunions at the hotel, and it was during the 2003 celebrations that the plaque was unveiled. He died aged ninety-five on the Isle of Man in 2010. (Various sources, including Smith & Rowbotham, *Commemorative Plaques of Cheltenham*)

SEPTEMBER 7TH

1932: On this day a sports meeting, organised by Burrow's Sports Club, took place. In addition to inter-business competitions between Burrow's and teams representing H.H. Martyn, the Gas Co., the Original Brewery, and the Corporation, a programme of club championships for the Cheltenham & County Harriers was also staged.

Another grand sports event had been held the previous week by the club. The very active sports organisation, maintained by the printing company Ed. J. Burrow & Co. Ltd, of Cheltenham and London, with their associated houses (Burrow's Press, Cheltenham Press, and Norman Sawyer & Co. Ltd), carried through the very successful evening's sports meeting at their beautiful ground in Moorend Grove.

Events included a ladies' half-mile walking race, a 100-yard ladies' hockey race and a tug-of-war. The very high degree of athletic prowess on show greatly emphasised the reputation for efficiency and quality enjoyed by this progressive firm in the production of guidebooks, travel publications and high-class colour printing. (*Cheltenham Chronicle and Gloucestershire Graphic*)

September 8th

1916: On this day the Gray family from Cheltenham suffered what was to be their first tragedy in the space of a few months. Beresford and Mary Jane Gray, who lived at Beresford Villa, Cirencester Road, lost their first son, Beresford John, aged twenty-five, when he was killed in action in France. Their second son, Ernest, who was twenty-four, was killed in action in Salonica on 5 November 1916. Both are commemorated on the Charlton Kings War Memorial and the Charlton Kings (St Mary's Church) War Memorial. Ernest is also commemorated on the Cheltenham War Memorial and the St Peter's Church War Memorial.

To lose one son in battle was bad enough but to lose two would have been hard to bear. Over 100 local families lost two sons. In one instance, twin brothers Edward and Harry Turner were killed in action on the same day on HMS *Good Hope*. William and Julia Souls of Great Rissington, Gloucestershire, lost five sons.

Someone else who lost a son on this day was Mrs Emma Brown of Libertus Road. Alan Francis Donald was killed in action on 8 September 1916; his brother Edmund Kenneth Wallace was later killed on 24 August 1917. (remembering. org.uk)

SEPTEMBER 9TH

1865: On this day the *Cheltenham Looker-On* reviewed the third Horticultural Exhibition of the season, which had been held in Montpellier Gardens on the previous Wednesday:

... when upwards of three thousand subscribers and friends of the Society congregated in the tents and grounds to witness the last Exhibition of the present year and to enjoy, once more, before the close of the Summer, the agreeable and fascinating promenade, more especially so on this occasion, when an opportunity was afforded to listen to the delightful strains of operatic and military music performed by the Band of the Grenadier Guards ... Unfortunate though the Society has been with many of its former Exhibitions in regard to the weather, Wednesday last proved an exception to the general rule, for a more genial Autumn day could not have been selected for a Floral Show, and, in consequence, every one present appeared thoroughly to enjoy themselves from the commencement to the close of the Fête. The gates were thrown open to the public at two o'clock and from that hour until half-past three crowds of elegantly-dressed ladies continued to arrive in the Gardens, and the space surrounding the Orchestra presented a very lively and animated appearance throughout the afternoon.

(*Cheltenham Looker-On*)

SEPTEMBER 10TH

1964: On this day the Rolling Stones, with their Cheltenham-born founder Brian Jones, played the Odeon cinema in Winchcombe Street. They had already played at the venue twice before. The show was compèred by Don Spencer, and the bands performing before the Stones were The Innocents, Mike Berry and the Mojos. As could be expected at any venue the crowds were enthusiastic, but in Cheltenham, because of Mr Jones, things threatened to get out of hand. The local paper reported:

> Police officers, security men, commissionaires and first aid men linked arms last night to prevent screaming fans from rushing the stage at both performances by the Rolling Stones at the Odeon Cinema. One girl managed to clamber onto the platform, but was quickly hauled down. During their lively act the Stones were pelted with sweets and other objects as tokens of affection … After the show crowds of fans waited outside in front of the cinema, but the Rolling Stones slipped out the back way with a police escort and went off in their own car.

(*Gloucestershire Echo*)

SEPTEMBER 11TH

1962: On this day the play *Billy Liar* by Keith Waterhouse opened at the Everyman Theatre. It starred William Gaunt who was a regular at the rep throughout the 1960s and went on to become a leading television actor.

Billy Liar was one of three demanding plays running back-to-back in which Gaunt appeared that autumn. Terence Rattigan's *Ross* opened on 25 September with Gaunt playing T.E. Lawrence; this was followed, two weeks later, by Harold Pinter's *The Caretaker*, in which again he played the very challenging lead role.

> I did those plays in an incredible period of six weeks playing the lead in each one. It was extraordinary. Very intensive work indeed, three enormous parts, playing one in the evening and rehearsing another during the day. In fact, it was during this time that the Cuban Missile Crisis took place but Ian Mullins and I were working so hard we completely missed it. The world could have ended and we'd never have known why. It was very hard work, that little stint, but it was a most enjoyable period for me. But I enjoyed all the productions I did in Cheltenham and I played a series of marvellous parts.

(Michael Hasted, *A Theatre for All Seasons*)

September 12th

1754: On this day Katherine Monson, a lady of whom few have heard but who had a significant influence on the way Cheltenham looked, was born in Lincolnshire. Being a woman and, what's more, a member of the aristocracy, she was Cheltenham's most unconventional builder.

Katherine, the second of Lord Monson's eight children, moved to Cheltenham while in her twenties. The first house she built in the late 1700s, Monson Villa off St Margaret's Road, was for her own use. The house was demolished in the 1960s to make way for the slightly less attractive Whitbread tower block, which was itself demolished in 2006 and replaced by an even less attractive multi-storey car park.

By 1805 Katherine had bought the plot of land adjacent to her own where she built herself a much larger house, St Margaret's. Buying up yet another plot of adjacent land, she built St Margaret's Terrace in 1820, a grand row of six houses which still stand today. She built about seventeen houses in Cheltenham and took an active role on-site even when she was well into her sixties. (Rebsie Fairholm, Cheltonia website)

September 13th

2011: On this day a spectacular robbery was reported in Cheltenham when a ruthless gang of three men robbed a helpless teenager in broad daylight.

The eighteen-year-old was walking along Roman Hackle Avenue, in Wymans Brook, at around 5.10 p.m. when he was grabbed from behind and had every penny he was carrying stolen – an amount believed to be in the region of 30p.

'I had my headphones on and someone grabbed me,' he said. 'There were two men there and then another came round the corner.' One of the muggers took his wallet and grabbed the bag he was carrying. 'All that was in the bag was clothes, some hair products and deodorant. The wallet was just full of receipts and had about 30p in it. I was surprised because nothing like that happens in Wymans Brook.'

He said that the three men, aged between nineteen and twenty, had run off down an alley in the St Paul's direction. But the youngster was surprisingly relaxed about the robbery. 'They tried to be violent, but they were not very good at it. They must have been the worst muggers ever. One of them punched like a girl and the other one tried to kick me twice and missed.' (*Gloucestershire Echo*)

September 14th

1877: On this day William Joseph Gale died near Nazareth in the Holy Land. His bust stands by the north door of Leckhampton Church. So, how did Mr Gale come to be remembered in a Cheltenham church, having died in the Middle East? No local paper made mention of the event, but *The Times* in London ran a story on 9 November 1877 headed 'Murder in Syria'.

Gale had been working on a farm in Haifa and sometimes acted in a semi-official capacity for the British Consul General in Beirut. The Consul was anxious to obtain information about some bandits that were causing trouble and sent young William to investigate. It was while he was making his way back to Haifa that he became separated from his escort and was never seen again. Remains of his body were found after an extensive search.

It seems that Mr Gale's connection with Leckhampton is probably through the retired Indian planter John Gale, who lived with his wife at Oakfield in The Park. They were the only Gale family recorded in Leckhampton at the time. William's younger brother Benjamin enrolled at the college in 1878 and in 1881 was recorded as living in Leckhampton with his sister. It could well be that they were responsible for the bust. (Eric Miller, CLHS Journal 23)

September 15th

1904: On this day Cheltenham's Winchcombe Street was rocked by a mighty explosion. The premises of Mr Challice, a taxidermist, all but disappeared as the result of leaking gas being ignited. So violent was the explosion that his shop door was later found in the yard of the Congregational Chapel which stood on the other side of the street. The explosion occurred at 7.30 p.m., so fortunately there were few casualties, although it is believed that several of the stuffed animals were a little worse for wear and one young woman passing by was hit by flying debris.

The shop completely collapsed but neighbouring buildings survived largely intact. Even Mr Challice's family home, Sudeley Cottage, which abutted the rear of the shop, survived more or less unscathed. It may have been a sad and tragic event for poor Mr Challice, but for the rest of Cheltenham it was the best free show in town and, in spite of the police cordons, the trams, which ran up Winchcombe Street, did a roaring trade in sightseers eager to see the scene of the disaster. (John Roles, *Cheltenham in Old Picture Postcards*)

September 16th

2011: On this day it was announced that notorious local criminal Kenneth Davis had been jailed for five years for a series of raids on homes in Cheltenham. The twenty-nine year old had been arrested on 20 August. Inspector Alistair Barby of the Gloucestershire police proudly stated that, 'Another burglar has been taken off the streets. ... Protecting the public from him is a priority.'

Davis, the father of a two-and-a-half-year-old daughter, was hoping to be a stay-at-home dad, but he had become addicted to morphine while in hospital and this led to his return to crime. Jailing Davis, Judge William Hart said he had sympathy for him because of his personal circumstances. But he added, 'I have never come across anyone who has got the record you have got for dwelling house burglaries. The public of Gloucestershire need to be protected from your further attentions.'

Jon Holmes, for the defence, described Davis as institutionalised. 'He is so used to being in prison that it has become a home from home, or perhaps the only thing he really knows. But it is also because his life in the community has difficulties he cannot cope with and he thinks life inside is easier.' (*Gloucestershire Echo*)

SEPTEMBER 17TH

1910: On this day the latest entertainment venue in the town was described:

The newest addition to Cheltenham's amusement centres is the Albert Hall, in North Street, which is now under the efficient management of Picture Entertainments de Luxe Ltd., Mr W. Roberts being in local control. The Hall is admirably adapted for this class of entertainment; it is large, lofty, well ventilated and furnished with every consideration for the comfort of its patrons. The moving pictures shown are of the admirable quality that the public demands now that cinematography has reached such a pitch of perfection, undreamt of when 'Picture Palaces' were more fittingly termed 'Flicker Theatres'. Dramatic episodes are now much in evidence, most of the films bearing unmistakable evidence of transatlantic origin, and this week a cleverly arranged series representing the life of Napoleon is the leading feature. A complete change will be made for next week. The pictures are interspersed with 'variety' performances by capable artistes. Two performances are given nightly and there are matinees on Wednesday and Saturday afternoons.

(*Cheltenham Looker-On*)

SEPTEMBER 18TH

2009: On this day the actor Peter Denyer died in Cheltenham aged sixty-two. He is perhaps best remembered for playing Dennis Dunstable in ITV's sitcom *Please Sir!* in the 1960s and '70s. Denyer started a long association with the Everyman Theatre in July 1978, soon after he set up home in Cheltenham. The first play he was in was *Double Edge*, directed by Michael Napier Brown. He then worked regularly at the theatre for several years. Roger Hendry, Theatre Service Engineer at the Everyman, has fond memories of Denyer:

> He was a good actor. After he first played the Everyman in the late seventies, Malcolm Farquhar, the Artistic Director, rather took him under his wing. He did other things but, because he lived in Cheltenham, he was often around the theatre and he directed a few plays.
>
> A group of us, including Peter and myself, decided to keep the Everyman name alive when the theatre was closed for rebuilding and to mount the pantomime at the Town Hall. The first one we did was *Aladdin* in 1983. It was a nightmare but great fun.

Peter Denyer cast the show with himself as dame. After that, Denyer specialised in producing and writing pantomimes. Even now, his shows are produced all over the country every Christmas. (Michael Hasted, *A Theatre for All Seasons*)

SEPTEMBER 19TH

1887: On this day a contract was signed which enabled the construction of some buildings in Winchcombe Street. Almost 100 years later, these became the much-missed Axiom Arts Centre.

The purchase of the site by Messrs George Stoddart Chapman and William Ride led to the establishment of W. Ride & Co., seed and corn merchants. The business was taken over in 1953 by W.J. Oldacre & Sons, another local corn merchant, but closed in the 1970s. In March 1979 the Cheltenham Arts Centre Trust was given permission to convert the buildings at Nos 57-59 Winchcombe Street into an arts centre. The Centre, as it was known, closed in the early 1980s. The venue opened a couple of years later as the Axiom. For the next decade it struggled to keep its head above water but, by the end of the '90s, the Axiom had achieved some stability and become a successful community arts centre. However, by 2000 the problems that had accumulated over the years finally forced its closure, amidst allegations of financial irregularities. (Klara Sudbury, CLHS Journal 20)

September 20th

2010: On this day it was revealed that a spy who worked at GCHQ in Cheltenham, and whose body had been found the previous month, was probably not murdered, as was first thought.

The body of Gareth Williams was discovered at a house in Pimlico in London on 23 August, stuffed into a sports bag where it lay decomposing for up to two weeks. It was believed he had died before being put into the bag, which was then placed in the bath.

Mr Williams, who was in his thirties, was on secondment at MI6. He had been due to return to Cheltenham to resume his position at GCHQ before he died. Scotland Yard said at the time that a post-mortem had been inconclusive in establishing a cause of death and further examination would be required. Three weeks later, having ruled out almost every other possibility, the police came to the conclusion that Williams had probably died as a result of some sadomasochistic game which involved climbing into the bag. It was unclear whether he did so on instructions from another person or was locked in the bag at his own request. It is likely that once in the bag, he died from suffocation and dehydration. (*Telegraph*)

September 21st

1874: On this day, the world-renowned composer Gustav Holst was born at No. 4 Clarence Road (then called Pittville Terrace) to a family of Swedish extraction. Since 1974 the house has been a museum containing many artefacts from Holst's life.

Holst was educated at Cheltenham Grammar School for Boys when it was situated in the High Street – a site now less academically occupied by a Wilkinson store. He attended the Royal Academy of Music and it was there, in 1895, that he met his life-long friend Ralph Vaughan Williams. In 1904 Holst took up his first teaching job in West Dulwich, South London, and the following year he became director of music at St Paul's Girls' School in Hammersmith. In 1907, Holst also became director of music at Morley College. He taught until the end of his life, but it is as the composer of *The Planets* suite that he is famous.

The Planets, written between 1914 and 1916, has been played by every major orchestra in every major concert hall in the world. The first complete public performance was given in London on 15 November 1920, with the London Symphony Orchestra conducted by Albert Coates. Gustav Holst died on 25 May 1934 in London, following complications after his stomach surgery. (Various sources)

SEPTEMBER 22ND

1913: On this day, Gillsmith's Hippodrome variety theatre opened in Albion Street. The proprietor was Mr Cecil Gill Smith and his theatre was in direct competition with the Opera House a few blocks away. The theatre was in the converted Conservative Club and retained its original Georgian façade. Nevertheless, no money was spared on its rebuilding and decoration. The theatrical newspaper, *The Stage*, reported:

> The new building is being erected on a corner site for Messrs Gillsmith Ltd. The architect is Mr Herbert T. Rainger of Cheltenham. Seating accommodation will be provided for close upon a thousand people, and in addition to this, there will be a spacious lounge, with full view of the stage, at the back of the circle, where afternoon teas will be served. The entrance foyer will be decorated in Tudor style in dark oak, and special attention is being given to the decoration of the auditorium. A novel colour scheme of copper flame rouge and French grey should give a delightfully restful, yet smart and effective, result. Indirect lighting is being adopted throughout the auditorium.

The Hippodrome later became the Coliseum cinema and, finally, the Springbok disco. The building was demolished in 2011. (*The Stage*)

SEPTEMBER 23RD

2011: On this day the Everyman Theatre reopened with a spectacular show by Ken Dodd. The theatre had been closed since the beginning of May 2011 for major restoration. The work, costing £3 million, involved completely repairing and repainting the auditorium in a style more reminiscent of that designed by its architect Frank Matcham.

Over the years layers of paint had built up, most of them seemingly pink. The most startling revelation when the paint stripper got to work was that the proscenium arch was made of marble. In fact, it was synthetic marble called scagliola, but the effect was stunning. The theatre's wonderful dome was repainted and repaired and all the cherubs and angles had their missing limbs replaced. Every visible surface was redecorated, all the carpets replaced, and most of the seats either replaced or recovered. All of the unsightly lighting gantries were replaced and a new control box was installed at the back of the dress circle. The two boxes, either side of the stage, which had not been used since before the war, were reinstated to provide a close, if not slightly distorted, view of the stage. The front of house also underwent a complete revamp. The dated bar and café were rebuilt and the curved staircase that connected them was replaced. (Michael Hasted, *A Theatre for All Seasons*)

SEPTEMBER 24TH

1932: On this day the comings and goings of many local clergymen were announced. The Revd Elphin Ellis from Plymouth was appointed to the Cheltenham Circuit of the Wesleyan Church and district. It was also announced that two other men of the cloth would be leaving town. Whether this was related to that event is not known.

The Revd R.E.A. Lloyd, who had been the curate of the parish church and St Matthew's Church for the previous two and a half years, made it known that he would shortly be taking up a new post in New Malden in Surrey. Prior to his leaving, a presentation was made to him by the Young Men's Club.

The final dog collar on the move was Revd W. Grist of Holy Trinity Church in Winchcombe Street, who had recently taken up the job of rector at the old parish church in Weymouth. He had been vicar of Holy Trinity for seven years, and he and his wife and daughter received handsome presentations from their parishioners before they left. (*Cheltenham Chronicle and Gloucestershire Graphic*)

September 25th

1919: On this day Cheltenham's second cemetery, at Charlton Kings, held its first burial service. The new cemetery was originally provided by the Urban District Council, but in 1974 it was taken over by Cheltenham Borough Council.

The town's main cemetery and crematorium are situated in Bouncers Lane, in the northern suburbs of the town. They are set in 65 acres of wooded landscape which include the gardens of remembrance and have beautiful views of Cleeve Hill in the distance. The first burial at the main cemetery took place on 19 November 1864. The crematorium was opened in 1938 and, perhaps surprisingly, was only the thirty-ninth such facility in Britain at the time.

There are two chapels at the main cemetery – the North Chapel (which can accommodate about sixty mourners) and the South Chapel (which can accommodate nearer 100). The crematorium chapel was renovated in 1995, with every effort being made to keep its original features and character.

The most famous person to be buried at Bouncers Lane is Brian Jones, founder and guitarist of the Rolling Stones, who died on 3 July 1969. (Cheltenham Borough Council)

September 26th

2010: On this day a major fire broke out in Millbrook Street, Cheltenham. The fire started in an abandoned factory at about 6.45 p.m. and was potentially so serious that local residents had to be evacuated. Flames, at one point, were reported to be over 30ft high. A great cloud of black smoke was visible over a large area and a series of small explosions were heard. Of the hundred-odd people evacuated, most were taken to a local school and some were put up at a nearby Territorial Army centre. The bridge near the Waitrose supermarket provided a good grandstand for the large crowd that gathered to watch the development of the fire. It took the fire brigade roughly an hour to get the blaze under control, and by 8.30 p.m. the evacuees were safely back at home. Part of the street remained cordoned off and firemen remained on-site overnight as a precaution. Arson was suspected and the police launched an investigation to determine the cause of the fire. (*Gloucestershire Echo*)

SEPTEMBER 27TH

1953: On this day, Alderman Daniel Leopold Lipson was created an Honorary Freeman of the Borough of Cheltenham.

The ancient title of Freeman was more than just ceremonial. In former times, freemen had a right to share in the benefits of any hereditaments or common lands in the borough, and enjoyed certain other privileges. The Honorary Freedom of Boroughs Act of 1885 empowered borough councils to award the 'Honorary Freeman' title to persons of distinction, and those who had rendered eminent service to the borough.

Lipson was a member of Cheltenham Borough Council, serving as Mayor during the 1930s, before being elected as an Independent Conservative MP for the town at a 1937 by-election. He was re-elected at the 1945 general election as a National Independent, but lost his seat, coming third at the 1950 election when long-serving Conservative William Hicks Beach was first elected.

Alderman Lipson died on 14 April 1963. A road on the Hesters Way estate was named after him. (Various sources, including CLHS Journal 24)

SEPTEMBER 28TH

1815: On this day the *Cheltenham Chronicle* contained an advertisement for a spectacle that was to take place at No. 70 High Street, opposite the Regent Library. The exhibition in question was the appearance of a seventeen-year-old lad who was 'near' 8ft tall. Purporting to be 'The Only English Giant', he was presented as 'One of the Seven Wonders'. Which seven wonders, the advert was careful not to say.

It was claimed that he had only previously been introduced to four persons of distinction, namely the Emperor of Russia, the King of Prussia, Count Platoff and Prince Blucher, who were said to be 'highly gratified at seeing *so* Gigantic a Youth'. One strange measurement that was given for the youth was that he was 26in from his foot to his knee, and that his foot was 15in long but that he was, nevertheless, 'well proportioned'.

The exhibition was open every day (except Sunday) from 11 a.m. till 10 p.m., with an hour's tea break for the lad at 4 p.m. The cost of viewing the spectacle was 1s. (CLHS Journal 24)

SEPTEMBER 29TH

1918: On this day, twenty-one-year-old Cheltenham war hero Lieutenant Douglas Woulfe Hay was killed in action at Villers Guislain; he is buried in the Villers Hill British Cemetery.

Douglas had attended Cheltenham College between 1911 and 1916, and thereafter the Royal Military Academy, Sandhurst. He was gazetted as a Second Lieutenant in October 1916. On being posted to France, he was attached to 6th Battalion Middlesex Regiment and was awarded the Military Cross for his part in the action on the Hindenburg Line in 1917, near Bullecourt. Lieutenant Hay was killed whilst leading his platoon against a German strongpoint at the Battle of the St Quentin Canal. He is commemorated on the Cheltenham War Memorial, the Cheltenham College Roll of Honour and in the Chapel of the Royal Military College. He is also remembered on a brass plaque in St Mary's Church, Cheltenham. (Graham Adams, taken from Joe Devereux and Graham Sacker, *Leaving All That Was Dear*; Cheltenham & Gloucester Branch of the Western Front Association)

SEPTEMBER 30TH

1929: On this day the Opera House was to undergo probably the biggest change in its history. The theatre was sold to a company called Cinema House Ltd, who intended to turn the building into a cinema now that the talkies had arrived. The *Echo* was invited to have a look:

> The first of the many additions our representative noticed on entering the Theatre was the large white screen across the stage for the pictures ... A glance at the rear of the stage reveals a new feature, for there are placed the two towers, eighteen feet high, in which are mounted the mighty loud speakers, with an aperture of 5ft x 4ft., through which the talking part of the talking picture business is done.

The new cinema evidently fancied itself as a cut above the rest and even issued theatre-like programmes for the shows. The girl attendants were resplendent in elegant scarlet frocks with blue facings and the men in uniforms of claret, gold and blue. To add even more class, a pageboy was employed as doorman to welcome the patrons. The entire changeover to cinema was said to have cost 'anything up to £15,000', according to the *Echo*. (*Gloucestershire Echo*)

OCTOBER 1ST

1891: On this day the New Theatre and Opera House opened its doors for the first time. Crowds in Regent Street jostled to catch a glimpse of the cream of Cheltenham society as the horse-drawn carriages drew up outside the brilliantly illuminated building. 'At enormous expense', Lillie Langtry, along with her 'powerful' Princess Theatre Co. from London, had been engaged to present the opening production, 'An original drama in four acts' entitled *Lady Clancarty*. But it wasn't just Mrs Langtry that thrilled the crowds. The building itself was the co-star that evening. The *Cheltenham Examiner* waxed lyrical about the auditorium: 'And now, the majority of the audience seated, and the multitudinous lamps casting their brilliant rays on the delicate Louis XV decorations of tier-fronts and boxes, and the gay draperies of the fashionable fair, the tableau curtain, of sumptuous amber plush, is drawn aside, disclosing an Act drop.'

The *Cheltenham Looker-On* was particularly impressed with the lighting, which illuminated not only the tasteful décor of the auditorium but the 'gay throng' within it. (Michael Hasted, *A Theatre for All Seasons*)

OCTOBER 2ND

1823: On this day Baron Charles Conrad Adolphus du Bois de Ferrières was born in Tiel in the Netherlands. The family was of Huguenot descent, but Charles' mother was English. His grandfather, General du Bois, had commanded Napoleon's French brigade in Holland.

Charles de Ferrières had been brought to England as a child. In 1851 he married Anne Sheepshanks and the couple moved to Cheltenham in 1860, where they spent the rest of their lives. Charles succeeded to the Dutch peerage, becoming 3rd Baron de Ferrières, in 1867 – the same year that he was naturalised as a British citizen. Ten years later the Baron became Cheltenham's second mayor, and in 1880 he was elected Liberal MP for the town.

One of his most visible legacies to the town was his gift of paintings to the art gallery. He had already donated £1,000 towards the building's construction. In recognition of his services and generosity to the community, he was made an Honorary Freeman of the Borough in 1900. His obituary stated that there was 'scarcely a society or charitable institution in the town that [had] not benefited from his support'. He is buried at St Peter's, Leckhampton, alongside his father. (Various sources, including Gwen Hart, *A History of Cheltenham*)

OCTOBER 3RD

1838: On this day a spectacular and unusual event took place in Montpellier Gardens. Thirty-seven-year-old John Hampton entered the history books by becoming the first man to make a successful parachute jump from his gas-filled 'Albion' balloon – there is no record of how many unsuccessful ones there were.

Balloons had become all the rage since the first flight by the Montgolfier brothers fifty-five years earlier. No large public event was complete in the first half of the nineteenth century without a balloon flight of some description. All the fashionable locations, like Vauxhall Gardens in London, vied to present the most spectacular event. Some of the best events were to be seen in Cheltenham.

Two days before his famous jump, Hampton displayed his 'improved safety parachute' in the Montpellier Pump Room – now the Rotunda. He made his jump using his 200lb umbrella-like parachute from a height of around 9,000ft and landed in Badgeworth about twelve minutes later. (Various sources, including Rowbotham & Waller, *Cheltenham: A History*)

OCTOBER 4TH

1857: On this day William Coote, a veteran of the Battle of Trafalgar, died aged seventy-six at his home at No. 15 Promenade. After ten years in the navy he had joined the sixty-four-gun ship *Agamemnon* in December 1804 and fought in her in the famous 1805 battle. The following year he was wounded at the Battle of San Domingo in the Caribbean and left the navy on a pension of £400 with the retired rank of Post Captain.

Another Cheltenham resident with connections to the battle was Revd James Saumarez, of Montpellier Lodge, Cheltenham. His father, Admiral Lord de Saumarez, although not at Trafalgar, was an intimate friend of Lord Nelson and served under his command, winning medals for his courage at the Battles of St Vincent (1797) and the Nile (1798). After his death in Guernsey on 9 October 1836, the Admiral was succeeded by his eldest son James. The new Lord Saumarez died at Montpellier Lodge on 9 April 1863, aged seventy-one.

There is, of course, also a Trafalgar Street in Cheltenham which runs behind Imperial Square. (Mike Grindley, CLHS Journal 20)

OCTOBER 5TH

1922: On this day the Daffodil cinema in Suffolk Parade showed its first movie, *Thunderclap*, starring Mary Carr. Although moving pictures had been shown in various halls and theatres around town since 1903, the Daffodil was Cheltenham's first purpose-built cinema. Its box office opened directly onto the street and one entered the cinema through a beautiful tiled lobby draped with red velvet curtains. The cinema was an instant success, always managing to fill its 750 seats. When the 'talkies' arrived in 1930, a sophisticated sound system was installed to replace the existing orchestral accompaniment.

In the 1950s the advent of television and increased competition saw ticket sales dwindle. The Daffodil had become little more than a seedy flea-pit and was finally put out of its misery on 7 September 1963 after a screening of *Cape Fear* starring Gregory Peck. The Daffodil then became a bingo hall until 1977, when the property was sold and became an antique furniture centre. This closed in 1989 and the building fell into disrepair until local restaurateur Mark Stephens decided to convert it into a restaurant. The Daffodil opened as one of Britain's most unique and dramatic dining rooms on 14 February 1998. (Various sources)

OCTOBER 6TH

1984: On this day a commemorative plaque was unveiled at No. 3 Priory Terrace to honour the renowned Cheltenham printmaker and publisher George Rowe.

Rowe was born in Exeter in 1796 and initially worked as a drawing teacher. His earliest known prints were of Hastings – *Twenty-Six Views of Picturesque Scenery of Hastings and its Vicinity* being published in 1823. He produced several more series of prints, illustrating views on the south-east coast and his home county of Devon.

Rowe moved to Cheltenham in 1832 or 1834 and became a significant figure in the town. He gave drawing and painting lessons with his wife Philippa, and sold artists' materials alongside his topographical prints. He produced the illustrations for two editions of *The Illustrated Cheltenham Guide*, which his company printed and published. Rowe was active in the politics of the town, being a founder member of the Cheltenham Liberal Association and serving on several committees. He was appointed High Bailiff of the Manor of Cheltenham and jointly owned the *Cheltenham Examiner*. He was also involved in property development, being a director of the Bayshill Estate Building Co. and joint owner of the Royal Well Spa, a site on which part of the Ladies' College now stands.

Following problems with his businesses in Cheltenham, Rowe moved to Australia in 1852, but he returned to his hometown of Exeter after about seven years and died there on 2 September 1864. (Various sources, including Smith & Rowbotham, *Commemorative Plaques of Cheltenham*)

OCTOBER 7TH

1927: On this day the Royal Navy minesweeper HMS *Cheltenham* was sold to Cashmore in Newport for scrap. The boat, of the Racecourse Class (sometimes called the Ascot Class), was built by the Ardrossan Dry Dock & Shipbuilding Co. on the north Ayrshire coast in Scotland and launched on Wednesday 12 April 1916.

This paddlewheel coastal minesweeping sloop weighed 810 tons and was powered by a 1,400hp inclined compound cylindrical return tube engine; she had a maximum speed of 15 knots and a range of 156 tons of coal. Her crew consisted of fifty men and she was armed with two twelve-pounder guns.

The ship operated only in British coastal waters, mainly between Harwich and either Portsmouth or Plymouth. In 1919 she sailed to Norway. HMS *Cheltenham* took part in the Spithead Fleet Review on 26 July 1924 and is the only ship to have carried the name Cheltenham. (Colledge & Warlow, *Ships of the Royal Navy: The Complete Record of all Fighting Ships of the Royal Navy*)

OCTOBER 8TH

1892: On this day William Swift from Badgeworth, near Gloucester, made one of his frequent visits to the Opera House in Cheltenham.

Swift, at this time headmaster of Churchdown School near Gloucester, meticulously kept a diary. He was a keen theatregoer and had often visited the Royal Well Theatre in Montpellier before it closed. He recorded a visit to the new Opera House, with his son, exactly a year after it had opened.

On the day in question they rode into Cheltenham and left their tricycles in Bayshill Inn yard, walking across the Promenade to Regent Street. Swift thought the decoration of the new theatre very beautiful, particularly the fine ceiling. He also admired the electric lighting and the gold and brown colour scheme. He wrote that he had paid 1s 6d for a seat in the Pit and had a drink in the 'subterranean refreshment bar' which was situated under the foyer. He did not record any of the rowdyism he had encountered in the final days of the old Royal Well Theatre a few years earlier. (CLHS Journal 8)

OCTOBER 9TH

1858: On this day the *Looker-On* announced that 107 acres, comprising up to seventy plots, were to be developed as a 'new town emulating Cheltenham in the number and quality of its fashionable residents'. Somerset Tibbs, George Ridge and William Bain had purchased the land, at a cost of £6,500, to build the Cheltenham suburb of Battledown. This new estate was to be as exclusive and desirable as Pittville and The Park. The advantage that Battledown had was its position, commanding as it does superb views over Cheltenham and its surrounding areas.

The name of Battledown was first recorded in 1598 as Badleton, and it's thought that its origin is Old English for 'Baedala's farm'. By 1692 the name Battledown was established. Local story goes that a battle took place in this area between the Royalists and the Parliamentarians during the Civil War, but any suggestion that the name commemorates a battle has been discredited.

The new housing project took some time to get off the ground and was a costly business. In the first couple of years, road-making expenditure alone amounted to over £3,700. Nevertheless, gradually the estate took shape and became one of Cheltenham's most desirable addresses. (D. O'Connor, *Battledown: The Story of a Victorian Estate*)

OCTOBER 10TH

1866: On this day a rather unusual event took place in Pittville Park – the Cheltenham lifeboat was launched. Now this may strike you as a little unnecessary, as there are very few shipwrecks on the lake and the water is only 4-5ft deep. In actual fact the boat was not setting out on a mission but was just to show the good people of Cheltenham what the money they had given to a public subscription had bought. No sooner was the boat launched than it was un-launched, put on a wagon and taken down to the RNLI station at Burnham-on-Sea in Somerset.

This launch was one of a number of events designed to bring the public into the park. During the season, which lasted from May to September, the waters were available daily but neither they, nor the attractions of the walks and rides of the pleasure grounds, attracted sufficient visitors. Consequently, a number of special attractions – like the lifeboat and the biannual shows of the County of Gloucester and Cheltenham Horticultural Society – were introduced in an attempt to draw the crowds. (John Roles, *Cheltenham in Old Picture Postcards*)

OCTOBER 11TH

1834: On this day the *Cheltenham Looker-On* reported the latest development in the ongoing story of the Napoleon Fountain. The sculpture, which had originally been the centrepiece of the Marble Fountain at the Sherborne/Imperial Spa, had first been unveiled eight years earlier. In May 1834 the fountain was moved to the newly opened Montpellier Gardens as one of its main attractions and placed on the lawn directly in front of the conservatories. A sort of rockery basin was built around the fountain's base, which was filled with water and stocked with a variety of ornamental gold and silver fish. A number of water jets were also added to enhance the attraction. According to 1842's *The Strangers' Guide Through Cheltenham,* the water was pumped to the fountains from the nearby Montpellier Laboratory. The *Guide*'s author, Henry Davies, claimed that, at full force, the water could shoot over 30ft into the air.

The fountain was removed from Montpellier Gardens in 1902 and, after being repaired, was placed in the Town Hall. In 1925 it was moved again, finding another home in the lobby of the Central Library, where it stayed until the 1960s. (*Cheltenham Looker-On*)

OCTOBER 12TH

1962: On this day Cheltenham MP Martin Horwood was born in the town. After attending Cheltenham College, Martin read Modern History at Queen's College, Oxford, where he was President of the Oxford Student Liberal Society. After graduating he worked first in advertising and then in the voluntary sector. In 1990 he moved to Oxford to work for Oxfam and in 1995, with his wife Dr Shona Arora, worked in India for a year. He was elected at the 2005 general election, but at one stage had ambitions to become a cartoonist. He said:

> My first love was art, drawing and things like that. I developed quite a good hand at cartooning, which I still do occasionally … I was amazed, when I was first elected, to discover there was a parliamentary art collection which MPs can borrow for their offices. Most of the important pictures had been snapped up but I found a pile of James Gillrays sitting in the basement. So, now I've got two of them on my office wall. Sometimes when I look at them I still can't believe it. He was the greatest political cartoonist ever.

(Interview in *The Cheltonian* magazine)

OCTOBER 13TH

1693: On this day a Court Baron was held before John Prinn, Steward of the Manor of Cheltenham. In those days each Manor held a Court Baron every three weeks or so. This dealt with the town's legal and social affairs and all villeins were required to attend. Villeins were peasants who were bound, under the feudal system, to the Lord of the Manor. They occupied a place in society roughly between slaves and freemen, the free peasants. Villeins, or serfs, as they were also known, were not able to leave the land without the owner's permission. Freeman tenants did not need to attend each court session unless they were involved in a legal dispute.

The courts had a jury, with jurors being drawn from among leading tenants. Their powers included being able to demand that the Lord carry out duties such as repairing the animal pound. Functions of the Court Baron included recording land sales, resolving disputes over property rights, damage and trespass, and regulating agricultural practice. Fines could be levied for failure to perform services. Failure to attend the court was considered an offence and was also punishable by a fine. (James Hodsdon (ed.), *The Court Books of the Manor of Cheltenham 1692-1803*)

OCTOBER 14TH

1926: On this day Sir James Agg-Gardner unveiled a commemorative plaque to Alfred, Lord Tennyson, on the house where the poet had lived at No. 10 St James' Square.

The thirty-seven-year-old Tennyson had moved to Cheltenham in 1846 after losing most of his inheritance and income in bad investments. Suffering from severe depression and hypochondria, he moved in with his mother and sisters in the house they rented in St James' Square. He was prescribed isolation and rest, as well as a course of Cheltenham waters to restore his failing health.

Perhaps Cheltenham was not the best place to find rest and isolation as it was still, at the time, the focus for the country's fashionable people. Tennyson though was not impressed, describing it as 'a polka, parson worshipping place of which Francis Close is Pope' – not a description that would have endeared him to Revd Close. Nevertheless, Tennyson stayed in Cheltenham for six years, using his mother's house to write most of his epic poem *In Memoriam*. When the poem was published in 1850, Tennyson succeeded Wordsworth as Poet Laureate. Tennyson died in 1892 aged eighty-three. (Smith & Rowbotham, *Commemorative Plaques of Cheltenham*)

OCTOBER 15TH

1962: On this day the Banbury to Cheltenham District Railway closed. The railway had opened in 1887 and was operated by the Great Western Railway. The BCDR remained a separate company until the GWR absorbed it in 1897. All services along the BCDR had to change direction at Kingham until 1906, when the GWR built a loop that bypassed the station.

British Railways withdrew all passenger services between Cheltenham and Kingham on 15 October 1962, between Kingham and Chipping Norton on 1 December 1962, and all freight services on 7 September 1964. The Midland & South Western Junction Railway line closed to passenger traffic in September 1961, and services on the Banbury to Cheltenham line were also withdrawn on 15 October 1962. (J.H. Russell, *The Banbury and Cheltenham Railway 1887-1962*)

OCTOBER 16TH

1906: On this day Dorothea Beale, founder and principal of Cheltenham Ladies' College, visited her doctor in London. She had been haunted for several months by the thought that she had 'some fatal disease'. The visit to the doctor confirmed it. She wrote of the fateful day in her diary: 'On Tuesday I went up to London hurriedly at 6.37, full of the thought of what was before me. I went straight to Dr. Aldrich Blake, an old pupil. She condemned me. … I looked into shops and felt giddy.'

On her return to Cheltenham, Dr Cardew confirmed Dr Blake's opinion, and it was arranged that Dorothea should enter a local nursing home on 22 October. After the operation, all went well until Sunday 28th, when she became obviously worse. She rallied somewhat, but then nervous prostration set in and after that there was practically no hope. Dorothea Beale died on 9 November at 12.15 p.m. during college hours. It was thought best that the girls should hear of her death before leaving. When all were assembled in the Princess Hall, the vice-principal said, 'It has pleased God to take from us our beloved principal.' (Ethel M. Barton (ed.), *Pioneers of Progress –Women*)

OCTOBER 17TH

1883: On this day, at the Corporation Water Works in Dowdeswell, the ceremony of turning the first sod was performed by the Mayor, Councillor George Parsonage.

The Dowdeswell Reservoir was constructed between 1883 and 1886, thus ensuring the town's future water supply. This was the first of a number of public amenities that were introduced or safeguarded during the first twenty-five years of the Corporation's existence, and these included significant advances in public health, leisure and recreation. The reservoir is currently owned and managed by the Environment Agency and is used as a 'balancing pond' for the water catchment from the east end of the valley. Severn Trent closed the water treatment works with the commissioning of the Mythe Treatment Works on the River Severn, and the reservoir itself became a flood storage reservoir for the River Chelt, in an attempt to protect Cheltenham from flooding from the east. (Various sources, including *Reserves Handbook: Nature Reserves of the Gloucestershire Wildlife Trust*)

OCTOBER 18TH

2004: On this day an obituary appeared in the *Telegraph* for Sir Robert Hunt, chairman of the Dowty Group.

Robert Frederick Hunt, always known as Bob, was born in Leckhampton on 11 May 1918. He was educated at Cheltenham Grammar School, but it was his time spent in a local garage after school that encouraged him to train as a mechanical engineer. In 1935 he joined George Dowty's works. Dowty was working on hydraulics for aircraft undercarriages and Hunt became a design draughtsman in the team which produced the landing gear for Frank Whittle's jet-propelled Gloster aeroplane: its first take-off in 1941 was one of Hunt's proudest moments.

In 1980 Hunt became a director (and in 1982 deputy chairman) of British Leyland which, at the time, was being transformed under the chairmanship of Sir Michael Edwardes. After Edwardes' era, Hunt remained a strong voice on the board until 1990, having seen it privatised as Rover Group and sold to British Aerospace. Hunt was also a director of Eagle Star and Charter Consolidated (the mining group) and a Deputy Lieutenant of Gloucestershire. He was appointed CBE in 1974 and knighted in 1979. He died on 17 September 2004. (*Telegraph*)

OCTOBER 19TH

2011: On this day reports were published concerning a police operation mounted in Cheltenham against brothel rings as part of a nationwide anti-slavery campaign. Senior figures from Gloucestershire police, who played a key role in the country's largest-ever swoop on vice dens, spoke about how they tracked down the masterminds behind the enterprise.

The operation, named Pentameter II, involved a series of co-ordinated raids and was the subject of hard-hitting Channel 4 documentary *The Hunt for Britain's Sex Traffickers*. As part of the national Anti-Slavery Day, a public meeting was staged to highlight the dangers of people-trafficking, which police say remains a 'significant' problem. Detective Inspector Sue Bradshaw, who played a central role in the investigation, was part of a panel of experts at the event.

In Cheltenham, officers carried out raids at brothels in Evesham Road, Normal Terrace and London Road. This followed several arrests that had been made for crimes linked to human slavery in the county earlier that year. DI Bradshaw added: 'Anti-Slavery Day was an opportunity to highlight this issue. Sex trafficking and other forms of slavery are not acceptable and action needs to be taken to end such persecution.' (*Gloucestershire Echo*)

OCTOBER 20TH

2008: On this day the usual bell-ringing practice took place at St Mark's Church. The church has a fine set of bells which peal out regularly either for services or for practice.

Despite being built with bells in mind, the impressive and imposing church tower and spire remained empty until 1884, when local resident, Mrs Murray Miller, a member of the congregation at St Mark's, donated five bells. The bells rang out for the first time on 12 February 1885. By the beginning of the 1990s the bells were known for their difficulty and the local band had begun to ring only for weddings and occasionally on Sunday mornings. The millennium was rung in but, soon after, ringing all but ceased. Local opinion was also, at times, not in favour of the bells. In 2003 several faults were found with the bells and a major restoration programme was undertaken which took five years to complete. (www.stmarkonline.org)

OCTOBER 21ST

1921: On this day the unveiling of the War Memorial in the Promenade Gardens took place, the ceremony being performed by Major-General Sir Robert Fanshawe. Since the idea of a memorial had first been raised, the suggested designs had varied considerably, with one suggestion being a classical circular temple with a domed top. At one point the council accepted a design to be built in red Scottish granite which included a golden crown illuminated by a concealed electric light. Fortunately, however, good taste prevailed and the simple but distinguished obelisk was erected in front of the main door of the Municipal Offices. The unveiling took place amid much pomp and ceremony, with military uniforms and old soldiers prominent amidst the onlookers. The Corporation Fire Brigade provided a guard of honour as they assembled on the steps of the Municipal Offices for the occasion.

A total of 1,266 men, who had either been born or educated in Cheltenham, died in the First World War. A service is held each year on Remembrance Day, which is attended by the Mayor, local dignitaries and representatives of the armed forces. (John Roles, *Cheltenham in Old Picture Postcards*)

OCTOBER 22ND

1881: On this day Oscar's Circus was in town and in full swing. Throughout the previous week it had been the favourite haunt of supporters of public amusements – especially on the Monday and Friday evenings, when the entertainments were patronised by Sir Francis Ford and the Mayor of Cheltenham. There was a very large attendance in the reserved stalls on each occasion. Mr Oscar introduced his two newly trained horses on the Monday, whose performances elicited loud applause from all parts of the house. Miss Lizzie Harmston's Chinese Dance was also well received at all performances during the week. On the following Monday it was announced that the circus was to be under the special patronage of Captain St Clair-Ford and, on the Wednesday after that, Captain Sumner was due to pay the entertainment a similar compliment. (*Cheltenham Looker-On*)

OCTOBER 23RD

1847: On this day, the first Great Western Railway station for broad-gauge track opened in Cheltenham near St James' Square. It was built on part of Jessop's Gardens, which was essentially a plant nursery and seed merchants but eventually spread over nearly 20 acres and effectively became a popular public park.

The original railway station was initially little more than 'dingy shedding', and it was not until 1894, after the old track had been converted to standard gauge in 1872, that it was transformed into the little Italianate gem with wrought iron and glass-covered carriage entrance that survived until 1966. The site behind the station, with its vast sidings, coal yards and other railway paraphernalia, stood abandoned until Waitrose rose from the ashes in 2002. The only reminders are a small green plaque on the front of the store, a pub called the Railway Arms in New Street, and the St James Hotel which served travellers using the station. (Various sources, including Rowbotham & Waller, *Cheltenham: A History*)

OCTOBER 24TH

1891: On this day:

… the hearty laughter heard within the Theatre was conclusive proof of the large measure of amusement afforded by the somewhat extravagant, but highly entertaining farcical comedy presented by Mr C. Hawtrey's company. *The Private Secretary* depends very largely for its success on two characters; one of which gives a name to the play, while the other, Mr Cattermole, is scarcely less important than the title role. Both were thoroughly well acted, the rendering of the Uncle by Mr Wyes, of the Comedy Theatre, who on Monday supplied the place of Mr Vernon, who was prevented from appearing by illness, was as natural as it was spirited. Mr Helmore made the most of *The Private Secretary's* peculiarities without running into extravagance of manner or action. The other players were equal to their parts; the female characters in particular being well represented.

The Directors came to a determination to reduce the price of the Orchestra Stalls to a half-a-crown for the second Monday, thereby enabling those who find the Upper Circle warm and otherwise inconvenient to have a seat in front of the house at a price which practically indicates that evening dress will not be necessary.

(*Cheltenham Looker-On*)

OCTOBER 25TH

1919: On this day, a columnist of the *Cheltenham Looker-On* was full of praise for the new *thé dansants* (tea dances) that had been established at the Town Hall:

> Cheltenham does not possess the reputation of moving with the times but these dances seem to indicate that a new spirit is abroad, or perhaps it is the influence of a Borough Councillor who believes in progress and 'push'. Whatever the reason may be, there can be little doubt that a long felt want has been supplied to the Town, and what is more remarkable there has been a realisation that decoration is an all-important factor of success.
>
> Excellent results have been achieved in the lighting scheme and the Town Hall had a far more artistic appearance than is usually the case, and the night effect has been produced with striking success ... The shading of the lights on the wall was admirable, but it would be a still greater improvement if the centre lights were similarly treated.
>
> In Cheltenham, as a general rule, hasty improvisation is the order of the day and the arrangements for the *Thé Dansants* clearly show that new ideas have come to the Town, and I am convinced that whoever is responsible for the decoration, music and general organisation has an intimate knowledge of the methods adopted in London at the various noted dancing resorts.

(*Cheltenham Looker-On*)

OCTOBER 26TH

1899: On this day Cheltenham acquired a fine-art gallery in Clarence Street, and the basis of its important collection of paintings, due to the generosity of one of its most public-spirited inhabitants, the Baron de Ferrières.

The Baron pledged to donate thirty paintings from his own and his father's collection, and gave £1,000 to pay for the erection of two galleries in which to display them, on the condition that the council would provide the necessary land. In the event, the Baron donated forty-three of his collection of mainly Dutch and Flemish paintings. As well as an art gallery, the building was intended as a venue for civic entertainments, like the mayoral banquet that followed the laying of the foundation stone of the new Town Hall in October 1902. The museum, which is now part of the same building, was not opened until June 1907, when the upper floors of the library were vacated by the Schools of Art and Science. (John Roles, *Cheltenham in Old Picture Postcards*)

OCTOBER 27TH

1701: On this day it was recorded in the Cheltenham Court Book that the local Quakers, or Friends, had been given permission to build a meeting house following years of religious persecution. Some Friends were actually sent to prison in 1685 and John Hayward was fined for refusing to pay towards the repair of the parish church.

The main persecution seems to have ended with the passing of the Toleration Act in 1689, and early in 1696 the Quakers were making plans for building a meeting house. The land for this was provided by Elizabeth Sandford (one of those imprisoned in 1685) and transferred to William Mason, John Pumphry and John Drewett 'to the only intent and purpose that a Quakers' Meeting House can be erected and built'.

At a quarterly meeting at Gloucester the following year, a two-man deputation of Cheltenham Quakers explained that they could not raise enough money to complete the building and were consequently granted £20. In 1703 the new meeting house was licensed for worship and shortly afterwards land was acquired for a burial ground in Grove Street. The meeting house was used by Quakers until 1836, when it was replaced by a larger building. The only trace of the Grove Street burial ground is a stone inscription above an old door in the wall. (Gwen Hart, *A History of Cheltenham*)

OCTOBER 28TH

1914: On this day the Prestbury Park racecourse received its first influx of wounded soldiers, having been converted into a hundred-bed hospital in the First World War. A fully equipped operating theatre was installed, complete with electric lighting. Belgian, British, Canadian and French casualties from the trenches were ferried by ship to Southampton, then on to Cheltenham aboard special trains.

Cheltenham has connections with several heroes of the First World War. Captain Anketell Moutray Read, son of Colonel J. Moutray Read of Cheltenham, was educated at Glengarth, Cheltenham and at the United Service College, Westward Ho. He joined the Royal Flying Corps in 1912 and went to France with the first Expeditionary Force in August 1914. On 25 September 1915 he was killed in action near Hulluch, France, and was awarded the VC.

Another Cheltenham First World War hero was Lieutenant-Colonel Richard Annesley West (VC, DSO and Bar, and MC) who was born in Cheltenham on 26 September 1878. He was awarded the VC following action on 21 August 1918 at Courcelles, France. He died on 2 September 1918. There is a plaque to his memory on No. 1 Oxford Street in Cheltenham. (Various sources)

OCTOBER 29TH

1925: On this day the celebrated actor Robert Hardy was born in Cheltenham. He is perhaps best remembered for his role as Siegfried Farnon in the long-running BBC series *All Creatures Great and Small*, which ran from 1978 until 1990.

Christened Timothy Sydney Robert Hardy, he was the son of Jocelyn (*née* Dugdale) and Henry Harrison Hardy, who was headmaster of Cheltenham College. He was educated at Rugby School and Magdalen College, Oxford where he gained a BA Honours degree in English. Hardy began his career as a classical actor. In 1959 he appeared as Sicinius opposite Laurence Olivier in *Coriolanus* at Stratford-upon-Avon. It was while playing Henry V that Hardy developed an interest in medieval warfare and he later wrote and presented an acclaimed television documentary on the subject of the Battle of Agincourt. He has also written two books on the subject of the longbow. In 1996 he was elected a Fellow of the Society of Antiquaries, and in 1981 he was appointed a CBE. (Various sources)

OCTOBER 30TH

1893: On this day Cheltenham's best-known landmark, the Neptune Fountain, was switched on for the first time. The fountain was designed by the borough surveyor Joseph Hall, who modelled it on Rome's *Fontana di Trevi*. It is pure decoration and does not commemorate anything in particular. The giant weeping willow tree that used to cast its shadow over Neptune and his horses was said to have been taken from the cutting of a tree that shaded Napoleon's final resting place on St Helena.

The fountain takes its water from the River Chelt, which flows underground beneath it. When the fountain was first built it stood outside the Imperial Rooms, which had originally been the pump room for the Sherborne/Imperial Spa. This spa had stood on the site of the Queens Hotel until 1837, when it was moved to the bottom of St George's Road to make way for Cheltenham's iconic hotel. The building was demolished in 1937 when the new Regal Cinema was built on the site. (John Roles, *Cheltenham in Old Picture Postcards*)

OCTOBER 31ST

2011: On this day the dust was beginning to settle from the demolition of a house near the Staverton/Gloucestershire Airport near to Cheltenham.

The demolition of Blenheim House – which the Head of Operations, Darren Lewington, described as a 'significant point in the project' – had started on the previous day and was the first act in the development of the airport. The removal of the building would, according to a spokesman, enable the extension of the existing runway, which would improve safety and allow larger aircraft to use the airport. The company that runs the airport also claimed that many jobs would be secured.

In the seven years since the scheme was first on the table, the airport had had to contend with a lengthy planning permission process as well as a well co-ordinated protest from local residents. The £4 million development scheme involved the construction of a new access road to the airport and improvement of many of the buildings and facilities on the site. It also included some new hi-tech equipment which would make it easier for aircraft to land in bad weather. (Various sources, including *Gloucestershire Echo*)

NOVEMBER 1ST

1963: On this day The Beatles played the Gaumont cinema in Winchcombe Street. The Friday night gig was the first venue on their Autumn Tour that year and was the group's first as undisputed headliners. The support acts were Rhythm and Blues Quartet, The Vernon Girls, Peter Jay & the Jaywalkers and The Kestrels. The Beatles had been on tour continuously for the past twelve months or so and this was their fourth tour of the year. Only two days before the Cheltenham concert, the band had returned home from a tour of Sweden. Their set ran barely half an hour and they played only ten songs.

The concert even made the daily papers. On 2 November, a report in the *Daily Mirror* carried the headline: 'Beatlemania! It's happening everywhere ... even in sedate Cheltenham.' This is thought to be the first use of the word in print, but within a few weeks it would be the normal way of describing the worldwide phenomenon that was The Beatles. (Various sources)

NOVEMBER 2ND

1868: On this day the Bishop of Gloucester consecrated the new All Saints' Church in All Saints' Road, Cheltenham.

The church was designed by John Middleton and is splendidly decorated, is very high ceilinged, and has an ornate wrought-iron screen separating the chancel from the nave. It also boasts a polished granite arcade and elaborate statuary in canopied niches. The spectacular West Door was carved by the largest firm of monumental masons in Cheltenham, R.L. Boulton & Sons. Built in the Early French Gothic style, the original design for the church included a 200ft-tall spire, but that was never completed. The stained glass in the church was designed by Edward Burne-Jones, a leading member of the Pre-Raphaelite Brotherhood.

Middleton was the leading church architect at the time and was also responsible for the churches of St Mark's, Holy Apostles, St Philip's and St James'. Spectacular though it is, All Saints' greatest claim to fame is that Gustav Holst's father was organist there and the young Gustav sang in the choir. (Various sources, including Rowbotham & Waller, *Cheltenham: A History*)

NOVEMBER 3RD

1863: On this day the Cheltenham & County of Gloucestershire Cricket Club (renamed Gloucestershire County Cricket Club in 1871) was formed. The club played for the first time at Lord's against the Marylebone Cricket Club in 1868, and the team included three brothers: E.M., G.F. and W.G. Grace. The first Cheltenham Cricket Week took place seven years later, organised by James Lillywhite, who was the college cricket coach.

William Gilbert (W.G.) Grace was born on 18 July 1848 at Downend, Bristol, and is widely acknowledged as one of the greatest players of all time. He played first-class cricket for a record-equalling forty-four seasons, from 1865 to 1908, during which he captained England, Gloucestershire County Cricket Club, the Gentlemen, MCC and several other teams. The brothers – W.G, his elder brother Edward, and his younger brother Fred – first played together for England in 1880; this was the first time three brothers had played together in Test cricket. Grace qualified as a doctor in 1879 and, because he practised as a doctor, was nominally an amateur cricketer. However, he is said to have made more money from his cricketing activities than any professional. (GCCC and *Gloucester Journal*)

NOVEMBER 4TH

1865: On this day, reviews of the previous week's plays at the Opera House in Regent Street were published:

The performances at the Theatre have been numerously attended during the past week, in consequence of the appearance of Miss Amy Sedgwick in several of her favourite characters, assisted by Mr Henry Vandenhoff, the well-known light comedian. On Monday, the comedy of *The Unequal Match* was performed, Miss Sedgwick taking the part of Hester Grazebrook, and Mr Vandenhoff that of Lord Arncliffe – the former character being especially adapted to the versatile talents of this accomplished actress.

On Thursday, the play of *The Hunchback* was represented, in which Miss Sedgwick, as Julia, and Mr Vandenhoff as Master Walter elicited repeated and deserved plaudits throughout the evening. The success that has attended the engagement of Miss Amy Sedgwick has resulted in a prolongation of her visit to Cheltenham and her appearance next week in three of her most popular characters, namely Lady Macbeth, Pauline and Mrs Haller.

(*Cheltenham Looker-On*)

NOVEMBER 5TH

1839: On this day, Revd Francis Close preached a sermon against the Roman Catholic Church. He was to repeat this address annually on that day for the next fifteen years.

Dom John Augustine Birdsall had arrived in Cheltenham in October 1809 and used his own money to build a chapel in Somerset Place, on the corner of St James' Square. While the building was under construction, he conducted Mass at the York Hotel on the Strand. Revd Close was opposed to all things Catholic and strongly opposed the Catholic Emancipation Bill of 1829. He even tried to persuade local Protestants to march to the chapel and destroy it. Father Birdsall left Cheltenham in 1836 to create a monastery in Broadway.

Despite the rantings and ravings of Revd Close, a fine, large and permanent Catholic church was eventually built in St James' Square. St Gregory's, designed in the Decorated Gothic style by Charles Hansom from Bristol, was opened on the site of the original chapel in May 1857. (Rowbotham & Waller, *Cheltenham: A History*)

NOVEMBER 6TH

2011: On this day, the plans for the 2012 Olympic Flame's visit to Cheltenham were officially announced.

The Flame was due to arrive in Cheltenham on 23 May, spending the night in the town before continuing its journey to Gloucester and beyond. A spectacular event was planned for the night of the 23rd at the racecourse. Councillor Andrew McKinlay, Cheltenham Borough Council's cabinet member for sport and culture, said: 'The facilities at the racecourse are second to none and provide the opportunity for many thousands of local people to come along and witness a moment in history.' The managing director of Cheltenham Racecourse, Edward Gillespie, said: 'We are delighted the racecourse has been chosen as the venue of the evening celebration for the Olympic Torch Relay in Gloucestershire. ... We shall be working closely with the Olympic Torch Taskforce and the local community to produce an evening that not only showcases the Olympic Torch, but also gives a taste of the true spirit of this great county.' (BBC News; Sky Sports)

NOVEMBER 7TH

1914: On this day the *Cheltenham Looker-On* thought it necessary to explain a few things about the new statue that had recently appeared in Montpellier, and which was the source of some confusion:

> The fountain and statue were conceived in the minds of the late Mrs Drew and her late husband of Hatherley Court. Messrs. Boulton were instructed to execute it in accordance with their views, which it must be admitted has been very faithfully and artistically done. The marble group represents the late King Edward as the Spirit of Peace, leading the Spirit of Mischief to the still waters. Perhaps, had Mr Drew lived until to-day he would have substituted a different Spirit of Mischief, the one that apparently only King Edward could hold in check or lead. The figures were modelled and carved by Mr Ambrose Neale, Messrs Boulton's chief who was also responsible for the Boer War Memorial in the Promenade. ... The generous givers expressed the opinion that there was no necessity to mention their names in connection with it. The then Mayor, Mr J. T. Agg-Gardner, M.P. thought otherwise and obtained sanction to disclose the identity of the donors. The statue is of Sicilian marble of the finest quality.

(*Cheltenham Looker-On*)

NOVEMBER 8TH

1886: On this day the great flat-race jockey Frederick James 'Fred' Archer committed suicide. Archer was born on 11 January 1857 in Cheltenham in a cottage off St George's Place. In his day, Fred was the most successful and acclaimed sportsman in horseracing. He is described by the National Horseracing Museum as 'the best all-round jockey that the Turf has ever seen'.

At the age of eleven Archer was apprenticed to Newmarket horse trainer Mathew Dawson, and eventually married Dawson's niece, Helen Rose Dawson. He won his first race in September 1870, on a horse called Athol Daisy, in Bangor-on-Dee.

Archer was Champion Jockey for thirteen consecutive years. He rode in 8,084 races, winning 2,748 of them. In 1885 alone he rode 246 winners, a record that was eventually broken by Gordon Richards in 1933. Archer won twenty-one classic races in all, including five victories in the Epsom Derby.

He was quite tall for a jockey and was constantly struggling with his weight. The effect on his health from his strict diet regimes and self-inflicted treatments, plus the depression he suffered after the death of his wife Helen after only a year of marriage, led to his suicide. Fred Archer shot himself at the age of twenty-nine. Several sightings of Archer's ghost riding a white horse have been reported at his old stables. (Various sources, including Rowbotham & Waller, *Cheltenham: A History*; www.newmarketracecourses.co.uk)

NOVEMBER 9TH

1881: On this day a wedding took place in All Saints' Church which was solemnised with a full choral service. The wedding march was played by the resident organist, Mr von Holst, father of Gustav. The breakfast and reception took place at the Crown in Upper Park Street and our old friend William Swift was there to record the family wedding in his diary. Swift noted that:

> ... soon after 12.40 we sat down to breakfast which lasted till 2.20 – cold chicken, ducks, roast beef, veal pies, fruit, ham, tarts, etc, etc, wine, sherry, port, beer ... In the afternoon the company amused themselves with music, singing, etc. then followed tea at five. At 5.30 the newly married departed amidst showers of rice by cab for the station on their way to Abergavenny. Dancing then began ... I played the concertina ... Spinning and trencher was the next game and forfeits, etc. Left at 9.

Swift made a note later that the party did not break up until 4 a.m. (CLHS Journal 8)

NOVEMBER 10TH

1978: On this day the first episode of the long-running and popular television series *Butterflies* was broadcast on BBC2. The comedy sitcom was written by Carla Lane and ran from 1978-83. The show starred Wendy Craig as frustrated housewife Ria Parkinson, with Geoffrey Palmer as her dentist husband, Ben. Their youngest son, Adam, was played by Nicholas Lyndhurst. The title of *Butterflies* superficially came from Ben's lepidoptery hobby, as well as being a metaphor for Ria's struggle against what she feels to be her captivity.

Most of the exterior shots for the twenty-eight episodes of the show were shot in and around Cheltenham. Often used were the High Street, Montpellier and Hatherley Park. The Parkinson house was situated on Bournside Road in Up Hatherley.

Carla Lane, Wendy Craig and the rest of the cast were reunited for a special one-off reunion episode produced especially for the BBC charity telethon Children In Need on 17 November 2000. It was so successful that it was briefly suggested that a new series could follow. But this didn't happen. (Various sources, including BBC)

NOVEMBER 11TH

1956: On this day the celebrated concert violinist Marie Pauline Hall died in Cheltenham. She was born in Newcastle-upon-Tyne in 1884, but settled in Cheltenham in 1911 after marrying her manager Edward Baring.

Her father, Edward Felix Handley Hall, played the harp for the Carl Rosa Opera Co., and initially taught her to play. When the distinguished French violinist and composer Émile Sauret heard Marie play at the age of nine, he suggested that she attend the Royal Academy of Music, where he was professor. Unfortunately, probably because her parents could not afford it, the offer was not taken up. In fact, it is said that, as a young girl, Marie would busk on the streets of Malvern while her mother collected pennies from passers-by. Nevertheless, from 1894 Marie was able to study locally with Edward Elgar, who gave lessons in the town. By the age of nineteen she was already giving concerts around the world.

Ralph Vaughan Williams wrote one of his most famous compositions, 'The Lark Ascending', for Marie Hall. She gave the first public performance of the orchestral version, playing the Viotti Stradivarius, at the Queen's Hall in London in 1921, with Sir Adrian Boult conducting the British Symphony Orchestra. (Various sources, including the Guarlford History Group; Smith & Rowbotham, *Commemorative Plaques of Cheltenham*)

NOVEMBER 12TH

1840: On this day one of France's greatest sculptors, Auguste Rodin, was born in Paris. But what is of interest to us is that on 12 September 1914 he arrived in Cheltenham.

To avoid the encroaching First World War, the seventy-four-year-old Rodin fled Paris with his elderly mistress Rose Beuret, along with Judith Cladel and her mother. Rodin had been friends with Judith's father, the novelist Leon Cladel, and Cheltenham was chosen by the refugees because Cladel's other two daughters lived there. After a long and difficult journey they took rooms in a small private hotel, Sussex House, run by a Mrs Gandy in Winchcombe Street near to Pittville Gates. Apparently the party was concerned that the landlady would discover that Rodin and Beuret were not married. But as they spoke no English and Mrs Gandy no French, their secret remained undetected. In fact, Rodin could not even pronounce the word Pittville so took to calling it *petite ville gaie*, pretty little town.

Rodin left Cheltenham at the beginning of October but his month-long visit left such an impression on Daniel Herdman, the then Borough Librarian and Curator, that he procured the loan of Rodin's most famous and iconic sculpture, *The Kiss*. The 4.5-ton sculpture was brought to the town in 1933 for the bargain price of £29 18s. It stayed in the museum for six years before being moved to London. (CLHS Journal 26)

NOVEMBER 13TH

2011: On this day international superstar Lady Gaga took Cheltenham wannabe superstar Kitty Brucknell for a consolation drink.

Lady Gaga had made a guest appearance on *The X Factor* during the episode that Kitty had been voted off. Twenty-seven-year-old Kitty, from the Reddings in Cheltenham, had overcome Guillain-Barré syndrome to appear in the show. She had spent nearly four months in a wheelchair after being struck down with the disease while on holiday in Corfu. Her mother said it was remarkable she could stand, let alone perform.

Kitty, like her idol Lady Gaga, wowed *X Factor* audiences over the weeks with her stylised, even zany, presentation of songs like Bjork's 'It's Oh So Quiet', which was set at the Mad Hatter's tea party complete with a giant rabbit. Bookies Ladbrokes and William Hill both had the singer at odds of 11/4 to be the year's winner. (*Gloucestershire Echo*)

NOVEMBER 14TH

2011: On this day the Salvation Army announced the result of its annual appeal in and around Cheltenham.

The appeal exists to offer ongoing shelter, companionship and life-changing support to homeless people, older isolated people and families struggling in poverty. A spokesman said: 'Despite the general economic circumstances, the generosity of the people in and around Cheltenham has still enabled us to raise a total of £7,833 14p for the Salvation Army Annual Appeal of 2011.'

In November 2010, the Salvation Army's hopes of raising money from their band playing to the Christmas shoppers in Cheltenham were dashed when the council refused to give permission, claiming the concerts would clutter the streets. Instead of the normal three open-air concerts, they were only allowed to perform one. Volunteer Beryl Scarborough said: 'Christmas is a vital time for us and not having our usual street presence will make it a lot harder. But it's about more than that. It is taking away the real message of Christmas.' (The Salvation Army; www.thisisbath.co.uk)

NOVEMBER 15TH

1885: On this day one of the most significant individual pioneers of British aviation, Frederick Handley Page, was born in Kings Road, a few yards from the gates of the Cheltenham cricket ground.

By the age of twenty-one he was chief designer of an electrical company, but in 1908 he set up as an aeronautical engineer and a year later, with a capital of £10,000, he established the first private British company of this kind in Barking, Essex. Handley Page Ltd was the UK's first publicly traded aircraft manufacturing company.

His military aircraft were significant enough – including the famous Second World War Halifax bomber and later the four-engined Victor jet bomber. But his role in civil aviation was equally important. He formed one of the earliest air freight companies, Handley Page Transport Ltd, in 1919, with routes to Paris and Amsterdam. This later became one of Britain's first international airlines: Imperial Airways. In 1939 this merged with the original British Airways to become the British Overseas Airways Corporation and in 1974, after more mergers, the newly reconstituted British Airways. Handley Page Ltd went into voluntary liquidation and ceased to exist in March 1970. (Various sources, including Smith & Rowbotham, *Commemorative Plaques of Cheltenham*)

NOVEMBER 16TH

1899: On this day Princess Henry of Battenberg unveiled a bust of Queen Victoria at Cheltenham Ladies' College.

The Princess was the fifth daughter and youngest child of Queen Victoria and Albert, Prince Consort. In 1884 she became engaged to Prince Henry, but Queen Victoria agreed to the marriage only on the condition that the couple made their home with her. On 22 July 1885, the Queen made Prince Henry a Knight of the Garter, and granted him the title 'Royal Highness' to give him equal rank with his wife in the UK. Beatrice and Henry were married at St Mildred's Church at Whippingham, near Osborne, on 23 July 1885. On the same day, a Bill to naturalise Prince Henry as a British subject was passed in the House of Lords.

Another statue of Queen Victoria had been unveiled at the college in April the previous year by the Duchess of Montrose. (Various sources, including *Cheltenham Looker-On*)

NOVEMBER 17TH

1956: On this day Cheltenham Town Football Club, the Robins, held one of their most important fixtures when they played Reading in the first round of the FA Cup. The Waddon Road ground had rarely seen the like since the club had started playing at the rather ramshackle stadium in 1932. In order to increase the (mainly standing) capacity, folding wooden benches were set along the touchline for the hundreds of enthusiastic kids – sporting their red-and-white scarves and crisp rosettes – to sit on. In fact, so many spectators crammed into the ground for the match that a record attendance of 8,326 was set. The current ground capacity (mainly seating) is only 7,400. Consequently, the attendance figure set on that cold Saturday will probably never be beaten.

Another maximum crowd turned up on 25 November 2007 to watch the Robins beat one-time top team Leeds Utd. The Robins won 1–0 thanks to Cheltenham striker Steven Gillespie, who scored the only goal in the last five minutes of the game. Not content with that win, the Robins also beat Leeds on the return fixture at Elland Road. Because of Leeds Utd's dominance in domestic and European football during the 1960s and '70s, the victories were all the sweeter and regarded by many as among the most satisfying in the Robins' long, though not always illustrious, history. (Cheltenham Town Football Club)

NOVEMBER 18TH

2010: On this day, *This is Gloucestershire* reported that a pregnant shop assistant who was kicked in the stomach and threatened with a meat cleaver was denied compensation – because she went back to work too quickly.

The woman, who worked in Bargain Booze in Coronation Square, Cheltenham was left battered and panic-stricken after two teenagers violently robbed the shop earlier in the year. She decided the best way to deal with her shredded nerves was to return to normality as soon as possible, but was furious when a government agency ruled that she was unscathed by the attack. 'They said because I didn't have a complete nervous breakdown, I wasn't badly injured enough to qualify for compensation,' she said. 'It was a horrible attack, but I didn't want to let them know that they had got to me. I thought it would be best to get back to work and get on with it.'

After reporting the robbery to police, the woman returned to work the following day and later applied for compensation from the Criminal Injuries Compensation Authority (CICA). However, she was told that her physical and mental injuries were not severe enough to qualify for the minimum payout of £1,000. (www.thisisgloucestershire.co.uk)

November 19th

1919: On this day a marriage took place at St Mary's Church, Charlton Kings, between Miss Joan Daubeney (daughter of the late Mr H.E. Daubeney) and Major K.B. Inman, MC (son of Canon Inman of Dorset). The Revd Edgar Neale, vicar of Charlton Kings, officiated at the ceremony.

The bride, who was given away by her brother-in-law, Mr Whitley, was attired in a beautifully draped gown of chiffon velvet and she carried a bouquet of Malmaison pink roses. Major Horne fulfilled the duties of best man. The wedding was a quiet one owing to the bride's recent bereavement, only immediate relatives and friends being present. After the ceremony the bridal party drove to Pyatt's Hotel, Cheltenham, where everything had been splendidly arranged and prepared for the wedding breakfast by Mrs Pyatt. The hotel entrance and the breakfast table were tastefully decorated with ferns and plants.

Later, Major and Mrs Inman left for London, the bride travelling in a smart navy tailored costume over which she wore a handsome fur coat. (*Cheltenham Looker-On*)

NOVEMBER 20TH

1823: On this day the *Cheltenham Chronicle* reported a dispute which had taken place in Montpellier involving members of a small French community in the area:

> On the night of Monday last the 'small boutique' kept by a young Frenchwoman and her mother immediately above the Sherborne Spa, yet near the entrance to the Montpellier Promenade and Pump Room, was broken into by some dastardly miscreants, and plundered of nearly all the store these poor creatures were possessed of. A quantity of eau de Cologne, several trinkets, toys, etc. – the very means of their existence – were stolen from them, and they are now reduced to very great misery.

A couple of weeks later more information was revealed about the incident. The owner of the 'small boutique', a Mme Rachael Wolff, had accused Jean-Jacques Le Roi of being the thief who had robbed her shop. It seems her only rationale for pointing the finger at Le Roi was that she considered him to be her only enemy in Cheltenham. Wolff later retracted her accusations after Le Roi received glowing references from important local dignitaries testifying to his good character. To compensate for his sufferings, a subscription fund was set up for his benefit. (CLHS Journal 23)

NOVEMBER 21ST

1882: On this day an eminent soldier who later lived in Cheltenham was listed in the *London Gazette*. Major-General Edmund Francis Burton of the Madras Cavalry became Supernumerary on the Effective List. Burton and his wife Georgina had nine sons, all of them soldiers. They lived at Hambrook House, Charlton Kings. There is an impressive Burton family tomb in the cemetery in Cheltenham. It commemorates the death of all nine sons, but the main inscription is to the first, who died tragically. It reads:

> In loving memory of Geoffrey, Cadet at the Royal Military College, Sandhurst, youngest son of General E.F. Burton and Georgiana his wife. Drowned saving his sister's life at Happisburgh, Norfolk 29 August 1893 Aged 18 years. This monument is erected by his sorrowing brothers in honour of his blameless life and noble death leaving us an example that we should follow his steps.

Another of their sons, Lieutenant-Colonel Arthur Robert Burton, died in Mesopotamia on 24 January 1918. He is buried in the Basra War Cemetery, Iraq. He left a widow, Florence Evelyn Hood Burton, and is commemorated on the Cheltenham War Memorial in the Promenade and on the Christ Church Roll of Honour. (Commemorations in Cheltenham Cemetery; Gloucestershire Regiment records)

NOVEMBER 22ND

1941: On this day, Cheltenham and District Warship Week was officially inaugurated to raise money for the war effort. Members of the public gathered in the Promenade for the opening ceremony, conducted by Mr W. Mabane, MP. The large and enthusiastic crowd then watched a mile-long procession of personnel from the army, navy and air force. A military band, along with a barrel organ, provided the music.

The front of the Municipal Offices, in the Promenade, was bedecked in flags, and a large banner above the central door proclaimed 'England Expects'. There was also an indicator, in the form of a model destroyer, to show the progress of the collection, which was unveiled by Mr D.L. Lipson, MP, on the following Monday.

Later that Monday morning, dignitaries were invited to a lunch at the Town Hall by the Mayor, A.E. Ward. The chief guest was Commander Oliver Locker-Lampson. (*Cheltenham Chronicle and Gloucestershire Graphic*)

NOVEMBER 23RD

1931: On this day the Repertory Theatre opened in North Street. *The Stage* said: 'The hall is excellently adapted to theatre purposes. The company had a hearty send-off.' The proprietor of the new venture was a Mr Rex Burchell who had, up until then, been putting on shows in Montpellier Gardens.

The North Street building had first opened in 1910 as the Albert Hall, putting on various events, including plays. It was soon taken over by the proprietors of the Coliseum, 200 yards along the road, changing its name in 1911 to the Royal Cinema de Luxe and later to the Theatre of Varieties and Cinema de Luxe. The venture was not without success and, in February 1917, the legendary Dan Leno appeared there in the *The Glad Idlers*.

Burchell's Repertory Theatre survived for a year or two but was doomed to failure. The theatre was taken over by a couple more companies, but it closed for the last time in April 1934. The building became a garage but was demolished in 1988 and is now a Job Centre. (Michael Hasted, *A Theatre for All Seasons*)

NOVEMBER 24TH

1964: On this day a new play, *Cabbages and Kings* by David Monico, was premiered at the Everyman Theatre, but not before overcoming a few hurdles. In those days theatre was censored by the Lord Chamberlain, and his famous blue pencil hovered like the sword of Damocles over all new writing. The text of every show had to be submitted to his office for approval before a licence could be issued for its performance. He had an issue with Monico's play and, on 5 November, less than three weeks before the play was to open, the assistant comptroller at St James' Palace wrote to John Ridley (the manager of the Everyman) saying:

> I am to inform you that the Lord Chamberlain cannot allow the dialogue given in the annexure to this letter and it must be altered or omitted altogether. In the latter case an undertaking must be given to that effect. Should it be your intention to substitute any dialogue, then the alteration must be submitted before it may be used.

The problem was on page 65: the word 'fart'. (Michael Hasted, *A Theatre for All Seasons*)

NOVEMBER 25TH

1846: On this day Sir James Tynte Agg-Gardner was born in Cheltenham. He was the town's longest-serving MP, representing the borough for the Conservative Party for a total of thirty-nine years. Although he was an early supporter of women's suffrage and was appointed a Privy Councillor in 1924, during the four terms he served between 1874 and his death, he only spoke twice in the House of Commons. He received his knighthood in 1916.

The family had been prominent in the town for many years, where his father, James Agg-Gardner, had purchased the Lordship of the Manor in 1843. After his father's death, the young James was made a ward of court. He was sent to Harrow School and was later educated privately. Although he gained a place at Trinity College, Cambridge, he opted instead, at the age of twenty-two, to stand for Parliament in the 1868 general election. His bid was unsuccessful and he decided to study law. In 1873 he was called to the Bar at the Middle Temple. He never practised law, although he did become a magistrate in 1875. He held directorship of many companies in the town, including the Brewery and the Opera House Theatre. He died on 9 August 1928 at the Carlton Club in London. (Gwen Hart, *A History of Cheltenham*)

NOVEMBER 26TH

1932: On this day, motoring enthusiasts in Cheltenham had the opportunity to try out a brand new car. For ten days only, the Victory Motor Co. of Winchcombe Street issued a special invitation to every family desirous of trying out the wonderful new Ford V8 motorcar. All they had to do was phone or write to arrange an appointment for a trial run. They were invited to try the V8 on any hill and be amazed at its extraordinary acceleration. It was claimed that the Ford V8 was the ideal car for all social occasions, being fast, powerful, comfortable, smooth and quiet. The V8 car was marketed as the Model 18, though it is commonly called the Ford V8, and, other than the engine, is virtually indistinguishable from the Model B. And the price? A mere £230. (*Cheltenham Chronicle and Gloucestershire Graphic*)

NOVEMBER 27TH

2011: On this day a young man called Lee spotted some flying saucers in Hesters Way. This is how he retold events that occurred at 8.15 p.m. on that fateful evening:

I was on my way to a party walking across King George playing field in Hesters Way. I was walking east looking towards Cleeve Hill, I saw one bright light about the size of a 5 pence at arms length appear … then another appeared next to it about an inch away and the first light went out … they did not move at all unless they were rotating which I could not discern. I watched them as I walked across the park [for a] duration of about 5 mins … I was looking nearly southward toward Gloucester at about 45 degrees to the ground I saw another light just as bright as the first just below the cloud base which seemed pretty high. I'm no expert somebody would have to check that out for me … I have always wanted to see some strange things in the sky … I love this subject and have always been and remain a skeptic [*sic*] about the origins of peoples sightings but this was strange and I would love an explanation ps the lights were not orange they were bright white ever so slightly golden in hue.

(www.uk-ufo.co.uk)

NOVEMBER 28TH

1853: On this day, two local policemen were prosecuted for taking a nap while on duty. On 30 November the *Cheltenham Examiner* gave details of the incident:

> On Monday last, a couple of 'guardians of the night' were brought up before the magistrates, on a charge of neglect of duty. It appeared that the active Police Sergeant Jeffs, in going his nightly rounds discovered that the policemen appointed to patrol the Tivoli and Park districts were *non est inventus*, and after a patient and diligent search he discovered the two truant 'Bobbies' comfortably snoozing in a fly [a two-wheeled, horse-drawn carriage] at the back of Lansdown Crescent. On telling them to 'come out of that' the affrighted peelers commenced rubbing their eyes and stammering forth excuses, the most characteristic of which was, that as the fly was left in that exposed situation they were afraid it would be stolen, and, therefore, got inside to protect it.

The magistrates thought the excuses exceedingly ingenious but not very probable, and rewarded them with a fine of 20s each and a promise that if they were ever 'caught napping' again, they would be sent to walk up the 'wooden hill'. This 'wooden hill' was the notorious treadmill in the Northleach House of Correction on which prisoners were forced to walk for many hours as punishment. (CLHS Journal 8)

NOVEMBER 29TH

2005: On this day, the regional heat of the sixth annual 'Target Two Point Zero: The Bank of England / The Times Interest Rate Challenge' was won by a team from Pate's Grammar School. A record number of entries were received from more than 280 schools and colleges across the UK.

Each team of four students competed in one of the forty-two regional heats. Like the Bank of England's own Monetary Policy Committee, these sixteen to eighteen year olds had to consider the factors affecting the UK's economic and inflation outlook. Then they had to decide what interest rate should be set to meet the government's 2 per cent inflation target. After outlining the main economic issues and giving their decision, the teams were questioned by a judging panel. The winning team from each regional heat went on to one of the six area finals to be held in February 2006, with the national final to be held in March at the Bank of England in London.

The team from Pate's Grammar School recommended an interest rate of 4.5 per cent, compared with the Bank of England's official rate of 4.5 per cent, set by the Monetary Policy Committee on 10 November. The team from the Cheltenham Ladies' College were runners-up, also recommending an interest rate of 4.5 per cent. (The Bank of England)

NOVEMBER 30TH

1896: On this day the Cheltenham Cricket Club staged a fundraising event which included a moving picture show. The club needed funds for laying and equipping a new ground, and a series of events were mounted at the Assembly Rooms in the High Street. Part of the entertainment was a presentation by a Mr Robert Paul of so-called 'animated photographs' using his newly developed projector called the Theatrograph or Animatograph. The very first public performance of moving pictures had been held less than a year before by the Lumière Brothers in Paris.

Mr Paul brought with him a selection of films. They fell into two categories: those depicting actual events (what we would call documentaries) and those showing rehearsed or acted scenes. One of the latter was a 'mirth provoking pantomime of the Soldier's Courtship'. Of the documentaries, pictures of the Paris Express arriving in Calais proved popular, as did film of the Prince of Wales at the derby.

The events were such a great success that the Cricket Club held a similar event the following year to help clear its debts. (CLHS Journal 23)

DECEMBER 1ST

1880: On this day Robert Bertram Mitford died at his house, Northumberland Lodge in Tivoli Road.

Robert was a member of the Mitford family, which included the famous sisters Nancy, Diana, Unity, Jessica and Deborah. The family had taken up residence in Tivoli Road around 1847. The house was then called Turbeyville Lodge after a previous resident, but in 1949 Mitford changed its name to reflect the county from which the family originated.

In the 1861 census Robert was described as a Landed Proprietor. He was a fellow of the Royal Geographical Society and a keen inventor. He was also a bit of a campaigner. He wrote a letter to the *Cheltenham Examiner* on 8 October 1857 with a suggestion to facilitate the apprehension of naughty errand boys who threw stones. He suggested that each errand boy should have a numbered badge stitched to their clothes, with the name of their employer printed on it. It didn't catch on.

After the death of his wife Anne in 1870, Mr Mitford stayed on at Northumberland Lodge until his own death. (Eric Woodhead, *The Mitfords of Tivoli*; CLHS Journal 21)

DECEMBER 2ND

1950: On this day Santa Claus arrived at his grotto in Ward's department store on the corner of North Street and the High Street where Primark now stands. That year an estimated 30,000 children queued up to sit on Santa's lap, have Ho-Ho-Ho bellowed in their little ears and be given a surprise present from Santa's giant sack. The basement grottos were very elaborate and wondrous affairs with, it seemed, no expense spared.

At Christmas, department stores in Cheltenham vied for Santa supremacy. It was a toss-up as to whether the Santa at Ward's was better than the one in Cavendish House. Ward's, which celebrated its fiftieth anniversary the following year, was cheaper and more downmarket than the posh Cavendish House in the Promenade. Ward's had a nice old-fashioned system of processing your money. There were no tills on the shop floor. Your money would be put into a capsule the size of a baked-bean tin and placed in a tube above the counter. It was then, at the pull of a wire, sucked away to some invisible accounts office in the store's nether reaches, where your money would be counted and your change and receipt placed in the canister which was then whooshed back to you. Secure it was; quick it wasn't. But people had more time in those days. (Various sources, including *Gloucestershire Echo*)

DECEMBER 3RD

1828: On this day, John Wornham Penfold, designer of probably Britain's best-loved red pillar box, was born in Surrey.

Cheltenham has more of his famous, but now quite rare, hexagonal postboxes than any other town in England, except for London. The distinctive six-sided design incorporates a decorative cap topped with a cast-iron acanthus bud, plus Queen Victoria's monogram on the front, below the collection times plate. There are eight Penfold letter boxes still in use in Cheltenham, including those in Hewlett Road, Bayshill Road, Lansdown Road, Evesham Road, Douro Road and Montpellier Walk.

Penfold submitted his designs for the pillar box in 1866. The Post Office had been attempting to standardise letter boxes throughout the country for some time, and had produced a national standard, but this was found to be wanting. With Penfold's box, the Post Office again attempted to establish an enduring national standard. The boxes were commissioned and continued in production for the next thirteen years. But the cost of producing Penfold's boxes was high, and a cheaper, plainer standard box was introduced in 1879. (British Postal Museum and Archive)

DECEMBER 4TH

1997: On this day an exchange took place during a debate in the House of Commons about the Government Communications Headquarters. Mr Baker asked the Secretary of State for Foreign and Commonwealth Affairs how many civilian and non-civilian staff were employed within GCHQ for each year from 1980. The Secretary of State, Robin Cook, replied that it was not their policy to provide detailed information on the staffing of the Intelligence and Security Services.

Mr Baker also asked the Secretary of State on what occasions since 1987 GCHQ has been involved in the surveillance of party political conferences. Robin Cook replied that the Intelligence Services Act 1994 requires the director of GCHQ to ensure that GCHQ does not take any action to further the interests of any UK political party. This was established policy even before the Act was passed. On a number of occasions GCHQ provided advice and assistance to the police at such conferences on the security of their communications. But GCHQ has not been involved in the surveillance of party political conferences. (Hansard)

DECEMBER 5TH

1963: On this day Cheltenham's only claim to Olympic fame, Michael Edwards, was born. Better known as Eddie 'the Eagle' Edwards, he was the first competitor ever to represent Britain in Olympic ski jumping and consequently became a national hero.

Eddie worked as a plasterer in Cheltenham but harboured a childhood dream of becoming a Hollywood stuntman. Despite Cheltenham's lack of snow he took up skiing and represented Great Britain at the 1987 World Championships in Oberstdorf, where he came ninety-eighth in a field of ninety-eight. He then took on the challenge of ski jumping and became Britain's first and only ski jumper and also, not surprisingly, the British national ski jumping record holder. His moment of glory came in the Winter Olympics in Calgary in 1988. Although he finished fifty-eighth in the 70m jump, he was in fact last as the fifty-ninth competitor was disqualified. Undeterred, he took part in the 90m jump, in which he was undisputedly last.

With his big, heavy-rimmed glasses which apparently fogged when he was jumping, and a keen and sarcastic wit, Eddie's moment of fame lasted quite a few weeks. He was a true eccentric and the media and public loved him. He now lives in Stroud and runs his own successful building and plastering company. (Various sources)

DECEMBER 6TH

1959: On this day the last performance took place at the Opera House in Regent Street. The old theatre had been on the decline for several years and the management called it a day in 1955. It was temporarily reprieved when it was bought in October 1955 by the Cheltenham Corporation.

Despite their high ideals, by April 1956 the theatre was having to resort to the old tried and failed format of presenting a season of variety. At the beginning of 1957 the council finally gave up and offloaded the theatre to a new company headed by Frank G. Maddox. Maddox fared no better and in 1959 it looked as though the theatre would become a warehouse or supermarket. There was a temporary reprieve in November that year when the Cheltenham Operatic & Dramatic Society staged their performance of Irving Berlin's *Call Me Madam*. The show closed on 6 December and so did the theatre. Surprisingly, a public that had not seemed interested or supported the theatre in its hour of need did not want to see it disappear forever. Such was the public outcry at the theatre's demise that only nine months later, due to the proverbial public demand, the theatre was reborn as the Everyman. (Michael Hasted, *A Theatre for All Seasons*)

DECEMBER 7TH

1975: On this day one of Cheltenham's greatest ever industrialists, George Herbert Dowty, died at his home in the Isle of Man. He had been born in Pershore, Worcestershire, but it was in Cheltenham that he made his fame and fortune.

After a series of jobs young Dowty joined the Gloster Aircraft Co., an off-shoot of the Cheltenham company H.H. Martyn. His special interest was aircraft landing gears and, over the following three years, he took out three patents on his designs. In 1931 he set up the Aircraft Components Co., his own one-man company, while still employed at Gloster Aircraft Co. In May that year he received his first order for six internally sprung undercarriage wheels from Kawasaki and built these in his workshops at No. 10 Lansdown Terrace Lane. A month later he left his job at Gloster in order to concentrate on his own company.

The new company was immediately and spectacularly successful and went public in 1936, but it was the Second World War that ensured his continued success. Twenty-eight different types of aircraft were fitted with Dowty equipment, which included 12,900 sets for the Hurricane, over 90,000 other undercarriage units, and more than 1 million hydraulic units. Plants were set up throughout Britain, as well as Canada and the USA. (Various sources, including Smith & Rowbotham, *Commemorative Plaques of Cheltenham*)

December 8th

1917: On this day, Lieutenant Edward William Bell of the Machine Gun Corps was killed in action in Palestine during the First World War. He is buried in Jerusalem War Cemetery. Bell, from Cheltenham, is commemorated on the grave of his father on the Cheltenham War Memorial, the Grammar School Roll of Honour, the St Luke's Church Roll of Honour and the Wesleyan Chapel Roll of Honour. On 3 June 1917, Bell wrote in *The Diary of a Sub*:

> Orders having been received – probably from the War Office, or some other Institution interested in the Great War – I am awakened at 5 ac emma by the noise of my batman cleaning the wrong boots, and rise to say once more good-bye to the old familiar scenes – and things can be most familiar in Marseilles – and the pretty 'rest camp', where the shattered nerves of three thousand 'survivors' have been slowly unshattered for a month. … The entire British Army having now embarked, and crowds of German spies having been kept back by the police on the quay, and the qui vive, sentries are posted at the gangways …

Lieutenant Bell left a wife and daughter at Cheltondale Villas, Cheltenham. (Laurence Housman, *War Letters of Fallen Englishmen*; Commemorations in Cheltenham Cemetery)

DECEMBER 9TH

1935: On this day a new theatre opened in the Winter Gardens in Imperial Square.

When the Opera House became a cinema in 1929 it left the town without a theatre, apart from the Coliseum which was mainly a music hall. In May 1931, Jessie Scrivener, a teacher at the Ladies' College, wrote to the *Echo* suggesting that Cheltenham should follow Bristol's example and establish a repertory company. She suggested that a space in the north wing of the Winter Gardens could easily be converted into a decent theatre. Rex Burchell, who later ran the Repertory Theatre in North Street, applied to run the new theatre but, in spite of the support of the Mayor, his application to set up a repertory company in the Winter Gardens was turned down by the council. Miss Scrivener's idea was not doomed though. One of her former pupils, Barbara Kent, in partnership with Ernest Cox and his wife Ellen Compton, put in a bid to the council for the Winter Gardens space. The council agreed on the condition that the new partnership converted the building and paid for lighting, heating and cleaning. Ellen Compton was part of the distinguished theatrical family that included Sir Compton MacKenzie and Fay Compton. (Michael Hasted, *A Theatre for All Seasons*)

DECEMBER 10TH

1881: On this day Mr Arthur Agg-Gardner, brother to the late MP for Cheltenham, took part in a disastrous balloon ascent which caused much anxiety throughout the country for the fate of one of its intrepid aeronauts, Mr W. Powell, MP for Malmesbury. The flight took off from Bath at noon in very foggy and unfavourable weather. Messrs Powell and Agg-Gardner were accompanied in the ascent by Captain J. Templer (Royal Engineers), who was in charge of the balloon on behalf of the authorities at Woolwich to whom it belonged.

Passing over Somersetshire, the aeronauts continued their course until within a mile of Bridport, when, finding they were rapidly drifting seaward, they attempted to descend. The balloon came down with great rapidity and, striking the ground with great violence, Mr Agg-Gardner and Captain Templer were both thrown out of the basket, the former sustaining a leg fracture and the latter being cut and bruised. Mr Powell remained aboard the balloon, which instantly rose with him to a great height and went out to sea. It was not seen again, although diligent search was made.

A report was circulated on the following Thursday that the balloon had been seen at sea by a Cherbourg fisherman but no corroboration of the fisherman's statement was received. (*Cheltenham Looker-On*)

DECEMBER 11TH

1940: On this day, or rather on this night, the worst German air raid on Cheltenham took place. At 7.30 p.m., after flares lit up the town, over 2,000 incendiary and 100 high explosive and oil bombs were dropped. Twenty-three people were killed and 600 made homeless. Half of Stoneville Street was demolished and ten people were killed when a bomb landed on the railway embankment at the end of the street. A gas holder at the nearby Gas Works was hit, as was the factory of H.H. Martyn. The beautiful art deco ticket office at the Black & White coach station in St Margaret's Road was also destroyed, along with other buildings in St Margaret's Villas. Further away, in Leckhampton, Pilley Bridge was destroyed. Other bombs that night fell on houses in Parabola Road, Christchurch Road, Lansdown Road and St Mark's.

This was not the only German air raid on the town. On 25 August 1940 a device fell in Hesters Way but failed to explode, and on 18 November 1940 eighteen delayed action bombs were dropped on Cheltenham, one of them smashing through the roof of a house in Pilley Crescent, but luckily this one also failed to explode. (Various sources)

December 12th

1914: On this day the *Cheltenham Looker-On* reported on a nice review that the town had received in a fashionable London magazine – *Queen*. The magazine stated:

> Cheltenham has long been recognised as one of the most favoured residential and educational centres in Great Britain, but the outbreak of war has brought the 'garden town' – as it is frequently styled – into special prominence, for through the closing of the foreign spas to English visitors the mineral waters of Cheltenham are being sought after by many who under ordinary circumstances would have taken a cure at Wiesbaden or elsewhere abroad. The town council of the Gloucestershire spa, with excellent foresight, installed a series of Aix douche, vapour, and brine baths a few years ago, and thus a complete course of medical treatment is provided by the administration of the Cheltenham waters. ... As a residential centre Cheltenham has many advantages, not the least being its pleasant climate at all seasons, while for education few towns in England can rival its choice of schools for boys and girls ... There are concerts daily – in the morning at the spa and in the afternoons at the Town Hall; there is a modern opera house, with representations by leading companies ...

(*Cheltenham Looker-On*)

DECEMBER 13TH

1886: On this day an important political and social event took place when the register opened for enrolment in Cheltenham's new Liberal Club. The new club opened in the grand Albion House in North Street. It was built in 1806 as a private residence and was one of the grandest private houses in the town.

To encourage membership of the club, the Liberals issued three exciting-sounding pamphlets guaranteed to get the fun-loving people of Cheltenham rushing to sign up. The first was entitled 'Disestablishment', which aimed to convince the public of the necessity to strip Queen Victoria of some of her powers. The second was 'Free Education', which speaks for itself really. The third was possibly the most politically inflammatory – 'Three Acres and a Cow'. This slogan was used among land reform campaigners of the 1880s, and was revived by the distributists of the 1920s. It refers to ideal land holding for every citizen.

However, the campaign did have its lighter side. The great music-hall performer Arthur Lloyd wrote a comic song of the same title and Jesse Collings, who had used the phrase as a slogan for his 1885 land reform campaign, became derisively known as 'Three Acres and a Cow Collings'. (CLHS Journal 22)

DECEMBER 14TH

1893: On this day Walter Guy Pearce was born in Cheltenham. Pearce was one of the leading make-up artists in the British film industry from the mid-1930s. In the early 1940s he went to Hollywood to continue his profession, where he was known as just Guy Pearce.

Some of the great Hollywood films he worked on include the 1941 five-times Oscar winner *How Green Was My Valley,* directed by the legendary John Ford. He was the make-up artist on the 1944 Otto Preminger classic *Laura* starring Gene Tierney and Van Heflin, *The Keys of the Kingdom* with Gregory Peck (which was nominated for four Oscars), and Orson Welles' *Jane Eyre* in 1943. He also worked with another British ex-pat, Alfred Hitchcock, on his 1944 film *Lifeboat.* Some of the other great Hollywood stars Pearce worked with include Victor Mature, Henry Fonda and Jack Benny, and he worked on several films with Betty Grable.

After the war he came back to the UK and worked on *London Town* in 1946. In 1948 he was make-up supervisor on Roy Boulting's film *The Guinea Pig*, starring Richard Attenborough. Walter Guy Pearce returned to live in America, where he died in 1979 aged eighty-five. (Various sources, including www.imdb.com)

DECEMBER 15TH

1942: On this day, England and Manchester City footballer Mike Summerbee was born in Preston. But it was in Cheltenham where he grew up, attending Naunton Park School. He first played semi-professional football for the then Southern League side, Cheltenham Town, the Robins, before becoming a full-time professional with Swindon Town in 1959, aged just sixteen.

He made more than 200 appearances for the Wiltshire club, scoring thirty-eight goals. In 1965 Manchester City manager Joe Mercer signed him for a fee of £35,000. In his first Manchester City season Summerbee started every single match – the only Manchester City player to do so that season.

Summerbee played a total of eight times for England between 1968 and 1972, and ended his footballing career as player-manager at Stockport County in 1978-79. In 1980 he played a single match for non-League Mossley in their FA Cup victory over Crewe Alexandra. He also starred alongside Pelé, Sylvester Stallone and Michael Caine in the footballing POW film *Escape to Victory* in 1981. (*Mike Summerbee: The Autobiography*)

DECEMBER 16TH

1962: On this day the Gaumont cinema in Cheltenham's Winchcombe Street changed its name to the Odeon. The architect of the former Gaumont Palace, which showed its first picture in 1933, was W.E. Trent. His cousin, N.A. Trent, designed the low-relief figures that can still be seen on the façade. As well as The Beatles in 1963, many other live beat groups and pop bands appeared there in the 1960s. The Rolling Stones topped the bill a number of times.

But it wasn't just music. Throughout the 1950s and early '60s the Gaumont/Odeon was a regular venue for the many variety shows that were still touring the country. The earlier shows were very much based on the popular radio shows of the time, like *Educating Archie* and *It's That Man Again* (*ITMA*). As television became more popular, it was stars like Mike and Bernie Winters, Max Wall and Norman Wisdom who took to the stage.

The venue also staged musical shows, with Ruby Murray appearing as Snow White alongside seven dwarfs in 1962. The shows had stopped long before the Odeon was divided up into a multi-screen cinema in the 1990s. The Odeon finally closed on 5 November 2006. (Various sources)

DECEMBER 17TH

1881: On this day, the *Cheltenham Looker-On* reported on the Christmas concert given at the college:

> The Amateur Concert, annually given by the Pupils and Masters of Cheltenham College to their relatives and friends on the eve of their Christmas Vacation, took place as usual last Thursday evening in the Classical School Room, which was filled with a throng of as gaily dressed ladies as was ever congregated within the same walls, protected in its rear by a phalanx of jubilant youths, whose enthusiastic applause of the vocal efforts – good, bad and indifferent – of their schoolfellows bespoke at once their kindly feelings and their delight at the advent of their holidays.

Pause for breath. The *Looker-On* was clearly not given to the use of a short sentence when a long one would do. But they must be commended for their discretion, as they seem to have been barred from the concert:

> The music programmed for the entertainment of the guests was of the ordinary popular and telling character but of its performances the *Looker-On* has 'nought to say', the Rev. Principal of the College having withheld the customary tickets of admission from its Editor …

(*Cheltenham Looker-On*)

DECEMBER 18TH

1882: On this day, a man whose name has been mentioned many times in these pages died. Dean Francis Close had been one of the most important and influential men in Cheltenham in the nineteenth century, and his legacy lives on in the town even now.

He was born in 1797 in the Somerset town of Frome, being educated in Midhurst in Kent and later at the Merchant Taylor's School. In 1816 he entered Cambridge University. There he met the evangelical cleric Charles Simeon, a meeting that would change his life and also the destiny of Cheltenham. Close was appointed the Anglican Rector of Cheltenham in 1826, a post he was to hold until 1856 when he was appointed Dean of Carlisle. The poet Tennyson dubbed Close 'the Pope of Cheltenham'.

Close was against all forms of public entertainment and found plenty to campaign against in 'The Pleasure Town'. He fought against theatres, stating after the Theatre Royal burnt down that no other theatre would establish itself in the town while he was there. He also crusaded against horseracing. He created an important teacher-training college in the town but his most lasting legacy is probably the school that bears his name. Dean Close School was founded in 1886, the most famous Old Decanians being the artist Francis Bacon and musician Brian Jones. (Gwen Hart, *A History of Cheltenham*)

DECEMBER 19TH

1902: On this day, Sir Ralph Richardson was born at No. 11 Tivoli Road in Cheltenham. Along with Laurence Olivier and John Gielgud, he was considered one of the greatest classical actors of the twentieth century.

Ralph was the third son and youngest child of Arthur Richardson, who was a master at the Ladies' College. When he was a baby, Ralph's mother Lydia left her husband and took Ralph with her to Gloucester, then to Shoreham-by-Sea. He was later apprenticed as an actor to a local theatre manager and then toured with Charles Doran's company for five seasons, gradually being promoted to larger parts, including Macduff in *Macbeth* and Mark Antony in *Julius Caesar*. In 1925 he joined Sir Barry Jackson's Birmingham Repertory Co., alongside eminent British actors such as Edith Evans and Cedric Hardwicke. But it was in the classics that he made his name. He is considered to have been the definitive Falstaff and Peer Gynt. Richardson was knighted in 1947 and worked right up until his death in 1983. When the Everyman Theatre reopened after major rebuilding work in 1986, the new studio theatre was named after him and opened by his widow, Meriel. (Various sources, including Ralph Richardson, *An Actor's Life*)

DECEMBER 20TH

1932: On this day a court case took place to establish responsibility for a derelict old tram which stood near the road in an orchard in Staverton.

The judge, A.R. Kennedy, heard submissions and claims regarding the ownership of tram No. 22. It was claimed that the tram was an eyesore, but nevertheless it stood on the same spot and became a bit of a landmark to those travelling along the A40 until it finally was removed in 1961. And the tram wasn't the only dilapidated means of transport that could be seen from that part of the Cheltenham to Gloucester Road. Until very recently, an old Gloster Meteor jet fighter lived in the corner of a field right by the side of the road, just opposite the Dowty factory. It had begun to look its age, and standing exposed to the elements did little to improve its appearance or condition. It disappeared sometime in 2010. (Various sources, including *Gloucestershire Echo*)

DECEMBER 21ST

1888: On this day our old friend and diarist William Swift was searching for a clergyman to conduct a funeral, and it seemed any clergyman would do.

One of Swift's duties as a churchwarden was to find a stand-in for the absent Dr Smith. It seems that he was literally tramping the streets looking for anyone wearing a dog collar. He tried everyone he knew. His first choice, Revd Cornford of Etchowe House in Lansdown Road, was unable to oblige due to a bout of lumbago. Swift's second choice, Revd Wosely Lewis who lived in Pittville Circus, was already booked. By this time Mr Swift was getting desperate and, with profuse apologies, accosted Revd Lyne in Bath Road. Luckily the vicar was free and agreed to conduct the service. Swift was grateful but was not impressed, describing him as 'a man over 50 years, a little mildewed with a rather shabby waistcoat and coat'. Still, he was better than nothing. Swift scribbled the details on a piece of paper and gave it to Mr Lyne, who bumbled off to Churchdown to carry out the funeral, despite falling in the mud en route and forgetting his spectacles. (CLHS Journal 8)

DECEMBER 22ND

1839: On this day John Nevil Maskelyne, one of the foremost illusionists of his time, was born in White Hart Row, now Whitehart Street, in Cheltenham. John became interested in conjuring after watching a stage performance by the fraudulent spiritualists the Davenport brothers. He saw how the Davenports' spirit cabinet illusion worked and stated to the audience in the theatre that he could recreate their act using no supernatural methods. With the help of George Alfred Cooke, he built a version of the cabinet. Together, they revealed the Davenport brothers' trickery to the public at a show in Cheltenham in June 1865.

Following the enormous success they had had debunking the Davenports, he and Cooke opened a permanent theatre/exhibition – Maskelyne and Cooke's House of Mysteries – in part of the Egyptian Hall in London's Piccadilly in 1873. He wrote a book on cheating at cards and created the Occult Committee of the Magic Circle to expose fraudulent spiritualists. He is credited as being the father of modern magic and illusion, but he was also an important inventor. One of his most widely used devices was the coin-operated public toilet which gave rise to the expression 'spend a penny'. (CLHS Journal 22)

DECEMBER 23RD

2010: On this day it was reported that some of the young ladies at the Cheltenham Ladies' College were perhaps not as ladylike as they should have been.

Comments made by girls at the college, as well as some of the other most prestigious schools in the country, were removed from a website which lets private school pupils post malicious rumours about their classmates. Parents, who pay £21,174 a year to send their daughters to the school, and teachers, were shocked by the viciousness of the comments. Extracts of posts left by teenagers at Cheltenham Ladies' College had been published in a national newspaper. One post read: 'Girl A rumoured to have bedded at least 45 guys …' Another read: 'Girl B is cheap and ugly and looks like a horse and needs some serious eyebrow work.'

A spokesman said the site was only intended for adult use and added, 'We are removing schools from the website as minors use the site despite all the disclaimers and warnings that we show to them.'

Principal Vicky Tuck said access to the site through the college's computer system had been blocked. She said, 'This site is objectionable and causes enormous distress to anyone who is mentioned on it. We abhor bullying in any form, educate girls to respect each other and take action when this is not the case.' (*Gloucestershire Echo*)

DECEMBER 24TH

1910: On this day, a local paper demonstrated that some of the adverts were more interesting than the news stories. For example, Maison Annette, Practical Corsetiére of Albion Chambers, Clarence Street, announced that stout ladies were their speciality. Meanwhile, Misses Laws and Price held classes in deportment, calisthenics and dancing for the daughters of gentlemen, while Herr Erik von Myhr (court violinist to the late King of Sweden) gave violin lessons at No. 45 Lansdown Crescent. He claimed an 'Astonishing method of concentration of the mind and relaxation of the muscles ... Splendid interpretation of all the master-works is taught to advanced pupils. Beginners are taught in Sevcik's famous semi-tone system.'

In an advertisement headed 'The Feet', Mr W. Prince Mumford, Surgeon-Chiropodist, offered his services and advertised his book *Painless Treatment of the Diseases of the Feet* for the price of 6*d*. For enthusiasts of the new-fangled motorcar, Alfred Miles, under the heading 'Motor Bodies', offered to design and build a 'New Broughamlette (open or closed), Entirely New and Unique for a mere 100 guineas'. (*Cheltenham Looker-On*)

DECEMBER 25TH

1854: On this day a rather embarrassing situation occurred at a mass baptism that had been planned. The *Cheltenham Examiner* revealed the details of the story a couple of days later, explaining that:

> At one of the chapels in the lower part of the town it had been arranged that a grand baptismal ceremony should take place on Christmas day, there being, we believe, from a dozen to twenty adult candidates for immersion. At the time appointed however, it was discovered that no water was to be obtained, in which to perform the ceremony, the whole of the wells in the neighbourhood being drained by the new sewers lately constructed. Under the circumstances the imposing ceremony had to be postponed until a more convenient season.

The *Examiner* did not reveal what everybody did after the ceremony failed to take place, but no doubt they would have preferred to be blue with cold rather than red-faced – or maybe not. (CLHS Journal 8)

DECEMBER 26TH

1960: On this day a terrible disaster struck at the very heart of Cheltenham. While people were still in bed digesting their Christmas dinners, a fire started that was to engulf one of the town's most famous and iconic buildings: the Municipal Offices in the Promenade.

The fire broke out in the early morning and the fire brigade arrived soon after 7 a.m. with the blaze well underway. One of the first firemen on the scene was Jack Simms. He recalled: 'We got the call at about 7 a.m. on Boxing Day. To this day I've no idea how it started, because everyone would have left the building two days before for Christmas. We were originally told the fire was in Royal Well, but when we got down there it became pretty apparent that it was in the Municipal Offices.' The fire, which raged for more than six hours, destroyed much of the central block and roof of the building. It is estimated to have cost more than £200,000 to rebuild – more than £3 million in today's money. (*Gloucestershire Echo*)

DECEMBER 27TH

2010: On this day the Playhouse Theatre presented its first-ever professional Christmas show. Ross Andrews' adaptation of the classic *Toad of Toad Hall* was presented by Dreamshed Theatre, headed up by Cheltenham playwright and director Bill Cronshaw. Online reviewer RemoteGoat was full of praise:

> It was like a relaxing stroll through familiar countryside; like slipping into a warm bath. We all know the story of Toad, whether it be from Kenneth Grahame's original 1908 book, [or] A.A. Milne's 1929 play based on the book.
>
> This production stuck largely to the Milne version, including the original songs and incidental music. The main protagonists were exactly as you might have imagined them. They each have a different character. Mole (Craig Roberts) was mild-mannered and self-effacing. Ratty (James Lark) was relaxed and outgoing. Badger (Bill Cronshaw) was rather gruff but looked upon as the senior statesman whereas Toad (John Martin Stevens) was pompous, impulsive and rich enough to be able to follow a whim.
>
> For special mention was the set design including props, which somehow had the quality of children's book illustration without being simply derivative, and the way in which the changes between scenes brought to mind the simplicity and naivety of a puppet theatre. I personally found it a delight.

(www.remotegoat.co.uk)

DECEMBER 28TH

1914: On this day, twenty-three-year-old Private William Thomas Bates from Cheltenham died from his wounds in France. He was a soldier in the 1st Battalion Gloucestershire Regiment which had been sent to France as part of the British Expeditionary Force, landing at Le Havre on 13 August 1914. Compared to the French and German forces the BEF was relatively small. However, the quality of their fighting soldiers, in all aspects of warfare, was said to be superb. Their gallant efforts at the beginning of the First World War afforded Britain time to recruit and train her new armies, but the cost was tragic.

Private Bates first went into action with the Glosters at Landrecies on 26 August 1914. The Germans entered the town disguised as French soldiers and, although fooling the Tommies for a while and outnumbering them three to one, they were eventually forced back. By November 1918 the Glosters had won thirty-one Battle Honours – but at a cost of sixty-two officers and 1,044 men dead, and many more wounded.

The Gloucestershire Regiment has a dedicated museum in the Gloucester Docks: the Soldiers of Gloucestershire Museum displays the remarkable story of all the Glosters who served since 1694 until the present day. The story is told through exhibits of uniforms, weapons, medals and much more. There are interactive displays as well as an archive of contemporary film. (Various sources)

December 29th

1890: On this day a grand social event took place in Cheltenham and:

> ... a more successful inauguration of the Winter Season could scarcely have been desired than was afforded by the Christmas Ball last Monday at the Assembly Rooms, which was so well attended as to recall the memory of bygone days when the series of Subscription Dances at the Assembly Rooms was attended by the élite of local Society.
>
> Rather more than a hundred and forty ladies attended, the number of gentlemen closely corresponding, to that the first element in a successful evening was present. With so gay a company in which each one did his best, the un-regarded hours naturally sped with quickness and the dances which commenced at a quarter to ten continued without interruption until a quarter before two, when the guests departed ... The guests on this occasion will find the one drawback to perfect enjoyment last week – a rather serious draft throughout the room – effectually removed. It arose in part from the new entrance into Rodney Road, but mainly from the circumstance that the ventilators in the roof had been left open in accordance with old practice and in forgetfulness of the change necessary in view of the altered method of lighting and heating. The door has been heavily curtained and the ventilators will be closed.

(*Cheltenham Looker-On*)

DECEMBER 30TH

1906: On this day, Josephine Elizabeth Grey died. This prominent Victorian feminist, born in Milfield, Northumberland on 13 April 1828, was especially concerned with the welfare of prostitutes. She led the long campaign for the repeal of the Contagious Diseases Acts from 1869 to 1886. She also held views on the Boer War, Irish Home Rule and many other important issues of her day.

Josephine married George Butler, a scholar and cleric, in 1852. Butler encouraged his wife in her public work and even suffered setbacks in his own career on account of his wife's notoriety. The couple moved to Cheltenham in 1857 when George Butler was appointed vice-principal at Cheltenham College. They lived in The Priory on the corner of London Road and Priory Road. In 1866 George was appointed headmaster of Liverpool College, and the family moved to Liverpool.

Josephine was also a passionate Christian and is quoted as saying: 'God and one woman make a majority.' She is remembered in the Church of England with a Lesser Festival on 30 May and 30 December, and is also represented in windows in Liverpool's Anglican Cathedral and St Olave's Church in the City of London. On 23 July 1983, a commemorative plaque was unveiled for Josephine on the site of The Priory in London Road. (Various sources, including Smith & Rowbotham, *Commemorative Plaques of Cheltenham*)

DECEMBER 31ST

1999: On this day a time capsule was buried in the foundations of the Regent Arcade by Councillor David Banyard (the Mayor) and the centre manager Colin Antrobus. Nobody seems quite sure what it contains, so perhaps one can speculate. What would represent Cheltenham and give some idea of what the town was like at the millennium? I would have thought an absolute prerequisite would be a phial of spa water and an MP3 player playing Holst's *The Planets* on an endless loop. They could also include a retired colonel, who would obviously need to be stuffed and preferably dead. The capsule should certainly include a Chamber of Horrors, containing the Eagle Star building and the High Street block that includes a Tesco and Wilkinson. It could also have a little gravestone on which is carved 'RIP the old Grammar School in the High Street, the New Club in the Promenade, the classy shops that used to stand in the Promenade and the High Street, and five beautiful old cinemas'. But, most importantly, the lid of the capsule should be booby-trapped so that when it is opened it explodes and destroys whatever is left of the Regent Arcade.

If you enjoyed this book, you may also be interested in…

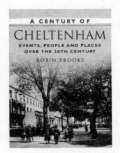

A Century of Cheltenham

ROBIN BROOKS

This fascinating selection of photographs illustrates the extraordinary transformation that has taken place in Cheltenham during the twentieth century. Drawing on detailed local knowledge of the community, this richly illustrated book recalls what Cheltenham has lost in terms of buildings, traditions and ways of life.

978 0 7524 7474 8

Cheltenham Then & Now

SUE ROWBOTHAM & JILL WALLER

In this superb collection of photographs, scenes of Cheltenham's yesteryear are contrasted with modern colour views to show what has been lost and what remains. This book offers an insight into people's daily lives and living conditions, and reveals the sometimes drastic changes which have taken place in the name of progress.

978 0 7524 6527 2

Not a Guide to: Cheltenham

TOM LOWE

Written by a local who knows what makes Cheltenham tick, this little book brings together the past and present to offer a taste of Cheltenham from the momentous to the outlandish. Learn about the movers and shakers who shaped this fantastic town, as well as Cheltenham's small wonders, tall stories, triumphs and tragedies.

978 0 7524 6883 9

Visit our website and discover thousands of other History Press books.

www.thehistorypress.co.uk